# The
# FREEWHEELING
# JOHN
# DOWIE

*With sincere thanks to*

PATRON
Stephen McNicholas

SUPER DONOR
Helga Dowie

# The
# FREEWHEELING
# JOHN
# DOWIE

John Dowie

**Unbound**

This edition first published in 2018

Unbound

6th Floor Mutual House, 70 Conduit Street, London W1S 2GF

www.unbound.com

Text Design by Ellipsis

A CIP record for this book is available from the British Library

ISBN 978-1-78352-480-8 (trade pbk)
ISBN 978-1-78352-481-5 (ebook)
ISBN 978-1-78352-479-2 (limited edition)

Printed in Great Britain by Clays Ltd, St Ives Plc

1 3 5 7 9 8 6 4 2

Dedicated to my mother J. Barbara Dowie
(née Hirst) on the understanding that
I'm not too big to be smacked

Dear Reader,

The book you are holding came about in a rather different way to most others. It was funded directly by readers through a new website: Unbound. Unbound is the creation of three writers. We started the company because we believed there had to be a better deal for both writers and readers. On the Unbound website, authors share the ideas for the books they want to write directly with readers. If enough of you support the book by pledging for it in advance, we produce a beautifully bound special subscribers' edition and distribute a regular edition and ebook wherever books are sold, in shops and online.

This new way of publishing is actually a very old idea (Samuel Johnson funded his dictionary this way). We're just using the internet to build each writer a network of patrons. At the back of this book, you'll find the names of all the people who made it happen.

Publishing in this way means readers are no longer just passive consumers of the books they buy, and authors are free to write the books they really want. They get a much fairer return too – half the profits their books generate, rather than a tiny percentage of the cover price.

If you're not yet a subscriber, we hope that you'll want to join our publishing revolution and have your name listed in one of our books in the future. To get you started, here is a £5 discount on your first pledge. Just visit unbound.com, make your pledge and type **dowie5** in the promo code box when you check out.

Thank you for your support,

Dan, Justin and John
Founders, Unbound

# *Contents*

# *PROLOGUE*

My comedy career began in 1971, which proves I have no comic timing. In 1971 there were no comedy clubs, no comedy agents and not much comedy future. There was, however, the Edinburgh Festival Fringe. I went there, aged twenty-one, making my professional debut and getting my first review, a bad one ('Fatuous' *Scotsman*) But a bad review was hardly surprising. Comedy requires practice and, with venues being almost non-existent, practice was hard to find. But I persevered, doing gigs where I could, in folk clubs, music venues, fringe theatres, universities and rooms above a pub. Things improved. By the end of the decade, I was working regularly and earning a living. In the 1980s, alternative comedy arrived, and with it more gigs, more money and a lot more comedians. By the 1990s, comedy was big business and about to get even bigger. It was then, with yet more comic timing, that I packed it all in.

It was as though my departure was just the break that comedy was waiting for. No sooner had I stopped than comedians were earning vast amounts of money performing in venues the size of small countries. I, meanwhile, was in a different sort of venue – a one-man tent. How did this happen? It happened because I have (I've been told) an addictive personality. This doesn't mean that once you get to know me you'll find me endlessly fascinating. It means that once I get hold of something I like, I do it to death. Which is what happened when I bought a bike.

I thought I could handle it. I'll just have the occasional ride, I told myself. Perhaps at weekends or when I feel stressed. What a joke. Soon I was having bike rides before breakfast. It got worse.

The more rides I took, the more rides I wanted. In a very short while I had sold my flat, was living in a tent, and riding my bike all the time.

As former contemporaries dined at the Ivy, I ate beans from a camping stove; as they drank cocktails at the Groucho, I drank wine from a plastic mug; as they snorted heaps of cocaine, I rubbed liniment into my legs. But the question is this: which of us was the happier? And the answer? Them. Obviously.

The bike rides I go on are not the kind enjoyed by the shave-your-legs-and-dress-yourself-in-Lycra sort of cyclist. I've got nothing against these people, but they're not my kind of cyclist. My kind of cyclist tends to be either very old or very young, riding rusty boneshakers or bikes with training wheels. The only thing they have in common is overtaking me with monotonous regularity. This is because I cycle less like a man and more like a snail, creaking along, my world on my back (actually, my bicycle's back), with no idea of where I'm going or how to get there. Which explains the slow pace. If you don't know where you're going, why rush?

Like my bike rides, this book meanders from place to place, sometimes takes a wrong turn and occasionally gets lost. Which might not be a bad thing. If it wasn't for getting lost we'd never know where we're supposed to be. Or so I like to tell myself. All the bloody time.

It's also a book that has no ending; at least, given that it's the story of my life so far, I hope it hasn't. I hope there are still a few more bike rides left: a few more hills to climb, a few more lanes to get lost in. But this is my journey so far. I hope you enjoy the ride. I did.

# CHAPTER ONE
## Birmingham

My first bike was a gift from my grandmother, given to me in 1963, on my thirteenth birthday. At eighteen, I gave it away to a rag-and-bone man, thinking that was the grown-up thing to do. What an idiot. I made an even bigger mistake three years earlier when I gave one of my teachers my teddy bear.

During the 1980s there was a series of TV adverts in which various celebrities nominated a teacher who had influenced them in a positive way. In a perfect world those celebrities, or anyone else for that matter, would have been able to nominate *all* of their teachers. However, this was the real world, and having only one good teacher put you ahead of the game. Mine was Mr Britton, who tried to teach me French, and succeeded, at least *un peu*. He succeeded totally, though, in treating me as an adult, treating me with respect.

In those days, the punishments my teachers inflicted on me were usually delivered with either a plimsoll or a cane. Or both. Mr Britton, an intelligent man, considered the beating of small boys to be beneath him. So, when I was shooting my mouth off in his classroom one day, instead of using his age, size, weight and authority against me, he chose to use his brain instead. Unfortunately for me. 'Come up to the blackboard,' he said. 'And on it write the word "extrovert".'

I stood, my face burning with embarrassment, a voice inside my head saying, 'I will never ever open my mouth in Mr Britton's classroom ever again', and then, in front of the entire class, walked up to the blackboard and on it wrote EXTRAVERT.

Some of the more literate children sniggered. Mr Britton could have encouraged them. He could have joined in. But he was better than that. Instead he said, 'Most people spell "extrovert" with an O. I see that you have spelt it with an A. That isn't wrong, just unusual. Rather like yourself. Now, would you like to sit down?'

Oh yes, I would like to sit down.

Mr Britton and I became friends, as much as a pupil and teacher can become friends. He not only encouraged my interest in writing and performing, he went further. An end-of-term school concert was coming up. 'You write something funny,' he said, 'and I'll help you perform it.'

I wrote a sketch. The sketch ended when a tin bath, filled with water, was brought on to the stage. I was then dropped in it. The school audience thought this was high comedy indeed – about as high as comedy can get – and reacted with laughter, cheers and applause. True to his word, Mr Britton joined me in the sketch. He also joined me in the bath. Following which, a white-faced head teacher spent twenty minutes trying to restore order. Then a girl from 3b came on and tried to play the flute.

Following this, it seemed only fair to reward Mr Britton in some way. I did this by giving him my teddy bear. As a joke.

That bear had been there for me when I was lonely, when I was upset, when I needed something to be close to in the midst of dark and scary nights. That bear had been the repository of a small child's love for years. And how was that bear rewarded? It was given away. As a joke. Because I had outgrown it.

If I have learned only one thing as I grow up, it is this: never grow up. Thinking that you have reached maturity is conclusive proof that you haven't.

\*

You'd have thought, following the Teddy Bear Tragedy, that I'd learned my lesson. I hadn't. Only a couple of years later, I gave away my bike, and didn't get another until I was in my fifties and living in London.

I'd been asked to direct an actor in his one-man show. Rehearsals were meant to take place in west London. I lived in north London. Getting from one place to the other using public transport meant an hour of commuter hell. Twice a day. My other option was to buy a bike and cycle along the towpath running beside the Regent's Park Canal. Not only did the route lead virtually door-to-door, but cycling the traffic-free towpath meant I'd avoid London's manic cars and belligerent buses. And not using public transport meant I'd avoid travelling with my nose in someone else's armpit, always a bonus.

And so I bought a bike, a folding model built by Dahon, a company that not only manufactures folding bikes but also attractive bags in which to carry them. I pictured myself cycling along the canal, rehearsing the show, having a few pints, then sauntering home, my bike packed in its bag and nonchalantly slung across my shoulders. I soon learned that a folded bike, even when put in a bag, still weighs as much as . . . well, a bike, basically.

I hadn't had the bike for very long, but it still hurt when it was stolen, the pain not lessened by the fact that I'd behaved like an idiot. I had ridden my bike to a supermarket. I had parked my bike at the bike stand. I had taken out my bicycle lock and carefully locked it to the bike stand. The only thing I did wrong in the whole complex process was forgetting to include the bike.

It's a terrible moment when you realise that your bike is no longer there. For a fraction of a second you see the shape of your bike in front of you, then reality kicks in and you realise that what you are looking at is the space where your bike used to be. Not the bike itself. No. That bike has gone. And gone for ever.

'When you ride a bike,' said a friend and fellow cyclist, 'a part of you rubs off on the bike. And a part of the bike rubs off on you. So when a thief steals your bicycle that thief is stealing a part of yourself. Not a large part, but a part of yourself nonetheless. And that is why,' he concluded, sensibly, 'all bicycle thieves should be hanged.'

Sadder and slightly wiser (if only in knowing how to lock a bike), I left a shop in north London now the owner of another bike, a non-folding Claud Butler Urban 200. A bike, I discovered, that was not just a bike. It was also a time machine.

Not long after I was born, my grandfather had advised my dad to buy a house, which, as it was being sold on a short lease, meant it was comparatively cheap. When the inevitable happened and my dad, his wife and children were made homeless, we moved into my grandfather's house, not only to punish him for handing out bad financial advice, but, as an unwanted consequence, to punish my father as well.

My grandfather found it pretty well impossible to live with my grandmother, and he'd volunteered for the job. My dad stuck it out for an unimaginable two years before he decided that it was time he took the advice of a 'bloke down the pub'.

Born in Belfast, my dad came to England when he was nine but never lost his accent, partly because he worked and socialised with men who shared not only his background but also his ambitions – to put paint on walls and beer down his throat.

For those men, the pub wasn't just some place that sold beer. The pub was the liquid pot of gold at the end of the working man's rainbow. No matter what hardships life threw their way, once they were in the pub those hardships were forgotten: strong men could be weak and weak men could be weaker; backs were slapped, shoulders were cried on, legs were pulled, deals were done and differences were settled with a punch-up in the bogs. The pub was the closest thing to heaven and a 'bloke down the pub' was the closest thing to a god.

So, when a bloke down the pub gave my dad advice on how to outwit the Housing Department of Birmingham City Council my dad not only believed him but also decided to act on it.

And there you have it – positive proof – alcohol ruins your judgement.

First, my dad gave my grandparents official notice that he was leaving, as he'd been advised to do. Then, at nine o'clock on a

Monday morning, family in tow, he went along to the Housing Department, insisting that they were responsible for putting a roof over their heads, and that he and his family were prepared to sit there all day until this happened.

That was the strategy the bloke in the pub had recommended. It had worked for him, apparently. He'd sat there all day and at five o'clock had been given the keys to a house. So had his mate. So, my dad sat and confidently waited until five o'clock, when, sure enough, he was summoned to an office where he was told that his wife and children were to be placed in a hostel for the homeless.

'And what about me?' asked my dad.

'You,' he was told, 'can look out for yourself.'

He then had to ring my grandparents and tell them what had happened. Not a good day for my dad.

However, two weeks later, Birmingham City Council relented and gave my dad the keys to a house, which meant he could finally get both my mother and her parents off his back. That is, until she and they saw the house – a terraced back-to-back slum in Balsall Heath, at the time one of the worst areas of Birmingham. But still better, as far as my dad was concerned, than living with his wife's parents.

Having acquired his house, all my dad had to do then was work for seven days a week from seven in the morning till seven at night. (His lucky number, he once told me, was seven.) As for my mother, she had it easy. All she had to do was raise four children, a dog and a cat in a house with no heating except for an open fire, and no hot water, only a single cold tap and a sink. We did have a toilet, however. It was outside and we shared it with two other families, who took a relaxed approach to both hygiene and aiming. My mother not only coped with all this but, as soon as all of her children were at school, got herself a part-time job.

My parents – what a pair of slackers.

Whenever my thoughts turn to my childhood, it is almost always to the house in Balsall Heath. I rarely, if ever, think about my grandparents' house, in Castle Lane, Olton, a suburb of Birmingham. I was only four when we moved there, six when we left, so I have few memories of that time. But I do have some, and was surprised one morning to wake and find them flooding back. I remembered the house, the garden, the shops nearby, walking to the station with my mother to meet her father on his way home from work. This bout of nostalgia was not only unusual. It was unusually acute. I felt a sudden longing to go to Olton and see it all again. Normally, that would have been the end of it. I'd have suppressed the desire and done something else. Such as go to the pub. But now, it occurred to me, all I had to do was put my bicycle on a train and in a short while I could do as much wallowing in nostalgia as I liked. If nothing else, it might be an interesting ride.

*

Olton station seems virtually unchanged since I'd last seen it, over forty years before. The platforms are still clean and litter-free, still decorated with wooden tubs full of plants and flowers. It is a bright and sunny day. The air smells fresh and new. It's hard to believe that grubby, noisy Birmingham is less than ten miles away.

I wheel my bike out of the station and start cycling, and, as I do, I find myself splitting into two separate parts, possessing the same soul but occupying different bodies – my present body and my childhood body. As the wheels turn, I travel through time as well as space.

I cycle past the first school I ever attended, Ulverley Primary, and see my mother, discussing my future with the school's head teacher. My five-year-old self, more concerned with the present day (and not finding it a good one), is wailing bitterly in the corridor outside, pressing himself against the cold, unyielding wall. A teacher appears and tells him to 'Stop making that noise this instant', and he does so, knowing instinctively that his life has changed, changed for ever, and not for the better.

I cycle on, following the route of the 127 bus, the first bus I was allowed to travel on alone. Only as far as the post office, my mother had told me, and that was an instruction I'd intended to obey, only somehow I'd missed it and travelled on to some strange hinterland beyond. I cycle through that hinterland now, watching my five-year-old self as he walks the long and lonely road that leads back to safety, to the familiar, to the post office; not having the heart to tell him that, although this may be the first journey he's got lost in, it won't be the last.

Then on to my grandparents' house. The low front wall has gone and a garage stands in place of the wooden door that led to a garden in which my grandfather spent hour after weary hour trying to teach me cricket, until I finally connected bat with ball and shattered a greenhouse window, quickly taking care of our cricketing relationship. At the front of the house is the bay window behind which my brother and I would sit while waiting for the 127 bus to pass, its bright red body occasionally graced with a black roof. 'Black Top' we would shout as the bus went by. This was 1955, when we had to make our own entertainment. We failed.

On the second floor is my former bedroom, in which I would lie awake, night after night, terrified by the picture that hung on the opposite wall, a picture of some horrifying man with bristling eyebrows and a dark and bushy beard, glaring at me through the glass. Years later I will remember this picture and mention it to my mother. 'Oh yes,' she will blithely say. 'It used to terrify me when I was a child.'

I cycle on through the suburbs that lead to my senior school where, appropriately, my whimsical fantasy ends and I find myself back in the real world. And not just the real world, but the fume-filled horror that is Birmingham's Stratford Road.

\*

In 1838 the city of Birmingham awarded itself the motto 'Forward' and inscribed it on a coat-of-arms. More appropriate wording might have been, 'It can't be done'.

When you were a school leaver in Birmingham in 1966 and you aspired to anything other than working in a factory or a shop or an office, 'It can't be done' would be all that you'd hear. I should know. I heard it all the time.

In 1966 I took a job in a branch of W H Smith.

'When you work for W H Smith,' the twenty-year-old in charge of the paperback department told me proudly, 'you've got a job for life.'

Apart from the chilling horror such a statement generates, how wrong can you get? In those days, W H Smith was a very different kind of shop from what it is today. In those days, you began by working on the shop floor, then becoming the deputy head of a department, such as books or records; then the head of that department, then you moved on to other departments, then you became the assistant manager of a shop, then the actual manager, then a sub-regional manager and so on until you scaled the dizziest of heights and became W H Smith himself. Nowadays all you do is wear a badge and stand by the till.

I lasted nine months at W H Smith before leaving, my exit prompted not just by the stultifying mundanity of the work, nor by the awful prospect of it being 'a job for life', but by encountering a man who might justifiably lay claim to the title 'comic genius'.

From the moment I sat in the back row of the Grand Theatre, Wolverhampton, in a seat furthest from the stage, and watched Spike Milligan strut his comedy stuff seemingly miles and miles below me, everything in my life changed, changed for ever, and changed for the better.

Spike was performing in a play, *The Bed Sitting Room*, co-written by him and John Antrobus. The play was set in London, nine months after the Third World War ('which, under a Conservative administration was the shortest world war on record'). I can't remember why I decided to go and see it, but I'm glad that I did, for from where I sat I could see not only Spike Milligan and the other diminutive figures on stage, but also the people who filled the rest of the auditorium. And every time Spike said something they found funny, their laughter caused their heads and bodies to bend towards him. Which, to me, looked very much like bowing.

After years of indifferent schooling and the prospect of a life that held no promise of anything that interested or excited me, I finally knew what I wanted to be: someone that people bowed down to.

I became obsessed by Spike and his play.

*The Bed Sitting Room* toured the Midlands and so did I. When it finally came to Birmingham I went to see it in the company of two friends. After the show they headed for the pub, me for the stage door. 'I'm going to speak with Spike,' I told them.

'Why bother?' they advised me. 'It can't be done.'

Half an hour later, my friends came out of the pub and saw me, still outside the stage door, talking with Spike.

I had read Spike's novel *Puckoon* and was singing its praises. 'Give me your name and address,' Spike said, 'And I'll send you some more of my books.'

I told him that I had no paper; I had no pen. Spike pointed to a chip paper lying in the gutter. 'There's a piece of paper,' he said. Then he reached into his top pocket, 'And here's a pen.'

I hadn't expected to receive any of Spike's books, and I didn't. But that didn't matter. Spending a few minutes in his company was more than enough for me. Plus the fact that, while we talked, he cracked a couple of jokes – jokes he had invented on the spot, jokes for my ears and mine alone.

That was in July. Five months later, I received a Christmas card. It came in a handwritten envelope and was signed 'To John Dowie From Spike (Milligan)'.

It's all very well wanting to become the next Spike Milligan – but where do you start? And how do you pay the rent while you're doing it? The answer to the second question came first. I was on a bus when a poster in the window of a dingy building caught my eye: 'Part time cleaner wanted'. The job required someone to work from 9 a.m. till lunchtime. Those hours suited my purposes perfectly. I could earn my rent in the morning then spend the rest of the day writing. Or, as it turned out, sleeping. I presented myself for an interview, got the job, and by the beginning of the following week was busily mopping a toilet in which, at frequent intervals, different men would ask the same hilarious question: 'Is this where the big knobs hang out?'

The toilet I was mopping belonged to British Relay, a firm that not only supplied television sets to various shops scattered around Birmingham, but also repaired them when they broke down, which they did annoyingly often.

In those days, a television set was not just an unpredictable object likely to break down for no apparent reason (rather like the people who appear on it today). A television set was also expensive. So much so that most people preferred to rent, rather than buy one. And that was just the standard black and white model. The colour sets, that were just beginning to come onto the market, were even more expensive and even more likely to break down. They were also in high demand.

During lunch breaks I would sometimes be asked to work an extra hour and deal with the telephone. 'And if any shop managers ring up wanting colour sets,' said Trevor, my boss, 'We've only had twenty come in and we can't give out more than two sets per branch. Got it?'

Then he would go away and the phone would start to ring.

'Colour sets?' I'd say to the panic-stricken branch manager on the end of the line. 'Sorry. I can't allow you more than two.'

'Two?' said each and every one of them. 'I've got orders for thirty. I've had customers who've been waiting *weeks*.'

'Sorry,' I'd answer. 'Two is the limit.'

'Let me speak to Trevor.'

'Trevor's gone to lunch.'

'So who are you?'

'I'm the cleaner.'

*

As to *where* you became the next Spike Milligan – I made my start at the Midlands Arts Centre in Birmingham. Some friends and I put together a show of sketches, poems and songs, helped in this by the Arts Centre's theatre director, David Gordon, a small, camp man who later became one of my closest small, camp friends.

The Midlands Arts Centre is situated in Birmingham's Cannon Hill Park. Every year the park held its Tulip Festival, which, as the years went by, became less and less about the tulips and more and more about the funfair that came with it. During the festival, the Arts Centre was roped off and guarded. This did not deter David who, returning to his theatre a little tipsily from the pub, simply hopped over the rope, causing a security guard to have a go at him.

Security guard: 'Where do you think you're going?'

David: 'Don't be a cunt, love. I work here.'

Security guard: 'Don't you call me love.'

It was thanks to David Gordon that I performed my very first gig.

An Asian Community Group was promoting an evening of entertainment in a cinema in Birmingham. They had contacted David to see if any non-Asian acts would be interested in performing. The only act that David knew about was me, so I went along.

The cinema was packed. I watched from backstage as the Asian equivalent of George Formby had the audience rolling – almost literally – in the aisles. He was strumming an Asian version of a ukulele, singing what was obviously a comic song and stopping every now and then to throw in some comic remark that had his audience howling. And I had to follow him.

I had a monologue prepared, a rhyming effort with the opening lines 'Have you seen my bird/I've lost my little bird/this morning he flew off into the sky'. To give the monologue more impact and to make it more visually interesting, I performed it while holding an empty birdcage.

My comedy has always contained a strong theatrical element.

I wasn't expecting much of a reaction from the audience, particularly because in my snobbish, middle-class, white person's way I didn't expect them to understand the subtle nuances of my humour. But I was happily surprised. They actually laughed. Not in any of the places I expected them to, but they did laugh. And a laugh is a laugh. I got through it and got off.

The only way out of the cinema was through the central aisle. As I reached the top of the stairs, a member of the audience reached out, tapped me on the shoulder and said, 'I hope you find your parrot, mate.'

Then I was out into the midnight streets of Birmingham where my post-performance euphoria was swiftly replaced by fear. This was a Saturday night in the late Sixties, and the streets of Birmingham would be full of aggressive young men with close-cropped hair, whose traditional way of spending a Saturday night was to seek out other young men, ones with shoulder-length hair, against whom they would vigorously defend themselves.

It was clearly my responsibility to provide the entertainment that the young men with close-cropped hair were hoping to find. All I had to do was walk from the city centre through the dimly lit streets that led to my home, and soon entire gangs of them would appear. And then the entertainment would begin.

Except it didn't. I made it home, unharmed, with no bones broken and no blood spilt. I couldn't understand why. Only later did it occur to me that any young men with close-cropped hair who saw me walking home would not have believed their eyes. 'Some Sort of Mirage' would have been their only conclusion. Not only was an effete-looking man with long hair walking through dimly lit streets in the middle of the night, but he was also carrying a birdcage. Weirder still, an empty birdcage.

*

In 1969, David Gordon left the Arts Centre and so did I. Two years before, a man called Jim Haynes had opened the Drury Lane Arts Lab in London, with the intention of providing 'a centre for the experimental arts; a community of creative young people in complete control of their physical and social environment; and to provide a realistic alternative to the commercialised arts'. In other words, a place to take shedloads of drugs and have sex.

Unsurprisingly, this idea proved popular with many young people. More arts labs were formed up and down the country, most of them dying out pretty quickly, but one that didn't was Birmingham Arts Lab, whose founders did not subscribe to the philosophy 'It can't be done'.

The Arts Lab was based in a run-down building about a mile from Birmingham City Centre. I made many appearances there, at one time sharing a bill with the jazz guitarist Davey Graham, at another appearing before the screening of a Marx Brothers film. (For a while I had, but sadly lost, a poster that read 'John Dowie & The Marx Brothers in Animal Crackers'.)

It was a good place to hang out. There was beer in the pub next door and marijuana everywhere, both of which were new to me, but not for long. Underground comics were being written, drawn and published; posters designed and printed; film and theatre shown on a regular basis. There were modern dance performances, which I enjoyed, and modern music concerts that escaped my comprehension. I went to one and watched a musician scrape his violin bow across his music stand, totally failing to understand (a) why he did that, and (b) why nobody threw bricks at his head until he stopped.

On the other side of Birmingham was Moseley Village, similar, in many ways, to New York's Greenwich Village. The main difference was that in the late 1950s and early 1960s, while Greenwich Village had the beat poetry of Alan Ginsberg and Jack Kerouac, a thriving jazz scene, comedians such as Lenny Bruce and Lord Buckley and folk musicians such as Bob Dylan and Joan Baez, in Moseley Village we had a pub.

The Fighting Cocks had a small upstairs room in which were held evenings of acoustic music, poetry, theatre, rock, and performances by people like myself. Except there were no people like myself.

Over the next two years, performances at the Arts Lab, the Fighting Cocks, other Birmingham venues and the occasional visit to a folk club, a fringe theatre or a college meant that I was slowly acquiring writing and performing experience. But not enough. I was performing sporadically but the comedy muscle needs constant flexing. I not only needed to do more gigs, I needed to do a run of them. The only way of doing that, in 1971, was by going up to Edinburgh and performing on the Festival fringe. All I needed was the money to book the hall and pay for the advertising, my travel and my accommodation. Luckily, the Festival was nowhere near being the comedy Mecca it would later become, so the costs were relatively cheap. But still beyond the pay of a part-time cleaner. So I supplemented my cleaning wages by getting a second job, collecting newspapers from the early morning train that brought them from London to Birmingham, sorting them out, then packing them onto vans. There was no public transport in Birmingham at three o'clock in the morning, so I had to borrow my brother's bicycle to cycle to work. I would have used mine but I'd given it away to a rag-and-bone man.

After three months of two jobs and very little sleep I managed to raise the money I needed – about £500. I took myself to Edinburgh, performed every day for three weeks, returned to Birmingham with a vastly improved act, got myself an Arts Council Grant and, I'm happy to tell you, haven't done a day's work since.

# CHAPTER TWO
## Hythe – Diss – Cornwall

Many stories begin when the hero or the heroine enters a new reality and their lives are changed for ever. It might be Alice falling down a rabbit hole, Mole abandoning his spring cleaning and heading for the river, or Lucy stepping through a wardrobe. My new bike didn't lead me into Wonderland or Narnia or happy encounters with toads and badgers. But it did take me to a Sussex graveyard where I woke up just before dawn with my underpants on my head.

But first I spent more time cycling in and around London. I discovered routes that didn't mean taking your life in your hands every time you ventured out. I also discovered Sustrans, a brilliant organisation with a terrible name (it's short for SUStainable TRANSport. I mean, come on). Sustrans create cycling and walking routes using old railway tracks, canal towpaths, green areas and seldom-used roads. They also publish maps of these routes, maps that are simple and easy to understand, which came as a relief to me. Having been advised to get hold of Ordnance Survey maps, I did so, and failed to make any sense of them whatsoever. All I could see were meaningless swirls, meaningless lines and meaningless hieroglyphics. I decided that I didn't need your fancy, complicated OS maps. Your plain, down-to-earth Sustrans maps are good enough for me. Or so I thought, as I set about planning my first major cycling trip.

Dr Syn, alias the Scarecrow, had been a hero of mine since I was a boy. A mild-mannered parson by day, he became the fearsome, supernatural Scarecrow by night, much like the Batman, another of my boyhood heroes, whose adoption of a mild-mannered identity to disguise his true appearance was a comfort to me and to people like me – nerdy, mild-mannered geeks who were regularly beaten up by bigger boys. Luckily, this eventually stopped. Not until we were in our thirties, but it did stop.

Dr Syn's adventures took place on Romney Marsh in Kent. They were written by Russell Thorndike, brother of the actress Dame Sybil, and inspired by a night spent in the Ship Inn, Dymchurch, in Romney Marsh. The Ship Inn, I discovered was not only still there but also open for business. A Sustrans route ran through Romney Marsh and I had a birthday coming up. Birthday treat and bicycle ride in one perfect package, I thought, demonstrating once again the triumph of hope over experience. I had organised a birthday treat for myself the previous year and it hadn't turned out well. Not well at all.

It was my fiftieth birthday. And I chose to celebrate it by sitting, flanked by my two small sons, staring at a horse's bottom.

It had seemed a good idea at the time, as bad ideas always do. How to celebrate this supposed milestone? Hire a gypsy caravan and go off with my kids. Of course. Fantastic. Would that some kindly soul had taken me outside and shot me then. This is positive proof that the older you get the more addled your brains become.

I'd forgotten that horses are big. I'd forgotten that horses come fully equipped with hooves and teeth and a bottom. And a horse's bottom is a fierce and terrible thing. I had expected it to empty itself occasionally. What I hadn't expected was that the horse would then use its tail to flick the contents of its bottom up through the air and into my face. And always *my* face. Never the faces of either of my sons, who were sitting beside me, trying to suppress their laughter and making a very poor job of it.

'What will you do if it bolts?' was the common question. A better one would have been: 'What will you do if it stands stock-still and refuses to move?' Which it did. About ten minutes into the journey.

Let me tell you something about horses. When you want to make a horse move, the following do not work: shouting, pulling, pleading, praying, and bursting into tears. Bursting into tears does not sway a horse in the slightest. What you have to do to make a horse move, I soon learned, is to whack its bottom with a stick. Which cheered me up. For a bit. But then we reached the campsite.

Now, I'm a city boy, me, from Birmingham, which is about as city as you can get. My idea of a quiet time in the country is listening to *The Archers*. When I'd heard the word 'campsite', I had visions of a place with buildings, containing things such as showers and toilets and Chinese takeaways. I hadn't expected an empty field.

But let's make the most of this, I thought, as we entered our field. This is idyllic. Grass for the horse to roam in and graze on, a stream running through for the horse to drink from; meanwhile, we can have supper at the picnic table so thoughtfully provided. Which we did. Well, nearly. I made supper. I placed the supper on the picnic table. And then the horse wandered up and ate it.

At least the horse experience had some laughs in it, if only for the horse. Before that my kids and I had been to Blackpool together, which provided no laughs for anyone at all.

'Miles and miles of golden sand', Blackpool declares about itself, as though this were something to be proud of. We went to look at the 'miles and miles of golden sand'. Never before have I seen two faces that so clearly expressed the phrase 'So what?' I mean, what are they supposed to do with all this sand?

'Sit on it,' I explain. 'Make sand castles . . . er . . .'

'Can we go home now?'

'No.'

'Why not?'

'Because we're here for a holiday.'

'Why?'

'Because Blackpool has miles and miles of golden sand.'

A pause to digest this information. Then a longer pause. Then:

'Can we go home now?'

Things might have been better if they hadn't just returned from a holiday with their mother in Disney World, Florida.

On our second day, we were walking the Blackpool streets in the face of a freezing gale hitting us direct from somewhere like Iceland. Now seemed the perfect time to wind up my children 'So,' I said, 'which is the better place for a holiday? Disney World, Florida? Or Blackpool, England?'

The youngest spoke first. 'Well, actually, Dad, we prefer Disney World, Florida.'

'Why?'

The older boy decided to help his brother. 'It's like this, you see, Dad,' he said, employing the I-am-talking-to-an-idiot tone of voice, which he has had to use for almost the whole of his life. 'In Disney World, Florida, you can be walking along and you can meet Mickey Mouse.'

'Or Goofy,' added the younger.

'I see,' I said.

We turned a corner. And there was Sooty.

Sooty was standing outside a theatre, handing out leaflets for his show. OK, the Sooty suit was looking a bit frayed. OK, he had cigarette burns in his fur. OK, he was clutching a can of lager and swaying a bit. And swearing. But it was definitely Sooty.

'There you are,' I said. 'Anything you could possibly want from Disney World, Florida, is also available to us, here in the north of England. Why not see if we can find ourselves a chip shop somewhere and celebrate. What do you say?' My sons said nothing. They looked at me in a pitiful, helpless sort of way. We left Blackpool an hour later.

*

Perhaps I thought, having survived both Blackpool and the horse experience, that organising a simple bicycle trip to Romney Marsh was within my capabilities. I was wrong.

I'd studied my Sustrans map and saw that I could take a train to Folkestone and cycle from there to the nearest town, Hythe, before reaching Romney Marsh itself. But why not take a train to Hythe? I thought. The only drawback seemed to be that, according to my map, no railway line ran to Hythe. This made no sense to me. Hythe is no less important than Folkestone, I reasoned. I couldn't believe that the people of Hythe could just sit there, at home in Hythe, knowing that their Folkestone neighbours had a railway station while they didn't. Perhaps, I thought, there *is* a railway line leading to Hythe but whoever drew the map either couldn't be bothered to put it in, or forgot. So, I checked with National Rail Enquiries and, sure enough, I could take a train from London Bridge and, in just over an hour, I would arrive in Hythe. And so I did. Only Hythe in Essex. Not Hythe in Kent.

*

I sit quite happily as the train takes me in the exact opposite direction to the one I want to go in. I don't bat an eyelid as I travel further and further north, through Shenfield and Chelmsford and into Colchester, where I have to change trains. It is only when we arrive in Hythe and I look around for the road that, according to my Sustrans map, leads from the centre of Hythe to Romney Marsh but which doesn't appear to exist, that I finally think: 'Something isn't right here.'

My first response is to blame whoever drew the map. Not only have they failed to include the railway line, and the railway station, but now they've gone and got the whole of Hythe wrong. For God's sake! It is as though I am in a completely different town!

A passing stranger, seeing I'm in difficulties, looks at my map and tells me that I am. My response is to blame him personally. I even say, 'What do you mean – a different town?' as though he'd planned the whole thing. Even I realise that this is not helpful. Not knowing what else to do, I go back to Hythe station (how I'm beginning to hate the word Hythe) and check the train times. My best bet, I decide, is to take a train to Ipswich, where I can buy some OS maps and work out where to go next.

I get to Ipswich, find a shop, buy some maps and, as I feared, they make no sense to me whatsoever. But they have to. I don't want to celebrate my birthday in Ipswich. If I can't stay at the Ship Inn, Dymchurch, I need to find somewhere nice nearby. I stare at my maps. By concentrating hard, and not letting all the swirls, lines and hieroglyphics throw me, I work out that I can travel by train to Diss, a small town just outside Norfolk. Maybe I'll find something there.

In Dante's Inferno there is, spelt slightly differently, another Dis, the sixth circle of Hell, described as 'a great plain of woe and cruel torment' where 'such dire laments issue forth as come only from those who are truly wretched, suffering and forever lost', which is more or less how the rest of my day goes.

For a start, I can't find Diss. To reach Diss you turn right out of the station. I turn left and very soon find myself in the middle of nowhere. I decide the best thing to do is carry on and hope for the best, a decision that accomplishes nothing except to lead me further and further into mile after mile of empty road, punctuated by signposts promising villages not too far ahead, which all turn out to be exactly the same. Rather than timbered country inns with crackling log fires and busty barmaids serving foaming pints of wallop, all I ever find are three or four houses with the curtains drawn and the lights off. And that's it.

It's close to midnight when I see the lights of a pub, standing at the top of one of the few hills in Norfolk. My thighs are leaden by now but I summon what strength I can, forcing myself up the hill to arrive just in time to see the lights go off. A churchyard bell tolls midnight. 'Happy birthday,' I think to myself with barely a trace of bitterness and wonder where the hell I am going to sleep.

The graveyard seems the logical answer. I push my bike through the churchyard gate and go inside, leaning my bike against a handy tombstone before lying on the dry, springy grass against a sheltering wall. This may not be too bad, I think. It's a warm night. The skies are clear. I have no blanket, not even a raincoat, but I do have a foolproof way of making sure I stay warm throughout the night.

'Heat escapes from the top of the head,' my mother had

told me, more often than I care to remember, and for reasons that I've never understood. That being the case, all I have to do is cover my head and I will remain warm all night, surely? I have no hat but luckily I do have a spare pair of underpants in my saddlebag.

With me, to think is to act. I take out the underpants, place them upon my head, and lie down. I am exhausted. Sleep is all I want. Sleep and the hope that I am up and gone before the church opens in the morning. The last thing I want to do is explain to some bewildered country vicar why I'm lying in his graveyard with my underpants on my head.

Mercifully, sleep comes. Mercilessly, it leaves. One hour later I am wide awake with freezing bones and chattering teeth. I tear my underpants from my head and curse my mother. And not for the first time. Not knowing what else to do, I decide to get on my bike and move on. Ten minutes later I see – oh joy! – an allotment. Now all I need is an unlocked shed where I can shelter from the cold and get some sleep.

The first shed has been padlocked by some sadistic swine with absolutely no fellow feeling for helpless cyclists with nowhere to sleep. But the second is not only unlocked but also filled with garden netting, which make a rudimentary mattress and a welcoming blanket.

And the miracles do not stop there. Having slept through the rest of the night I set off the following morning and pass a public toilet which is not only open, but has hot running water and paper towels. I wash myself. I dry myself. I clean my teeth. I get back on my bike and cycle, in a day of increasing sunshine, through roads that lead me, downhill all the way, to the pretty coastal village of Orford where the King's Head Inn charges me £11.50 for The Best Fucking Breakfast I Have Ever Had.

I was enjoying my bike rides and wanted to do more. The only thing standing in my way was my insistence on cycling around the countryside with a blindfold on. Which is what my inability to learn how to read a map amounted to. I'd buy maps, look at them, then put them away, deciding I'd learn how to read them tomorrow. (I'm the kind of man who's never known the meaning of the word 'procrastinate' and never got round to looking it up.) That I was eventually able to read a map – a proper map, with swirls, lines and hieroglyphics – was due to a trip to Cornwall, a hill too steep to climb, and the apparent death of a writer.

*

The writer in question was Colin Wilson, who achieved literary success in the 1950s with the publication of his book *The Outsider*. He was appearing at a literary festival in St Germans, Cornwall, and so was I. I had wangled an invitation to read some of my poems and was due to follow him. I stood at the side of the stage as Colin Wilson gave his lecture.

You'd think, having written a book with the title *The Outsider*, he might have had a bit more knowledge about what things are like when you go outside. But no. Given the weather, his choice of clothing was shockingly inappropriate. It was a blisteringly hot day and Colin Wilson had chosen to wear a thick, woollen polo-neck sweater, a blazer, heavy-looking trousers and, as the only concession to the near-tropical heat, a panama hat.

I waited in the wings for his lecture to end. The subject of his talk was 'Unified Consciousness' and his conclusion was that it would, if ever achieved, be somewhat similar to the World Wide Web. Having made this point he then sat in a chair placed close to the microphone and appeared to die. His head slumped forward and he sat, unmoving. This was of no interest to the compere who simply shuffled past his immobile form to get to the microphone and introduce me.

During my days as a stand-up comedian, I performed in many inappropriate places, from bars full of boozed-up students to rooms full of spitting punks, but even I draw the line at performing comic verse while standing next to the corpse of a recently deceased giant of post-war English literature. Say what you like about me, but I have standards. I made frantic signals to the compere, pointing at Colin Wilson's apparently dead body. The compere broke off from whatever he was saying and began issuing requests for the 'St John Ambulance People to come to the stage'. They came. Two of them. Bowing and waving modestly to the crowd, before doing one of the worst things you can possibly do to a man who has just fainted, which was to push his head between his legs, thus preventing further blood flow to the brain and helping to bring about a possible seizure. Luckily, an ambulance arrived before they killed him, and Colin Wilson was stretchered onto it, still unconscious, and carried away. All of this being quite happily watched by the literary audience, until a Festival organiser requested the crowd to 'Please give Mr Wilson some privacy, I mean, for God's sake, people, come on', and they drifted away.

Given they were meant to be my audience also, I now had the afternoon free. Thank you, Colin. I had brought my bicycle with me, along with an OS map of Cornwall, even though I still couldn't read it. I decided that, as the heat was so intense, a ride to the Cornish coast would be a sensible thing to do.

I set off, and very soon found myself travelling down a hill of terrifying steepness. And not only a hill of terrifying steepness, but one that was seemingly endless. One thing was clear: assuming I didn't kill myself on the way down, there was no way I'd be able to cycle back up.

I reached the bottom. I had no idea where I was and there wasn't a signpost to be seen. Consulting my map was my only option. After many puzzling minutes, I managed to work out that I could cycle along a road that led to a ferry, which in turn led to a road on which was a railway station where I could take a train that would take me back to St Germans.

Cycling on I realised, with mounting excitement and total astonishment, that all of my map-reading predictions were coming true. I was so excited by this revelation that I decided to carry on for another five miles to nearby Plymouth and the railway station there. A decision somewhat spoiled by a drunken man lurching out in front of me, causing me to jam on my brakes, narrowly miss him, and nearly fall. 'I'm just trying to get home,' he shouted as I cycled away, before adding, 'you wanker.'

Wanker? I thought. Me? A wanker? Well, yes. Possibly, but at least a wanker who can read a map.

# CHAPTER THREE
## *Getting on My Bloody Bicycle*

It was 2003 and I'd had enough. I'd stopped performing stand-up comedy nearly a decade before. Since then, I had written scripts for the theatre, for the radio and for television. I had directed other performers. I had written and performed shows for children. But one by one these activities had withered away and died, leaving me with no aspirations of any kind.

This is not to say that my life and my days were empty. Far from it. I had a rigorous, some might say punishing schedule, which I stuck to with almost fanatical devotion.

It went like this: wake with crippling hangover, drag aching bones to shop, buy Alka-Seltzer, go home, attempt breakfast, push breakfast away, light first cigarette, smoke that, start on second, struggle with crossword, look at clock, nearly lunchtime, remember pub down the road is selling Guinness at £2.50 a pint and if people like me don't give pubs like these the support they deserve how on earth can they hope to make any kind of a living, reach for hat and coat . . .

Three or four pints of Guinness would take me through the afternoon and a couple of bottles of red wine would take care of the rest of day, until sleep, and then the next morning and all the weary work to do again.

Clearly, I couldn't go on like this. I needed to get hold of some dope.

Nothing to do. That was my problem. The only thing that gave me any pleasure was riding my bicycle.

Let us look at the silly man, sitting in his isolation, surrounded by his bottles of wine and his beer and his cigarettes, saying to himself over and over again, 'What shall I do? All I enjoy is riding my bicycle.

'What shall I do? All I enjoy is riding my bicycle.

'What shall I do? All I enjoy is riding my bicycle.'

How many times did the silly man sit there thinking this thought before the voice of reason intruded?

'GET ON YOUR BLOODY BICYCLE THEN.

'Instead of sitting there nursing a hangover,' the voice of reason continued, 'you could be riding your bike around Europe.'

'I can't afford to—'

'Rent out your flat,' the voice interrupted. 'That would pay for the travelling and the campsites . . . '

'Campsites?' I said. 'I can't stay on campsites! Campsites mean camping and camping means freezing cold nights and wet miserable mornings and fires that won't start and food that won't cook and insects and discomfort and waking up at dawn to discover a madman with a meat axe has got into your tent . . . '

So, what finally tipped the balance in the campsite's favour?

My drug dealer.

Perhaps when you read the words 'drug dealer' you imagine a dimly lit smoke-filled room and some cadaverous, croaking figure sitting on a low sofa at a table festooned with cigarette papers, ash trays, a burning joss stick and a mountain of black sticky resin. And you would be right. That is pretty much every drug dealer I have known and loved throughout the years. My present drug dealer, however, was different. For a start, he was a health fanatic. He wouldn't allow cigarette smoke in his flat, defending his marijuana inhalation as being an extension of his yogic breathing. He refused to deal non-organic drugs of any kind and only sold high-quality home-grown grass. He also rode a bicycle.

'Cycling and camping?' he said to me, once I'd mentioned my plans. 'It's the best thing in the world, man. When you want a cup of tea,' he continued, 'you stop and you make yourself a cup of tea.

It's Zen, man. It's Living in the Now.'

'Hmm,' I thought. 'Living in the Now . . . sounds interesting. I might try it for a couple of weeks and see how it goes.'

'Also,' he continued, 'how many hotels can you smoke in nowadays?'

And that was, more or less, the argument that swayed me. The final point was the question of my diet. I'm vegetarian. And if I relied on being fed by restaurants and cafes in meat-mad Europe, I thought, then the chances were I'd starve to death. Europe's idea of a vegetarian meal is ham.

*

If you're contemplating becoming vegetarian yourself, then here's a phrase you'd better get used to. You'll be hearing it a lot. 'Carrots scream when they're pulled out of the ground.' I have been told this more times than I have eaten carrots.

I stopped eating meat in 1966 and did so for three reasons: I didn't like the concept. I didn't like the look of it. I didn't like the taste. A simple issue of dietary preference, you'd have thought, but no. It was as though I'd declared war on the entire human race.

It's vegetarians who have the reputation for proselytising, for prissily criticising other people's dietary habits. That being so, why is it that every time I find myself at a dinner party there's always some meat eater prepared to have a go at me? All I ever want to do is keep my head down and enjoy my bowl of gravel on a bed of lettuce. Instead I get: 'So, why don't you eat meat, then?'

Once that question is answered (never to anyone's satisfaction), out come the predictable inanities: First, I'm informed about the vocal abilities of root vegetables. Then the conversation goes like this.

'So, what would you do if you found yourself trapped on a desert island and there was nothing to eat except meat?'

'Well, what would you do if you found yourself trapped on a desert island and there was nothing to eat except a dead baby?'

'Now you're being ridiculous.'

I decided to follow the advice of my drug dealer and the needs of my vegetarian stomach. I would buy a tent, I would camp and I would cook for myself. But first, I needed to rent out my flat. But before I did that, I had to do something about its contents. Most notably the three or four hundred vinyl albums that filled a good part of it.

*

I have a friend, Martin, who deals in second-hand records. I rang him. 'I need to get rid of my vinyl,' I told him.

'Oh,' said Martin. 'Why?'

'Because I'm renting out my flat. Would you move into a flat that had my record collection in it?'

'No,' said Martin. 'I've seen your record collection. I wouldn't want to live with it.'

He wasn't joking. The bulk of my collection consisted of Marc Bolan's early whimsical bleating and bootleg recordings of Bob Dylan trying to get his car started, the wheezing of his dead engine sounding not unlike his singing. Also, most of my records were in appalling condition: bent, scratched and covered in ash and candle-wax droppings – which is what will happen to vinyl when it's been listened to in a dimly lit smoke-filled room by some cadaverous, croaking figure sitting on a low sofa at a table festooned with cigarette papers, ash trays, a burning joss stick and a mountain of black sticky resin.

At first I thought that getting rid of the vinyl I'd been collecting since the Sixties would be a wrench. But, with each cardboard box that Martin packed, carted off and placed in his car, I felt a lightening of the spirit. It lightened even more when he paid me. Several hundred quid. I was astonished. I'd been hoping for a tenner.

'There's actually a record in your collection that's worth something,' Martin told me. 'And I bet you can't guess what it is.'

I couldn't.

'"Elephant Rider,"' Martin informed me. 'By the Hush.'

I'd bought 'Elephant Rider' by the Hush for 10p when I came across it in a junk shop somewhere, but only because I'd liked the title. I'd played it once, hadn't liked it, put it in my singles box and forgotten all about it. It turned out that while the A-side was worth approximately somewhat less than 10p, the B-side, 'Grey', a Sixties psychedelic classic, was worth, Martin told me, a lot more.

'How much more?' I asked him.

'Enough to cart away this worthless load of junk you call a record collection,' he said, and was gone before I could reopen negotiations.

*

Selling my vinyl collection had proved not only profitable, but also spiritually pleasing, as though I were shedding old skin. This made it easier to contemplate the next step – getting rid of my comic books.

One of the benefits of living in a slum in Birmingham was that, opposite the terrace in which we lived, was a shop that not only sold second-hand comics, but also had an arrangement – take two comics back and your third comic was free. It seemed like a good deal at the time. How I regret it now.

One of the many comics I bought in that shop was the one in which Spider-Man made his first appearance, a comic now worth about $40,000. I also bought the very first comic featuring The Fantastic Four, now worth $35,000.

Nowadays, when comic-book collectors buy comics, they wrap them in a plastic bag, tape the bag shut, place the comics upright in an acid-free cardboard box then store them in a cool, dark place away from direct sunlight. But I didn't do that. I took mine back to the shop and swapped them for copies of *Archie and Jughead*.

After a while, I did start saving my comics. I didn't wrap them in plastic or store them in airtight containers, but I did put them in boxes so I could take them out and read them whenever I felt like. Which was often. Consequently my comics had yellowing pages, faded colours and rust stains from the staples that held the dog-eared pages together. All the things that devalue comic books, mine had in abundance. I also had about five hundred of them, including Batman editions going back to the mid-1950s, so I was hoping for a good price for them, despite their condition.

I'd arranged for two separate comic-book dealers to come and look my collection over. The first picked up a battered comic, flipped open the pages, stuck his nose inside and inhaled deeply.

'Know what I call that smell?' he asked me. 'I call that *love.*'

And then he began rooting through my collection, beginning with my Batman comics, flipping with increasing speed back through the late Fifties, when the publishers, desperate for story ideas, had Batman undergo one dramatic transformation after another: Merman Batman ('Yes, Robin! I've become a human fish!'); Rainbow Batman ('I must, Robin – I must wear a different-coloured Batman costume each night!'); Phantom Batman, Rip Van Batman, Invisible Batman, Negative Batman, faster and faster his fingers flew before coming to a sudden and disappointed halt.

'No Zebra Batman,' he sighed. 'Thought you might have a copy. Can't find it anywhere.'

I felt bad. Very bad. What sort of comic book collector doesn't own a copy of Zebra Batman?

The second dealer came. He was older and overweight with bad breath and slippered feet. With him was his assistant, a Thing dressed in black with greasy hair flopping over his pale face, looking like something out of H. P. Lovecraft. He said nothing, but simply crouched over my collection, like a vampire bat, checking the price of each comic against a trade paperback. Neither of them opened one of my comic books and inhaled the aroma. Instead, the older one lit a cigarette and told me, 'Anything he wants, he gets. I make sure of that.'

He then offered me £400 for my collection. The first dealer had offered me £350. I knew to whom I wanted my collection to go. But I'd promised myself I'd sell to the highest bidder.

But then again, did I want to sell my collection to someone who'd wrap them in a protective plastic bag, tape the bag shut, place the comics upright in an acid-free cardboard box then store them in a cool, dark place away from direct sunlight never to see the light of day, much less be read? Let alone loved?

I accepted the smaller offer. The first dealer came, paid me, boxed up all my comics, placed them in the back of his car then turned to me and said, 'If ever you want to . . . '

'What?' I said. 'Come and visit them? I don't think so. They're yours now.'

He drove off and I went inside. I was fifty quid down but happy. My comics had gone to a good home. They had gone to the right guy.

Later, I told this story to a friend who works in the comic-book world. He knew both dealers and told me that I couldn't have got it more wrong. The second dealer paid his bills on time and could be trusted. The first dealer never paid his bills on time and couldn't be trusted at all.

I'd sold my precious comics to the wrong guy. But for the right reasons.

*

When the promoters of cycling list the many benefits that riding a bike will bring, they're almost always to do with health. You'll be as fit as someone ten years younger, they say; you'll be less stressed, your sense of balance and co-ordination will improve, your joints and muscles will be stronger and more efficient. They hardly ever mention the important stuff – i.e., buy a bike and you get to do some serious shopping.

Once you've bought your bike, you buy a pair of panniers. Then you cycle to your nearest bike shop and fill them. And not just with mechanical stuff – pumps and tools and lights and bells. There's also clothing – helmets, gloves, leg warmers, arm warmers, jerseys, socks, shorts, sweat-wicking shirts – the list goes on and on. But be careful of what goes on that list. Particularly if you're a man. There are some things – some items of clothing – that no man should even consider owning.

I'm talking, obviously, about tight-fitting cycling shorts.

I bought a pair once. By mistake. Thinking they were the baggy sort of shorts, I bought them, took them home, tried them on in front of a mirror, then realised, with horror, that these shorts were, in fact, tight; and they clung. I'm not saying they had a great deal to cling to, but what they did cling to was mine, and private, and I preferred to keep it that way. This, I realised, as I stared at my ghastly reflection, was why Superman wore his underpants on the outside. He'd clearly had enough of people looking him up and down and saying, 'I didn't know you were Jewish.'

But no matter how much shopping you can do as a cyclist, it's nothing compared to what you can buy if you're going camping. Tents, obviously. Also sleeping bags, sleeping mats, bivouacs, dry bags, stuff sacks, hand torches, head torches, gas-burning stoves, paraffin-burning stoves, stoves burning a variety of fuels – and this is just the basic stuff. There's also the more esoteric offerings – a four-slice folding toaster rack, for example, which I really, *really* want, despite such problems as what about the butter? How will I cope with butter in blazing hot sunshine on a campsite covered in grass? Or a lightweight, plastic, six-egg storage box, which I also really, *really* want despite the fact that I don't eat eggs. Then there's the *REALLY* good stuff – by which I mean the Swiss Army penknife, starting with the basic three-blade version (knife, corkscrew, bottle-opener) before finishing with the magnificent, 32-blade version which can do everything you could possibly imagine, from opening a can of beans to stripping wire, scaling fish, sawing through metal, magnifying objects, picking your teeth, filing your nails and tweezing out your nostril hairs. The only thing it can't do is remove stones from a horse's hoof, but that's only because there's no such blade and there never has been.

I was happily poring over catalogues full of this kind of stuff when the friend who was staying with me came into the room, looked over my shoulder, and said, 'Isn't it a bit early for camping porn?'

Another day ruined.

He later made up for his heartless remark by giving me a gift – a guide to the museums and art galleries of Europe. I threw it away.

Many people, before setting off on a cycling trip, would have been grateful for such a book. They'd have an itinerary – places to visit, places to stay, trains to catch. Not me. As far as I'm concerned, 'trains to catch' is a contradiction in terms. Nor did I want to visit museums or look at art. I wasn't on a voyage of self-discovery. I wasn't hoping to find myself, or even somebody like me. I didn't want to make new friends; I didn't even want to keep the old ones.

I was only interested in three things: solitude, silence and scenery.

I decided to take a leaf out of Spike Milligan's book. Before beginning one of his stage shows – an impromptu performance of poems, sketches and songs – Spike would always say, 'This show has not been rehearsed. Therefore, it can't go wrong.'

My trip would be the same.

I decided to begin my journey in Holland, choosing the Netherlands for three reasons: it was flat; most Dutch people spoke English; and it wasn't far away if I had a nervous breakdown. My flat had been emptied of all possessions and rented out. My world had been reduced to a bike, four bags and a tent.

It was time for me to live in it.

# CHAPTER FOUR
## Holland

I first went to Holland in 1973. I was performing a solo tour, not only my first abroad but my first anywhere. I had hair then, which came down to my shoulders, and I carried a big red suitcase full of comedy props. The suitcase had a broken lock, which meant it was held together by tightly knotted string. Neither my hair nor my suitcase presented any problems when I left England. They did when I came back. To the untrained eye, I was just some long-haired hippy with a crap suitcase. But to HM Revenue and Customs, I was, clearly, an international drug smuggler.

'Open the suitcase as quick as you can,' a customs official informed me, 'Or I'll cut the string.'

I did as he asked, and watched as he made his way through the contents of my case, amusing his colleagues by taking out my comedy props and using them to perform comedy routines of his own. He picked up the rubber monkey head with the movable mouth, which I used in my ventriloquist sketch, and did about three minutes with it. Which was two minutes more than I ever did.

He was starting to get on my nerves.

Finally, he reached the bottom of the suitcase. And there was the large, brown paper parcel he'd been hoping to find. He placed it on the counter in front of him and said, 'Would you mind telling me what's in this parcel?'

At that time, I used to perform a comedy song during which I'd toss a paper cup full of glitter over my head. A paper cup full of glitter did not come cheap in Birmingham in the early 1970s.

But it did in Amsterdam, where I found a shop that sold a kilo of it at an astonishingly low price. This was what was in the parcel. As I told him.

'It's a kilo of glitter,' I said.

'Oh?' he said. 'A kilo of glitter, eh? Well, let's just have a look at this kilo of glitter, shall we?' He then opened the packet and poured the contents onto the counter.

This is what happens when you pour a kilo of glitter onto a counter: a portion of the glitter, about 10 per cent, will happily fall onto the counter. The rest of it likes to take the more scenic route, floating up into the air before coming down and gently settling on the head, shoulders, ears and eyebrows of whoever did the pouring. And once it's settled, it likes to stay there.

There was a long, horrified silence as the customs official registered what he had done to himself. The silence was broken by one of his colleagues who informed him that he now resembled 'a member of the homosexual community engaged in the act of fornication'.

But not in those words.

*

There is no sign of the customs official when I arrive in Harwich over three decades later. Presumably, he's still in hiding, trying to get the glitter out of his hair. I'd arrived in plenty of time to catch the ferry, so before boarding I decide to look for a shop to buy emergency food (having no idea what might be available on the boat) and, more important, emergency wine (i.e., cheap). I spot the lights of a supermarket and I'm happily cycling towards it when I see something that makes me come to a halt. It's the last thing I want to see. My stomach turns to water. I am afraid. Very afraid. Standing between me and the supermarket, silhouetted in the light of an overhead streetlamp, is a gang of teenage girls.

I've only been afraid of teenage girls three times in my life.

When I was younger than them.

When I was the same age as them.

And ever since.

'It's my grandad,' a particularly vicious fourteen-year-old informs her cackling friends as I speed by, trying to appear both nonchalant and deaf. Then into the shop where I buy wine, bread, cheese and fruit before cycling back through more unwanted abuse ('Hey, Grandad – are you lost?') and boarding the ferry.

There are two restaurants on board: the European version – where sophisticated diners are served elegant meals on sparkling bone china. And the British section, where semi-human scum stuff their tattooed faces with chips and beer. Pop music plays in both venues. I take myself to my cabin, shut my door, drink my wine, eat my food and spend the rest of the night trying to think of phrases that might intimidate a gang of teenage girls.

There aren't any.

Next morning, I wheel my bike onto Dutch soil. Holland is wearing a bright blue sky with a matching yellow sun and looks as though she'd been designed by Noddy. It is nearly nine o'clock and everyone in Holland, it seems, is cycling through the pale sunshine, either on their way to school or to work. A granny cycles by. A toddler sits behind her, another is perched in a basket hanging from the handlebars, and, to complete the set, she has a baby on her lap. This, I decide, is the perfect place to be. Holland is where bicycles go when they die.

I see a sign to Delft, and arbitrarily set off in that direction, cycling happily on a traffic-free path. This is cycling at its best. There is no animosity here. Car drivers have their precious roads to themselves and can race up and down them at their ridiculous speeds, slamming into each other as much as they like. Cyclists, meanwhile, enjoy a quieter, slower journey, sharing the path not only with other cyclists, but with parents pushing prams, people in mobility scooters and people in wheelchairs, all coexisting in friendliness and harmony. Unless you pat them on the head when you cycle past. They hate that.

In Delft, I find a VVV – the tourist office. There I buy maps before finding a campsite not far from the centre of town. It is a joy. Not only is it on the edge of a nature reserve, with canals and rivers that merge into small lakes; not only is there an animal compound with pigs, goats and chickens; not only are there ducks and herons and bullfrogs everywhere; but there's also a pub. Things can't get any better than this, I think. But I am wrong. They can. The pub opens at nine in the morning and doesn't close till midnight.

I spend three happy days in Delft, before I leave and begin cycling and camping my way across Holland. I am having a pleasant time, until I make a massive mistake and cycle to Rotterdam.

The cycle track runs alongside a motorway which is still being built, so it's dust, filth and noise all the way there – the journey made worse by the fact that Rotterdam is rebuilding large parts of itself, so it's dust, filth and noise when I get there. This would have annoyed me less if Rotterdam hadn't been rebuilding itself the last time I was there, over thirty years ago.

The people of Rotterdam are clearly addicted to dust, filth and noise. It's got into their systems and now they can't live without it. They spend all their waking hours tearing down Rotterdam, building it back up, then tearing it down again, all the while blaming the whole thing on the Germans and the Second World War. Having spent a noisy, dust and filth-filled hour in Rotterdam, I decide I can't take any more, and leave. From then on, I spend my time in the quieter parts of Holland, cycling from one tiny campsite to another, campsites in which I am, quite often, the only camper.

My fear, before setting off on this trip, was that I wouldn't enjoy camping and I'd end up spending money, which I couldn't afford to spend, on hotels and the like. Instead, I found myself loving the whole camping experience.

My day has a pattern. I arrive at a campsite, usually in the late afternoon. I unload my gear and inflate my mattress. While less experienced campers might faff around with bicycle pumps and such, old hands like me simply unroll our self-inflating Thermarest mattress and let it inflate itself. This gives us time to erect our one-poled tent, which, having only one pole, is easy to do and takes little or no time at all. And hardly any swearing.

Having erected our tents, we then unpack our lightweight aluminium Trangia stoves, fuelled by methylated spirits, which are available everywhere, unlike gas canisters, which change shape and size every time you cross a border. Plus the meths will come in handy if the wine runs out. We chop an onion, fry it in oil, add vegetables, lentils, a stock cube and water, sit back and let it simmer. This takes about three-quarters of an hour, which gives us plenty of time to sit and drink wine, while watching the sunset through our brand-new and wonderful varifocal spectacles.

Before I bought my brand-new and wonderful varifocal spectacles, I had two pairs of ordinary spectacles: one for looking at things close up and one for looking at things far away. Which meant that looking at road signs and maps was not fun. I'd look at my map, swap spectacles, look at the road sign, then forget what the map had said, swap spectacles, look at the map, then forget what the road sign had said, swap spectacles, and so the day went on in a never-ending short-sighted circle. No longer. Now, with my brand-new and wonderful varifocal spectacles, if I want to look at something, I just look at it. Sometimes I look at things whether I need to or not. Just for the hell of it.

Sunset, wine and supper done, I climb into my tent, where I might read by the light of my head torch, which not only illuminates everything but leaves my hands free for more useful things: such as finding my head torch. It also has an amber shield, which fills my tent with a cosy glow, similar to the glow that I bathe in, knowing that all this comfort is only possible because of the practical choices I've made; choices based on careful, painstaking research. Or as some people call it, 'camping porn'. When I've finished reading, I hang my head torch from the handy hook dangling above me, place my precious spectacles into one of the tiny pockets in each corner of my tent, then drift off into a smug, self-satisfied sleep.

I wake at sunrise or, as some people mistakenly call it, cockcrow. How the cock got the credit for being the first bird up is beyond me. The cock is the laziest bird in the business. All the other birds have had their early worm and are contemplating lunch before the cock has even cleared its throat. I seriously doubt that 'cock-a-doodle-doo' has anything to do with the sun coming up at all. I don't speak the Language of Birds, obviously, but given the cock's basic function my feeling is that 'cock-a-doodle-doo' translates as 'Time to fuck a hen.'

I'm squeamish. And I'd thought that anything to do with the creepy-crawly section of society would mean my camping trip would be ruined. But no. Creepy-crawly creatures didn't bother me at all. Perhaps because I was entering their world, rather than they entering mine. I can't complain about insects in a field when it's their field to begin with. A field that they have to share with many forms of life.

Once, camping at the side of a river, I wake at three o'clock in the morning to the sound of two Dutch women having a row. I can't understand what they could possibly be having a row about, why they have to have it outside my tent, and why they keep using the same words over and over again. This goes on for about half an hour before I realise that they're geese.

After a day of unrelenting wind and rain I arrive in Gouda, damp and dispirited. Luckily, there is a street market in progress, with almost every stall selling waterproof cycling gear. I buy a pair of waterproof trousers for a very cheap €12.50. No sooner have I handed over the money than it stops raining.

I set up my tent in a campsite about ten miles west of the town, before heading for the showers. On the way, I pass a man, mid-seventies perhaps, sitting outside his caravan.

'Goedenavond,' he says.

'Goedenavond,' I reply in my faultless Dutch.

'Ah,' he says. 'You are English?'

We start chatting. He asks me if I'm on my way to Amsterdam. I tell him that I am. He then gets very excited and tells me I must visit the Flower Auction, some sort of Dutch activity that doesn't interest me at all. He gives me a leaflet. As I leave, I wave the leaflet and say, 'Dank u wel.'

He is astonished. 'You know "dank u wel"?'

'Alstublieft,' I said airily. He looks as though he is going to faint. It turns out that he is a retired businessman who has spent a lot of his life working with the English and not one of them could be bothered to learn even a phrase as simple as 'please' or 'thank you'. They couldn't even pronounce his name. 'Houffman is my name,' he says, sorrowfully. 'You know what they call me?'

'No.'

'Hoffman.'

The unfeeling arrogant English bastards.

Later, I'm outside the laundry room, waiting for my clothes to dry and looking over my maps. Houffman appears, sees my maps and is astonished all over again. 'These are the best maps you can buy,' he says. Then he notices that one of my maps is of Zeeland – now he is *really* excited.

'You are going here also?'

I tell him I hope to cycle around as much of Holland as I can. He looks as though he's about to burst into tears. Another of Houffman's experiences of the English is that if they come to Holland at all they make straight for Amsterdam and that's it. He then spends half an hour showing me routes I might enjoy and campsites I should stay on.

'And Zeeland you must visit,' he says. 'Is very beautiful there.'

I tell him I am thinking of visiting Utrecht and his face falls. In practically a whisper he tells me that, 'Utrecht . . . it is not so nice.' I am torn between taking his advice or ignoring it and going there anyway – after all, how bad can it be? I mean – I've been to Liverpool.

Next morning I leave and cycle past Houffman, standing outside his caravan. He sees me as I pass.

'Goodbye,' he shouts and waves.

I wave back. 'Goodbye, Hoffman.'

\*

Still undecided as to which way to go, I stop at the library in Gouda to check my emails and find this in my inbox:

Hi there, this is a dutch musician from the band palinckx (www.palinckx.nl), improvised rock/theater is our thing, we are looking for a copy of your song "british tourist" because we are considering to perform it, me and our drummer remember the song well but the rest of the band does not know it, I would like to be able to play it for the band so they can decide whether we work with it or not, if we do so we naturally respect your author rights, we are a small band, doing lots of live performances, the odds of our version of your song to be pressed and released are very small but if this happens you will be properly notified. If this is all right with you, please mail back an mp3 or send a cd to

Arjen de Vreede
Utrecht, Holland.

'British Tourist' was released by Virgin Records in 1977. It was meant to satirise the stupidity of racism by vilifying the Dutch, the most inoffensive race imaginable. The only consequence of the release of my record was that I was vilified for being a racist. I was hoping the song would become a one-hit wonder. Instead, it was a miss and no wonder. It did nothing in England but it was a very different story in Holland, where it was frequently played on Dutch radio to a lot of extremely angry Dutch people, who all reacted by raising an eyebrow a quarter of a centimetre and saying, 'This we think is not so very amusing.'

BRITISH TOURIST
I'm a British Tourist and I'm very, very rude.
I hate the stinking foreigners, hate their stinking food.
I don't like French or Germans or care for Belgians much.
But most of all – worst of all – I hate the Dutch.
The Dutch! The Dutch! I hate them more than dogs.
They live in little windmills and mince about in clogs.
They don't have any manners. They don't say 'thanks' or 'please'.
All they eat is tulips and stinking Gouda cheese.

I'm a British Tourist with a countenance severe.
I love to strike the foreign type and box each poxy ear.

But there's one dirty dago that I cannot bear to touch –
The slimy crawling stench-appalling snotty grotty Dutch.
The Dutch are mad – their fingers stick in dykes.
They use the wrong side of the road and ride around
on bikes.
They don't have any manners. They don't have any brains.
There's only one race worse than them – and that's the
fucking Danes.

I wrote the song while touring Holland with my 'comedy/rock' band, the Big Girls Blouse. I'd formed the band, in Birmingham, following three years of performing solo. I'd started writing little comedy songs on the piano and felt the need to flesh out these songs with a musical accompaniment. I also felt like having some company.

A friend of mine, a musician, told me about the time he acquired his first electric guitar. He unpacked everything, took the lead, plugged one end into the guitar, the other end into the amplifier, switched on the amplifier, struck his first chord and thought, 'Everybody in the world should have one of these.' Similarly, everybody in the world should be in a band. Apart from the constant pleasure of working with musicians (particularly on songs you have written yourself), there is a camaraderie in working and playing together, particularly while touring, that's rarely found anywhere else. After a while, of course, camaraderie turns to conflict, friendship turns to friction, and the band breaks up due to 'irreconcilable musical differences', i.e., hating the sight of each other.

The act I performed with my band combined allegedly humorous lyrics with an ear-splitting din. The ear-splitting din was provided by the lead guitarist, who, like all lead guitarists, possessed an instrument with a volume control that only worked one way. Which wasn't down. At one particular sound check, despite the protestations of everybody within earshot, he told us that his guitar was 'not too loud it just sounds too loud'.

My band didn't last very long, but during its short life played some of the popular rock venues of the time, such as Dingwalls, the Marquee, the Greyhound in Fulham and the Hope & Anchor in Islington. But the tour of Holland marked the beginning of the end of my time with the Big Girls Blouse. Not one member of the band could understand why I chose to tour there. 'They won't understand a word we're saying,' they said. 'They speak better English than we do,' I replied. Then we stopped at a bar and ordered five beers. The waiter brought us four boiled eggs.

\*

Staggered by the coincidence of receiving an email from a man in Holland while actually in Holland, I reply to Arjen's email, telling him I am on my way to Utrecht, so why don't we get together and I'll teach you the song myself?

I find a campsite not far from Utrecht, then cycle off to a bar in the city centre, where Arjen and I have arranged to meet. I thought I'd be meeting a young punk who plays in a band in front of twenty people a night. Instead, I meet a man in his thirties who exudes the kind of quiet, calm confidence that comes from being in one of the biggest bands in Europe. A band, he tells me, that is also popular in South America and the USA. Not so popular in England he adds, but then, 'It is such a small market that it is somewhat hard to care.'

Arjen drives us to his studio in the Utrecht suburbs. I'm nervous. I haven't touched a piano in over ten years and I was rubbish when I did. I needn't have worried. Arjen is a real musician and he wants to get the job done, so he puts his energy into accomplishing that, rather than criticise someone else's cack-handed playing. We complete our demo of 'British Tourist' in about four takes and with hardly any swearing. Afterwards, we leave his lovely little studio, and share a pot of tea in his equally lovely kitchen.

'Well,' said Arjen, 'we got it done.'

Indeed we had. The recording we made surfaced a few years later, performed not by one of the biggest bands in Europe, alas, but by one of Arjen's more obscure projects and was, if anything, even more hideous than the original. I haven't seen Arjen since, and it's highly unlikely that I ever will; but I'll always remember our afternoon together with fondness and affection, as though it had been spent with an old and valued friend. Which it had.

*

Neither Utrecht nor the camping site close by has it in their power to persuade me to stay. (Houffman was right.) I decide to head towards Amsterdam, after which I'll go south towards Belgium and France. I find a campsite in nearby Haarlem, choosing to stay there, rather than Amsterdam itself.

I'd been taken to Haarlem in 1973, to meet the parents of a Dutch girl I'd met. Her parents lived in a part of Haarlem that was quaint, old-fashioned and charming. As were they. Her father wore a tweed suit with plus fours. Her mother dressed in twin-set and pearls. Iced lemonade was served on the lawn. Once it was established that I spoke no Dutch, they spoke only in English, which I thought was an act of astonishing politeness. At one point, the conversation turned to me and I was asked what it was that I did. I haltingly tried to explain the nature of my comedy performances. 'Ah yes,' said the mother knowledgably, then added what I took to be, 'Bunteruntjaff.'

'I'm sorry,' I said, 'I really don't know any Dutch at all.'

'No, no,' she repeated. 'Bunteruntjaff.'

Seeing my blank look, she excused herself, went indoors, returned with a large English–Dutch dictionary, opened it and pointed to the phrase, 'banter and chaff.'

'Ah yes,' I said. 'Banter and chaff. Yes. That is exactly what I do.'

*

Her daughter had appeared backstage, boyfriend in tow, following a gig during my first visit to Holland. I'd been invited to tour the

45

Netherlands by De Lantaren, a theatre/arts centre in Rotterdam that provided minimal fees and even more minimal accommodation – a mattress on the floor of the coffee bar. Which closed at 2 a.m. This was an improvement on the accommodation I'd been offered at the Melkweg – none at all. I was in the dressing room after the show, wondering where I was going to sleep that night, when she appeared (with her boyfriend) and offered me accommodation.

But it wasn't just accommodation she was offering – or, rather, it was. The finest accommodation a woman could offer a twenty-three-year-old virgin who had never been accommodated before. Sex was going to happen, I was certain. My certainty helped by the fact that, while her boyfriend went to the bar to buy drinks, I put my hand up her skirt. What inspired such a bold step I have no idea, but it wasn't rejected. 'Later,' was her comment. The future looked promising. We went back to her flat, me wondering what was going to happen with regard to her boyfriend, while at the same time knowing what was *not* going to happen with regard to her boyfriend. I didn't know the Dutch for 'threesome' and I didn't intend to find out. I needn't have worried. The only thing he wanted from me was to act as his audience. Not to any sexual activity. Though that would have been grisly enough, the reality was even worse. He was a mime artist. And he wanted me to watch him doing it. Too late to run screaming into the night. Too late to wonder if this was the hideous price I had to pay for hoping to access his girlfriend's vagina.

And so the long night began. I sat, a fatuous, insincere smile plastered to my face, as he escaped from a glass box, walked into the wind, climbed a ladder, flew a kite, became the kite, then a bird, laid an egg, became the chicken poking its way out of the egg, grew into a hen, clucked its way around a farmyard, then was picked, up, slaughtered and eaten by a man who found himself trapped inside a glass box . . . the whole thing only lasting for hours and hours and hours.

Next morning he left for work and I went to work also, as a result gaining (a) manhood, (b) a girlfriend, (c) a place to stay, and (d) a bitter enemy in the shape of a dumped mime artist.

I don't know what it is about Dutch mime artists but when their girlfriends dump them in preference to English comedians, they get all talkative. And in English. 'I will never let an Englishman into my house ever again,' he sobbed, waving a small knife in my direction, while his ex-girlfriend helpfully pointed out that actually it wasn't his house and the two Dutch policemen called by a neighbour told him not to be a tit.

I also gained something else – something that failed to manifest itself until I returned to England a fortnight later. 'It's gonorrhoea,' said the cheerful male nurse at the Birmingham Clap Clinic, who, for the purposes of taking a smear test, had just inserted a metal object into the end of my astonished penis. The gonorrhoea diagnosis came as news to me. I'd assumed that the discharge from my penis, the ferocious burning whenever I urinated and the fact that my testicles had swollen to the size of tennis balls were merely symptoms of the tremendous amount of sex I'd been having.

'No, it's gonorrhoea all right,' the cheerful nurse continued. 'Or as it's known in Holland, Mime Artist's Revenge.'

\*

Memories of my Dutch girlfriend cause me to become all nostalgic. It's an itch that must be scratched, which is apt. I take a train from Haarlem to Amsterdam, and spend a happy day wandering around, hoping to find something that will trigger a memory.

Isn't that where we—?

No.

Wasn't that the place where—?

No.

Later, tired but happy, I take the train back to Haarlem. I've made many visits to Amsterdam over the years but this, I feel intuitively, will be my last. As the train pulls away, I watch Amsterdam recede into the distance, sprawled across the horizon like some old tart lying on a couch, past her prime, her waist thicker, her face more jowly, her breasts now sagging, but still attractive, still sexy, but ageing and fading until, finally, she is gone.

*

I spend a final night in Haarlem, then pack and cycle north to a gorgeous little town, Urk, gorgeous in part because it is blessed with a lighthouse (a lighthouse automatically bestows gorgeousness on wherever its located), followed by a hideous thirty-mile journey south alongside a motorway. I reward myself with a night in a hotel before continuing south through Apeldoorn to Arnhem.

Until then, I have travelled alone. But as I approach Arnhem I find myself with a writer on my back.

When learning of my proposed bike ride, well-meaning friends and relations would ask, 'And will you be writing about your travels?' to which I'd reply, 'I hope not.' In my mid-twenties I'd cured myself of premature ejaculation by singing about it on stage, which is not a method I'd recommend to everybody. Since then I'd been, as we say, exposing myself on stage on a regular basis. One of the purposes of my bike ride was to get away from all that. I wanted to enjoy the journey for what it was and not to treat every event as potential chapters in the All-Engrossing Story of My Life. Having said that, I did take notes. Not the most literary of notes, though, mostly consisting of entries such as 'Cycled to Delft. It was nice.'

This all changes as I cycle into Arnhem, the scene of one of the bloodiest battles of the Second World War, immortalised in the film *A Bridge Too Far*. As I cycle across that very bridge – now renamed the John Frost Bridge, in honour of the army officer who commanded the men who died defending it – the writer appears, settles on my shoulders, and begins whispering unwanted platitudes into my ear: ' . . . it was here that eight thousand gallant men laid down their lives so that . . . '

But it is the following morning, as I cycle to the nearby

Airborne Cemetery in Oosterbeek, where close to two thousand Allied servicemen lie buried, that the writer's voice is at its loudest, its most insistent, and its most unwanted.

'Above the gravel path that leads to the cemetery the sheltering boughs of cathedral-like trees reach towards the solemn skies that cast their dark shadows on the . . . '

Oh do shut up.

I don't know what to expect, still less what my reactions will be, as I open the wooden gate of the cemetery and step inside. I soon find out. I glance down at the first grave to catch my eye, that of a private, 'Aged 18 years'. The same age as my eldest son. It is then that the tears begin to pour down my face.

And continue to pour as I walk through the cemetery grounds, passing grave after grave after grave. All of them the graves of young men.

The field is so small; the graves are so many.

After a while I begin playing a kind of ghoulish game. Can I find a gravestone of someone in their twenties? And, if I do, can I then find a grave of someone in their thirties? The older the person whose grave I seek, the more rare that person becomes.

From time to time I come across gravestones that read simply 'An Officer', the bodies presumably being so badly burned that they could be identified only by insignia. This does not help in the stopping of my tears. Nor does finding the graves with headstones that read, 'Known Only To God'.

My game ends with the discovery of the grave of an NCO – a sergeant. He was in his forties. How old he must have seemed!

In a corner of the cemetery I find a bench and sit and wait for the tears to stop. As I sit, I watch a man mowing the cemetery lawn and, looking around, I notice how beautifully tended everything is, every grave adorned with fresh flowers. I assume this must be the work of whichever Oosterbeek department maintains the cemetery, but no. As I am leaving I happen to glance into a red brick arbour, built, a plaque informs me, by the British and Polish Veterans of 1944. Set into the wall is a memorial stone. It reads:

In lasting gratitude to the people of this neighbourhood
for their loving care of the graves of our comrades
who lie here and in other cemeteries nearby
and to the children who honour them with their flowers.

*

The next morning, cycling towards Nijmegen, I discover that
something has gone wrong with my eyesight. I stop, rub my eyes,
squint, rub them again – but the problem remains. The road
ahead of me, rather than being flat and straight and disappearing
in a point towards the horizon, is somehow rising high above me,
as though reaching towards the sky, defying all sense of logic and
perspective. Then I realise what is happening. I'm looking at a hill.
Then another hill. And then another. As I cycle on, I realise that
I'm surrounded by dozens of them.

It is as though whichever god created Holland decided to take
all the hills available and shove them all into one place – Nijmegen.
And now I have to cycle them all. I start struggling up the first,
using muscles in my thighs that hadn't just been off work for a
day or two; they'd retired, packed their bags and gone to live at
the seaside. Several hills later, I stop and look at my map. There's
a campsite about halfway down one of three roads ahead of me.
Characteristically, I choose the wrong road. The scenery flies past
in a quickening and terrifying blur. This is one hell of a hill. I
reach the bottom and recheck my map. I should have passed the
campsite halfway down. There had been no sign of it. And now
it's turning dark, there's the hint of rain in the air, and the last
thing I feel like doing is turning around and climbing back up a
bloody big hill, especially when I'm out of practice in climbing
bloody big hills.

I'm studying my map in the hope of finding a second campsite
when there is a shimmering blur of colour and a racing cyclist
appears from nowhere, coming to a halt beside me and jabbering
in Dutch. I look at him blankly. He has turned away, and is sitting
astride his bike, staring into the distance. I try my usual, 'Spreekt

u Engels?' Without moving or even turning his head, he says, 'I think you will find that I am capable of communicating in English perfectly well', then goes back to staring at nothing and saying less. Given that he'd spoken first, I'd have thought he could have made more of an effort. We sit in an uneasy silence, which I break by saying, 'I'm trying to find this campsite', and showing him my map. He glances at it briefly, then says, 'You are on the wrong road.' He looks away again. My heart sinks. He then says, 'I have a spare bed that you can use. It is only eighty kilometres from here.'

Only eighty kilometres? As far as I'm concerned, eighty kilometres is a three-day ride. And even if it isn't, even if by some immense stretch of the imagination I am able to complete eighty kilometres in whatever is left of the day, how is this cycling relationship going to work? It's not. Not unless he's the kind of bloke who likes to take some old dog for a walk, having to stop every three yards and wait for the poor wheezing beast to catch up, all the while thinking, 'It would be an act of kindness to have him put down.'

And then I begin to wonder what exactly this man's motive might be. Is this some kind of homosexual encounter? Is this bronzed super-fit muscle-bound glamour boy trying to get off with me? Well, of course he is. He's Dutch. They have no morals. Or scruples. Or taste. These are the thoughts that run through my head as we slowly cycle on, both of us with sinking hearts, until, from out of the gloom, a wonderful and welcoming sign appears: 'Camping 300 metres'. Neither of us has to face an impossible journey. We are both relieved. We both pretend not to be. I stammer out some thanks for his generous offer. He says, 'It is ok. I hope to see you again.' And then, with a wave of his hand, he is gone, vanishing as quickly as he came. I turn and enter the campsite, grateful beyond all measure for his offer. And even more grateful that I didn't have to take him up on it.

Next morning I cycle into Nijmegen itself. There isn't much there of interest to me except for one thing: the fairly unique and wholly magnificent geek treat that is the Velorama Nationaal Fietsmuseum, which, in English, translates as (you may be surprised to hear) The National Bicycle Museum. Three storeys of . . . well, bikes, basically. Beginning with a working model from a design by Leonardo da Vinci, there are three floors of bikes of every description, from steel-rimmed wooden boneshakers of the past to the modern-day low-slung recumbents so enjoyed by cyclists who like to end their lives flattened beneath the wheels of lorries.

On the second floor of the museum is the only representation of a human being in the entire building. It's a portrait of James Starley, 'the father of the bicycle'.

*

James Starley was born in 1831. At the age of nine he invented a device, using the rib of an umbrella and a piece of wood, to trap rats with. As a teenager, he created a self-rocking baby's cradle, a one-stringed window blind, an adjustable candlestick and a device that allowed ducks to go through a hole in a fence but kept rats and foxes out. He then began mending and improving sewing machines before creating the Penny Farthing, followed by the chain-driven tricycle and perhaps his greatest invention, the Differential Gear, which was to make his name and somebody else's fortune. Among many other inventions, he went on to design a bike for riders who had lost the use of their legs. His final creation, patented in the spring of 1881, was a folding tricycle, marketed as the 'Challenge'. Though whether the challenge was in riding it or folding it, I'm not sure.

His nephew, John Kemp Starley, entered the family business and devised 'the Safety', a bicycle with the then innovative but now standard 26" wheels. John Kemp Starley had a son, John Kemp Starley (imaginative, these inventor types), who married one Florence Ada. She gave birth to two children, John Kemp Starley (there we go again) and Gwendolen Lillian Starley. Gwendolen Lillian Starley married Wilfred Hirst, a journalist from Skipton in Yorkshire. They had two children, Michael and Barbara. Barbara Hirst married my father, Harry Dowie, and that's where I come in.

When I was little, my mother would take my brother, my two sisters and me to a park in the nearby town of Coventry, where we would look at the statue there of James Starley. In Birmingham, in the 1950s, this was considered a day out.

My mother also possessed strange beliefs concerning blood and its genetic properties. When my brother got on a bike for the first time and, in my mother's words, 'just rode it straight away without any training or anything', she ascribed that to 'the Starley blood'.

That same blood runs through my veins and I fell off my newly acquired bike every day, consistently, for the first six weeks. And still do.

However, if James Starley is the acknowledged Father of the Bicycle, then, it follows, I must be the Great Great Grand Nephew's Cousin Once Removed of the Bicycle. Or something. Either way, whatever I am, the bloke who charges entrance fees for the Velorama Nationaal Fietsmuseum would not give me a refund on the strength of it. The bastard.

*

I thought I'd take the advice of my good friend Houffman and cycle to Zeeland, where a ferry in Vlissingen would carry my bike and me over the water to Belgium. What Houffman had failed to tell me was that the wind would be in my face for the entire journey. Also, there would be virtually non-stop rain. I get as far as the tiny town of Goes, where I find a cheap and cheerful campsite run by a cheerful farmer and the only man in Holland to ever make me laugh.

I address him with my usual 'Spreekt u Engels?' He replies with the usual, 'A little bit.' As we walk into his office, I bang my head on the doorframe. He makes sympathetic noises. I rub my head saying, 'Don't worry. There's nothing in it.' To which he replies, 'Well, I didn't want to be the one to say that.'

I set up my tent. No sooner have I finished than the heavens open. And stay open for the next three days.

For some reason, this doesn't bother me. In one of the infrequent dry spells I cycle into Goes, enjoy some quiet bars and do some shopping. I find a second-hand bookshop, which, surprisingly (Goes being quite small and out of the way), has a large selection of English books. I splash out on a relatively expensive Iris Murdoch hardback (€7.50), take it back to the campsite and read it while the rain comes down. The next day, during another dry spell, I return to Goes and swap Iris for a Doris Lessing and a Margaret Atwood. Back to the campsite for more rain and reading followed by another dry spell in which I trade Doris and Margaret for a Muriel (Spark) and a David Lodge (nice, finally, to have another man in the tent).

After four days the weather clears up and I clear off. Fine to begin with, the weather soon turns nasty again, and I find myself battling against what I confidently believe is called a howling gale. It is like cycling into a wet and windy wall. It's as though the whole of Holland is some sort of boisterous dad, his hand pressed hard against his child's forehead, roaring, 'Try and hit me! Go on! Try and hit me!' i.e., the kind of father every child hates, After about four gruelling hours of this, I reach a little town, Kapelle, see a railway station and think, 'Fuck it. I'll take the train.'

There is nobody in the station except for a man mending a broken ticket machine, who tells me that I can buy a ticket on the train. The conductress does not share his opinion. I am liable to pay a €30 fine, she tells me, asking for my address. When I tell her it's in London she does an impressive volte-face and says I can travel for free. Not because she's a big fan of London, or me, but because there's no way she or the train company can enforce the fine. So, Holland is €30 down and me and London are €30 ahead. Lucky us.

I get off the train at Roosendaal, setting off in a vague south-easterly direction, hoping it will take me towards Belgium. It's getting late, but then I come across a campsite, set in the middle of a forest. It's expensive but they have a shop on-site, which will provide me with everything I need for the night, such as food and, more important, wine.

Here's a tip for anyone thinking of camping in a forest – don't get drunk and then, as soon as it's dark, wander off for a walk around the campsite thinking you'll spend a happy few minutes enjoying the birdsong. If you do decide to do this, your drunken foot will stick itself underneath a tree root, your drunken body will try to walk forward, your drunken foot will bring you crashing to the ground, your drunken body will go one way, your drunken ankle another, and you will be in hideous pain for the rest of your drunken night.

Luckily, you can dull the pain with more alcohol.

I go to bed fearing the worst and next morning the worst is what I get. I cannot put any weight on my ankle. Luckily, I can still cycle, so I ride into Roosendaal and the Tourist Office. They look through a phone book, find a local therapist and give him a ring, only to be told that he has broken his arm. This does not bode well. They find another therapist, but there is no appointment available until 3 p.m. Which is a lot better than 'Come back in a week', but still leaves me with five hours to kill and only one ankle to kill them with.

I find the local library, do some emails, cycle to a café near to the therapist, have a crap cheese *tosti*, an ok coffee and not bad frits, and read, writhing in occasional agony as something annoys or exacerbates the pain in my ankle. Such as breathing. Finally three o'clock comes around and I hobble into the therapist's surgery.

I once stepped off a train, missed the platform, and fell down onto the track. Next morning I had a knee the size of a football and a show to do that evening. A sports therapist zapped my knee with something futuristic and not only was I able to walk again but that evening I could perform my show. I was hoping for something similar in Roosendaal. Instead I get a man in tweeds and a bow tie, with a plastic skeleton hanging off a hook in his surgery. He examines my foot, moves it about, then applies a crepe bandage and charges me just under €40. I'm convinced I've been ripped off and that the therapist with the broken arm would have done a better job. But just before I leave, he asks me to walk about. I do. I can walk, and I feel no pain. No pain at all. Which makes me feel like a heel. Appropriately.

Next morning I pack and prepare for my journey into Belgium. I have no idea what to expect when I cross the border, but I have my passport to hand and a collection of receipts from campsites and hotels to prove to the Belgium border guards that I'm not some beatnik bum. More important, I have buried my tiny lump of Dutch hash at the bottom of one of my panniers, next to some cheese. This, I am confident, will baffle and bewilder any Belgian sniffer dogs. A long dull road leads through flat, boring countryside. I'm hungry, can't find any shops, so press on until I reach the nondescript town of Wuustwezel. I call into a supermarket, buy fruit and yogurt and am surprised to find no liquorice for sale. This is unusual. If there is one thing that the people of the Netherlands like, then it's their liquorice. Supermarkets devote whole aisles to it.

Outside the supermarket, I take out my map and try to work out exactly which part of Holland I am in. But I'm not in Holland. I'm in Belgium. And nobody told me! So much for all those border guards and their machine guns and sniffer dogs. The only clue to my having crossed the border into Belgium was that Belgium shops don't sell liquorice.

Which makes the whole passport thing look somewhat redundant, doesn't it?

What is the point of a passport? What purpose does it serve? To prevent acts of terrorism? I don't think so. Are terrorists who are capable of commandeering planes and flying them into New York landmarks somehow unable to forge a passport? Or does every terrorist about to enter a country and do some terrorising apply for a passport, but on the application form, write: 'Occupation: Terrorist'? Why am I unable to leave or return to the country I was born in without a passport? Oh wait. Because I have to pay for it. Now it makes sense.

I cycle further into Belgium, but some sense is telling me that something, somewhere has gone wrong. I stop and check the map. No. Everything seems to be fine. I put the map away. I move off, and, as I do, my front wheel hits the edge of a pothole in the road in front of me. I know immediately, and instinctively, that this is not a good thing. I am right. Two seconds later there is a clunk, clunk, clunk from the front wheel. I look down. Flat tyre.

I'm not a complete idiot. I know that one of the first rules of cycling is 'Always carry a puncture repair kit', and I do. Knowing how to use it is another matter. I do know how to use a pump, though, so I decide to try inflating the tyre. I might have succeeded but the valve is missing. How the valve went missing, I have no idea. With no other option, I start pushing. My only hope is finding a Belgian bike shop. A fellow cyclist comes along and offers me the use of his pump. I thank him, then point out the missing valve. He tuts and shakes his head. I ask him if he knows where the nearest bike shop is. He says, 'Zundert – but is five kilometres.'

I say, 'Oh well . . . '

He says, 'It is the game.'

I say, 'Thank you for stopping.'

He says, 'No problem.'

And then he leaves. I check the whereabouts of Zundert on my map. It is then I discover that, rather than heading into Belgium, I have been cycling back into Holland. I am furious. Will this Dutch bitch never let me go? With no other choice I decide to push on, finally seeing a sign – Zundert, 3K. Not far now, I think. Then, moments later, to my happy astonishment I come upon a bike shop! I go inside. They do repairs! A man comes out to examine my bike. I point to the absent valve. He says, 'I replace,' removes the front wheel, takes it away, and comes back a few minutes later, my wheel restored. He replaces my wheel, we shake hands and he tells me to settle up with his boss.

His boss is standing at the till. He gives me the bill. I don't have enough cash and, it turns out, his till won't accept my card. I offer to leave my luggage behind as security while I cycle to a bank. The boss, speaking little or no English, hands me over to a mad cyclist in Lycra who is hanging around the shop, as mad cyclists in Lycra tend to do. He directs me to the nearest bank, saying, 'You cycle for five kilometres then opposite a church you will find a bank.' He then adds the dreaded words 'You can't miss it' which, historically, means, 'You will miss it.'

He then says, 'Also, a short way past the church is a cemetery. Here is buried the brother of Vincent Van Gogh. It is a very peaceful place. You should visit it.'

'Oh, I will,' I say, having no intention of doing any such thing. If it was Vincent Van Gogh himself and I had time to kill I might have contemplated visiting his grave. Maybe. But his brother? Do me a favour. Nobody is interested in anything to do with a famous person's brother. If you don't believe me, ask James Belushi.

I cycle into town, find a bank, get the money, cycle back. The Lycra-clad cyclist is still there. 'Very peaceful,' I tell him, 'A very beautiful grave.' As I am paying my bill, the mechanic comes over, and he, the owner, the Lycra man and I have a pleasant little chat. I tell them what I've been up to and what I'm hoping to do next. They look pleased to have helped me on my way. I leave to three cheerful cries of 'Tot ziens.'

Later, I was to discover that if I'd continued pushing my bike into Belgium in the hope of finding a bike shop, I'd have been pushing it for at least thirty kilometres. While I had been berating Holland and calling her a bitch, she, like some faithful dog dragging its abusive master away from the edge of a cliff, had been hauling me away from the Belgium border and back to the last bike shop in Holland. The very last.

Dank u wel, Nederland! Dank u wel!

# CHAPTER FIVE
## Belgium – France – Dubai – France

If ever you want to feel as though you're being booted up the backside every fifteen seconds, then buy a bike and ride it around Belgium.

For some reason, the Belgians have decided that what their country needs to liven it up is a thin strip of tar laid across their roads every hundred yards. But this is no ordinary strip of tar. No ordinary strip of tar would send a shock wave up the wheel, through the bicycle frame, into the saddle post then straight up the bottom of whichever poor bastard is sitting in the saddle.

Kerthunk.

Kerthunk.

Kerthunk.

Every fifteen seconds.

Kerthunk.

Kerthunk.

Kerthunk.

And when you've had enough of that, you can cycle into one of Belgium's many attractive towns and villages, all of which are paved with cobblestones. Small wonder then, as I cycle through Belgium, that I am increasingly and genuinely convinced that my teeth are falling out.

Or at least the middle teeth in the bottom row. I wake each night, half asleep, with the uneasy feeling that my teeth have shifted out of position. And then, still half-asleep, I hear a clicking noise as my tongue pokes them back into place. Or do I? Am I dreaming all this or is it really happening? I don't know. And I'm worried. Worried I might wake up and find my teeth in my sleeping bag and a hole in my face. This is not good.

*

I had decided to begin my Belgium travels with a visit to Antwerp, where I hoped to buy maps and guidebooks. I get there by following road signs that take me along a long, flat and tedious road, through a hideous industrial section, before arriving in Antwerp itself. My first impression? This is Rotterdam with a frock on. Antwerp, like Rotterdam, is big. Unlike Rotterdam, Antwerp has examples of architecture that others might drool over. But not me. I'm too preoccupied with finding a way out of it. I had bought my maps and decided to head towards Ghent, but no matter which route I take from the centre of Antwerp, I find myself back on a horrible and massive road leading to a horrible and massive roundabout full of horrible and massive lorries. After an hour of this, I give in and head for the railway station. I find it and buy a ticket for Ghent. The train runs alongside the road I was hoping to find. I'm not sorry to have missed it. It's long and flat and tedious. Exactly like the one I came in on.

I spend a few hours wandering around Ghent, one thing quickly becoming clear: the people of Ghent love their cathedrals. There are cathedrals on every corner. Also buskers. I stop briefly to watch two old guys; one is playing a violin, the other an accordion. In different keys. I can't decide whether this is bad busking or Belgian jazz. As they segue from 'My Way' into 'Yesterday', I do the sensible thing and run like fuck. In the town square some sort of performance is taking place. A poet is performing in front of a two-piece band. He's reciting his works in Flemish so I have no idea what he's on about. But it doesn't take me long to work out that he's not very good. He performs like every other bad poet I've ever seen: head down, no eye contact with the audience, body moving out of time to the music, appalling microphone technique – popping every 'p' – and turning his head every time he turns the page so that half of his sentences go missing. Which may not be a bad thing.

As I watch, I am reminded of a poetry group I joined when I was sixteen. Against all sense of rationality and judgement the person running the group suggested we each read aloud our latest work. One of the group, who called himself Zak – I wouldn't mind betting that his parents had christened him something entirely different, such as Kevin or Brian – read a poem that began 'And I fucked her in the park'.

It was the word 'and' that intrigued me. What, I wondered, might have happened before?

'I gave her twenty quid and . . . '

'I killed my mother and . . . '

'I bought myself a rubber sex doll/Only for a lark/I blew her up while on the bus . . . '

I leave the Flemish poet to it and wander off, deciding to treat myself to lunch in a nearby restaurant. It has been raining hard all day. I take off my soaking wet jacket and waterproof overtrousers before I go in and sit at a table, whereupon the waitress comes over and spills a jug of water down my leg.

The next morning, after another night of dental nightmares from which I wake, sweating and fearful, I force myself, appropriately, to bite the bullet and get my teeth looked at. The Tourist Office gives me directions to a dental hospital. I make my way there, lock my bike, enter, and, the moment I do, an elderly woman accosts me in either Dutch, French or Walloon. I don't know which, so I do my 'Spreekt u Engels?' bit. She does. I tell her my story and she snaps into impressive action. First, she informs me that I need to be in an entirely different building. Then, instead of waving vaguely in the appropriate direction and telling me that I can't miss it, she leads me to it herself. Once there, she takes me to the reception desk and interrogates the receptionist on my behalf, before escorting me to the appropriate department where she makes me an appointment for 1.30 p.m. that same day. She makes sure I know exactly where to go and what to do. I presume she is a volunteer helper, filling her days of retirement in a useful and practical manner. One thing is certain: I love her and I want her to be with me always, finding out what I want and making sure I get it. She is what God should be like.

I return to the hospital shortly before 1.30, sign in, then sit in the waiting room, wondering if I'm going to be hanging around all afternoon. But no. I am not in England. Shortly after my arrival I am taken to a room. Moments later the dentist arrives. I tell him my concern. He puts on huge magnifying glasses that look like something out of a 1950s science fiction movie, stares through them at my teeth, gives them a wiggle, then reassures me. Yes, they are loose, and, yes, they will come out, but there's something he can do about it – he can fit a brace linking the loose teeth together. 'Rather like,' he informs me, 'a party of drunken men who keep each other upright by wrapping their arms around each other's shoulders.'

As he fits the brace he informs me, chattily, that he always uses the 'drunken men' analogy when treating the British because 'they seem to understand it so well'.

Newly braced (in both senses of the word) I go back to the campsite, where, as if to compensate for the fact that my teeth have been saved, I discover that my phone has died.

Next day I cycle to Bruges and I'm disappointed. I was hoping to enjoy the company of two Irish gunmen, a pair of manky hookers and a racist dwarf, before remembering that although two Irish gunmen, a pair of manky hookers and a racist dwarf appeared in the film *In Bruges*, they aren't necessarily to be found in Bruges. Hence the disappointment. They are the main reason I'm here. This may also be true of the hordes of tourists that fill every inch of the place. Why are you here? I feel like asking. If it's because of the film – move on. The film is over. If it's because of cathedrals and architecture, then go to Ghent. They have plenty of both and no tourists.

I take my broken phone to a man in a phone shop who looks at it and says, 'It is dead', before selling me another. At €25 it's cheap but texting friends is hard work as the keys are tiny. Luckily this is not a problem, as I have no friends. Heading back to my campsite, I pass a second-hand bookshop, buy some books, and spend a pleasant day reading, only to have it completely ruined when my dead phone comes back to life.

Next day I cycle for about fifty kilometres to Ypres, where I'm told the campsite is closed for refurbishment. What kind of logic is this, I wonder, closing a campsite in the middle of summer? Isn't that what the winter is for? Ypres looked like an interesting place to visit, which I would have liked to do. Instead, I have to cycle another ten kilometres to the next campsite where I'll be way too knackered to cycle back. And too angry. Accordingly, I find myself in the little town of Kemmel, the centre of which is being rebuilt. Every road leading in or out of the town appears to be closed off. You can't get in and you can't get out. Not if you drive. Clearly, this part of Belgium has gone barmy.

I find a campsite. It is vast but only costs a reasonable €10. I shower then mooch into town to find the supermarket is shut. I resign myself to going back to the campsite and making do with whatever foodstuffs I have left in my panniers, but instead I stumble across a splendidly insane restaurant – Het Labyrint Kemmel.

Given that the rest of Kemmel appears to be closed, and closed permanently, I am amazed and thankful that the restaurant is even open. I am even more amazed when I go inside. The place is crammed with countless plaster statues and portraits of Jesus, all displaying the same basic Jesus look: long, beautifully shampooed hair, parted in the middle; blue eyes and an expression that seems to say: 'I know I look gay but I'm not. I'm straight. And a virgin.' As well as Jesus, there are rocking horses scattered about and, behind the bar, a long row of handbags – but not handbags that are in any way special. No. Just handbags. Ordinary handbags. On the walls are collections of clay pipes, plates, lanterns and, in keeping with the Jesus theme, old woodworking tools. There are also toys for children to play with. Sadly, there are no children. Happily, there are no adults; I am eating alone.

Music is being played from behind the bar, but not the usual ubiquitous pop. Instead I listen to a mixture of classical, sacred, folk, and jazz. All of the tunes are either bizarre or beautiful or both, and no tune outstays its welcome. Take note of this, almost every restaurant everywhere else. Looking somewhat shocked at the prospect of a customer, a waiter appears and hands me a menu. Astonishingly, there are several vegetarian options. Several! I order a goat's cheese salad, sauté potatoes and a half-bottle of rosé. The food arrives fifteen minutes later. It is fucking fabulous.

I am now torn. The French border is close. On the other hand, perhaps Belgium has more to offer than being just a bit of land stuck between Holland and France. I decide to cycle to Mons and find out. I'm on my way there, when I call in at a cybercafé and find another email has arrived, making my decision for me. It is from someone I used to know during my time in Birmingham.

Her name was Debbie but everyone called her Dubai, because that's how she pronounced it. The Birmingham accent is an accent I've always hated, but that hadn't stopped me fancying Dubai. And I wasn't alone. Everybody fancied Dubai. She had a look much loved at the time – Sixties Rock Chick Chic, i.e., long blonde hair, the maximum amount of mascara and the minimum amount of skirt. This was an effective look. Hard-core heterosexual women, married for forty years and with six kids, would take one look at Dubai and rapidly rethink their sexual orientation. The only problem with fancying Dubai was her boyfriend, Al the Bastard, a 'man with a van'. Al the Bastard made a living moving students from one bedsit flat to another. He was not only one of the biggest men in Birmingham, but also the one with the shortest temper. A dalliance with Dubai was one thing. Having something heavy dropped on your head – such as a van – was another. Consequently, nobody made any moves in Dubai's direction, certainly not me.

But that was the past and this was the future and who knows what opportunities might be available to me now?

I reply to her message, saying something along the lines of, 'Nice to hear from you,' and am pleased, and excited, when she responds almost immediately, with, 'Are you still in Brum?'

'I'm in France,' I type. 'Where are you?'

'Porto Torres,' comes her reply.

'Which is where?' I type.

'On the coast of Sardinia,' she explains. 'Across the channel from Marseille,' she continues. 'Why not pop in for a visit?' she propounds, at which point my penis pushes my brain aside and announces that it is now in charge of all negotiations and any further decisions.

I sign off, saying I hope to see her in Porto Torres soon. My only problem now is getting there.

## INTERLUDE: DEBBIE/DUBAI

I have to travel from Mons to Marseille where I can take a ferry to Sardinia. This means travelling from the top of France to the bottom. And my penis has decided that this needs to be done as quickly as possible. I cycle into Mons, where I have no time for anything other than a bag of Belgian chips and the chance to admire the way young Belgian boys greet each other with a peck on the cheek. Make this activity compulsory in Britain, I think, and say goodbye to fighting in the street. Then I am off on a seemingly endless journey of cycling, unpacking, camping, packing and cycling again, until I reach Laon, where I hope to take a train to Paris, followed by another to Marseille.

The ticket seller in the Laon station speaks no English but I manage to learn, using my primitive French, that there is only one train to Paris that will also take my bike, and that it leaves at 6.30 a.m. the following day. I book myself a ticket then cycle to a campsite about a half-hour's ride away. All I have to do next morning is get up at 4.30 a.m., pack away all my gear, cycle through dark and unfamiliar streets and arrive in Laon in time to catch the train. This, astonishingly, I manage to do.

In Paris I am told that if I want to take my bike on a train to Marseille, I have to first remove my panniers, then my pannier racks, then turn the handlebars 90 degrees, remove the front wheels and the pedals and put it all into a box. Where I get the box from is another matter; as is the question of how I'll be able to actually carry my bike-in-a-box, my four panniers, my handlebar bag and my tent. And then, somehow, fit it all onto a train.

What I need is a train with a guards van – *un fourgon*. There are no *fourgons* on any of the trains from Paris to Marseille. There is, however, *un fourgon* on the train from Paris to Nice. And in Nice I can take a ferry to Sardinia. So I put myself and my bike on board a train, leaving Paris at 15.20, arriving in Nice about six hours later.

Normally, a train journey of anything over an hour would drive me mad with boredom and impatience. But not this journey. I have been living in a cyclist's world, travelling at a cyclist's pace, and not a fast cyclist at that. Now, sitting in a comfortable seat, protected from the elements, watching scenery fly past at miraculous speed, I am entranced. And remain entranced for the entire journey, which is over in what seems like moments. Alas.

In Nice, I cruise the streets and find a hotel.

The next day is a Sunday and, annoyingly, there are no ferries from Nice to Sardinia. But I can take a train – with the all-important *fourgon* – to Marseille and catch a ferry from there. All I need to do is wait in Nice for another five hours until the train leaves.

Well, there are worse ways of killing time than wandering up and down the promenade in Nice watching the idle rich get skin cancer. I do this before returning to the station in time for the Marseille train. On the platform I look in vain for the *fourgon*. I do find a carriage with a steel door, which is locked. The conductor and two assistants are standing by it, laughing and smoking. I say, '*Bonjour Monsieur. Où est le fourgon?*' The conductor indicates that it is behind the steel door, then turns back to his mates. Assuming there is a problem with the door, I haul my heavily laden bike further along the platform, then up three steps on to the train, before wheeling it down the corridor towards *le fourgon*. Halfway there, I find myself facing a queue of French people, who not only block my passage but stand, gazing at me with interest, as if expecting me to somehow make a bicycle magically vanish. At which point I lose my temper, and, pointing to the *fourgon* bellow, in French, 'I Go There!' Their dumb brains finally grasp the concept that I'm not lugging this bike around as some sort of fashion accessory or good luck charm but I'm trying to get into the carriage that was built for such a purpose and they get out of my way.

The train is packed. Looking for a seat, I put my head into a carriage, which is empty except for the conductor and his two cronies, refusing entry to all others, smoking illegally and laughing at the idea that I should ever find a seat. I refrain from comparing them to a penis and a matching pair of testicles. But only because I lack the language. And the courage.

As the train pulls into Marseille, I chat to another cyclist who also had to struggle to get his bike on board the train. He tells me, in broken English, that the conductor had no intention of opening the *fourgon* door, as it would mean having to get off the train, unlock the door, and then get back on again. In other words, this stupid French prick took deliberate pleasure in making someone else's life just that little bit more difficult than it needs to be. I feel like getting hold of this boorish bastard and telling him that my grandfather lost a leg fighting in a war to save this country – and by extension his filthy French skin – and if my grandfather had known of the conductor's behaviour, he, my grandfather, would have given me his artificial leg and let me use it to boot his, the conductor's, fat filthy French arse from Marseille to Morocco.

Instead I fall back on the English Way of Doing Things and get off the train looking miffed.

Marseille smells of excrement. I ignore this and follow signs to the ferry port. There's a queue of cars whose drivers, I presume, are waiting for the ferry office to open in the morning. Several people have made makeshift beds on a nearby verge. It is a warm, cloudless night and I decide to join them.

Next morning, I am first in the queue at the ticket office. The ferry is full. It is also full the next day and the day after that. However, I can buy a ticket and hope for either latecomers or cancellations.

I do this, and get to the port a good two hours before the ferry is due to leave, then spend the next ninety minutes walking up and down, smoking and praying until, at 4.30 p.m., my name is called. I have a ticket!

Before boarding the ferry, I call Debbie/Dubai and let her know I'm on my way. She gives me directions to a bar near to the port, where we arrange to meet. Before hanging up, she asks, 'Do you still drink? And smoke?'

'Yes and yes,' I say.

'Good,' she says, then adds, 'In that case we should get on fine.'

'How fine?' I wonder.

'How fine?' echoes my penis.

'It'll end in tears,' says my brain.

My brain was right.

*

Some people are terrified of Death. I'm not one of them. I welcome Death. Dead people feel no pain. Dead people don't have to worry about the vile and unpleasant things that the living have to cope with, such as anal polyps and people who talk in the theatre. No. When you're dead, the world's a much better place to live in.

Like Death, Time also carries a scythe; but not a scythe that frees us from this world. No. What Time likes to do with his beastly scythe is to carve deep and unforgiving lines in our faces; to strip us of the hairs that grow on our heads while ignoring the ones that bristle from our noses and our ears. Time adds pounds to our stomachs, sags our breasts, bends our spines, brittles our bones, removes our teeth and eyesight and robs us of the ability to dance at our children's parties without being mocked by them and their mates.

It isn't Death that terrifies me. It's Time.

As I wait in the Porto Torres bar where we've arranged to meet, I wonder what Time had done to Dubai.

I am pleased to see that Time has been kind.

Her figure is fuller. Her once-blonde hair has turned to grey and been dyed a variety of pinks. Around her neck, spectacles hang from a rhinestone chain. Dubai looks fine and well and I'm sure I would have enjoyed her company. But there is a problem with Dubai. The problem is the man who comes with her. A man called Philippe.

The first thing I notice about him is his deep and abiding love of garlic. Whether he chooses to eat it raw or simply rub it directly into his sweat glands, I cannot say. But love it he clearly does. He is also a gourmet and has decided to share his love of food with the rest of us. By eating it with his mouth open. He does this with the complimentary bowl of peanuts at our table (all of them); with the sandwich he orders (which I pay for); and with the meal we share later (which I also pay for). Any attempt by Dubai or myself to reminisce, or chat about old friends, is thwarted. Philippe commandeers the conversation in a low, guttural French that I find impossible to understand. Eventually I leave him to it, contenting myself by staring at Dubai while wondering, *'What do you see in him? What on earth do you see in him?'*

With the meal finally over, we return to Dubai's flat, which, luckily for me, is stocked with plenty of wine. The best way of my coping with the rest of the evening, I decide, is to get drunk as quickly as possible, which I do. I then stagger off to bed, spending the rest of the night listening to their voices floating up the stairs, as they argue both loudly and bilingually. The following morning I wake with a hangover and the realisation that I have got to get out. My disgusting plan is to sneak off before they get up, but Dubai surprises me, emerging from the bathroom as I tiptoe downstairs with my luggage. For a moment we stare at each other, both speechless, while phrases such as 'text message – dead parents' flash across my mind; eventually I simply blurt out, 'Sorry, got to go,' then I load my bags onto my bike, wheel it out of her flat, then I'm on it and I'm off, heading I know not where, caring even less, embarrassed by my behaviour while exulting in my freedom, cycling furiously through Porto Torres until I see a sign to the ferry, reach the ferry office, book myself a ticket for the next available crossing, collapse over a coffee in a nearby café and wait for my panic-stricken heart to stop its relentless thumping.

And through it all, my smug brain reminds me that none of this is its fault. While inside my underpants my chastened penis lies still and keeps its silly mouth shut.

*

The journey from Porto Torres back to Marseille is, as I expected, tiresome. Until the end of the evening when the bar closes, people drift away, and two guitar players begin playing together. A third drifts over and joins them, swiftly realising he may have made a mistake, as the fluid fingers of the others race up and down their fretboards, almost defying him to keep up. He manages, but only just. A couple of other passengers come over, and for about an hour we are treated to an acoustic concert of some of the best live music we have ever heard. Music played by musicians, not for money, but purely for the pleasure of playing together. And playing together nicely.

I once read an article in which a journalist described being in a pub in Southern Ireland, watching just such a jam session, the band comprising virtually all the virtuosi of Ireland's folk world. He sat in open-mouthed awe at the talent performing only a few feet away. He had a harmonica in his top pocket. One of the musicians pointed at the harmonica and said, 'Why don't you join in?' He was about to reply 'Not good enough' before realising that being good or bad was not the point. It was playing together that counted, not how well you played.

This is how the best musicians are. It's the bad ones that criticise another person's skills – or lack of them. The good ones know better.

\*

The ferry reaches Marseille at 7 a.m., and, disembarking, I am treated, again, to the smell of human shit. This, I discover, is entirely appropriate. Marseille is a shithole. A shithole full of shit people.

I decide to grab a coffee in a café before heading for the station. There is nowhere to leave my bicycle, so I prop it against the café window, where I can keep an eye on it. The owner wanders in off the street and asks whose bicycle that is. I tell him 'Mine'. He responds with a curt 'Move it'. I decide to move it all right. To another café.

I take a seat outside. It's still early, so the place isn't busy but I still have to wait for a good fifteen minutes before the waiter saunters to my table. I ask him, politely, for 'Un café, s'il vous plaît.' He looks at me contemptuously before snarling, 'Eh?'

I then head towards the toilet. Apparently it is occupied. A man stands outside the toilet, stopping others from going in. He could have stopped me with a polite, 'Excuse me, sir, but I regret to inform you that a friend of mine is occupying the toilet at present.' Instead he puts his hand to my chest and pushes me back, growling, in French, 'Wait.'

I leave the café and head towards the station. As I do, a front pannier rack breaks off and falls to the ground. I am furious. I throw it away, strap my front pannier onto the back of my bike, and carry on. But now with a wobble. I make my way to the station where I hope to get a train to another town that doesn't smell of human shit but does sell pannier racks. At the station I find a ticket seller with a Union flag in her window, indicating that she speaks English. I tell her I want a train to Avignon '*avec un fourgon*' in which to put the bike I am standing beside. She sells me a ticket for the 11.30 train. I only have to wait for three hours, so I am pleased. Until the train arrives and I am told that is has no *fourgon*. Back to the ticket office. I let others in the queue go ahead of me as I wait for the same woman to finish serving her customer. She does. I step forward. She closes her window.

Well, I am not having that. To my astonishment, my mouth opens of its own volition and I find myself bellowing, 'I am English and you sold me the wrong ticket!' Luckily, she decides to deal with me, due to astonishment of her own, tinged perhaps with fear. It turns out there is no train with a *fourgon* until 8.30 in the evening. I decide to wait. Partly because I can't face cycling on a badly balanced bike. And partly because I have decided that I want to take a train to Avignon and nothing is going to get in the way of my pig-headed ambition.

I then spend a miserable day hanging around Marseille. It's baking hot and I cycle fruitlessly around trying to find somewhere pleasant in which to kill time before I catch my train. Eventually I find a suburban area with a café, outdoor tables, and a touch of greenery. I'm seated at a table when a beggar woman appears, a nine-year-old boy in tow. They go from table to table. Most people wave them away, but a young girl slips the nine-year-old a coin, which he takes. The mother turns, sees what has happened, and, enraged that her son has accepted a coin that could have gone to her, rips her jacket from her shoulders, throws it to the ground, and starts to curse him. She then takes hold of her son in order to strike him. I find myself shouting, '*Non!*' as people at nearby tables rush to intervene. Then the manager of the bar appears and hustles the woman and her boy away.

What breaks my heart is the expression on the face of the boy. It isn't just fear. It's also shame.

Sickened by what I have seen, I decide to spend the rest of my time waiting at the station. I don't know why I chose to do this, but it definitely meets the approval of some of the people who live and work in Marseille. As I wait for my train, these people help themselves to my phone and all the cash in my wallet. Something I don't discover until later, when I arrive in Avignon.

The route to the campsite is clearly signposted, and a cycle lane takes me there, so I am in good spirits until I discover the absence of both phone and money.

I thought that would be an end to my bad experiences, but there's one more to come.

The following day I wash some clothes, including my sweat-stained baseball cap, hang them out to dry, then set off into Avignon to get some cash, to report the loss of my phone, and to find a bike shop selling, I hope, pannier racks.

Two out of three isn't bad. After about two hours at the police station I am handed a copy of the statement I gave (in my limited French) to a policeman (who spoke no English). I read the statement and am astonished at my fluency. I get some cash and then, at the Tourist Office, I'm given a helpful map and a list of bike shops. Two of them turn out to be motorbike shops; the third has closed down but the fourth looks promising: it actually sells bicycles. I go inside. They do not sell pannier racks. Instead, they recommend another shop. How do I get there? They show me on a map. I cycle there. They do not sell pannier racks either. Luckily, they can recommend a bicycle shop. How do I get there? They show me on a map. It's the one that sent me here.

After a long and fruitless day I crawl back through Avignon's baffling one-way system to the campsite, where I find that someone has stolen my baseball cap.

This is unforgivable. If somebody wants to help themselves to my mobile phone, fine. It's insured and I can replace it. Likewise, I can't fault whoever robbed me of my cash. How else are the pickpockets of Marseille meant to spend their time and practise their skills if not by hanging around railway stations and educating tourists into the foolishness of walking around with wallets full of money? But whoever stole my hat – from a campsite that I'm assuming we both use and would like to feel secure in – that person is a creature of pure evil. Even worse, a creature of pure evil in a stylish hat.

In Avignon I receive another email that will dictate the course of my journey.

At one time, a friend of mine had illustrated poems I'd written and published them on a website. One of the poems was a tribute to Izzy the Cat, a family pet which had died.

> Poor old Izzy
> She kept herself busy
> She ran around the room
> And made us all dizzy
> But now she is dead
> And we're ever so sorry
> But poor old Izzy
> Is Wozzy

At about the time I was being pickpocketed in Marseille, a French friend of mine, Isabelle, known to her friends as Izzy, had been ego-surfing the web, came across my poem, and sent me an email. Learning I was in France, Isabelle then invited me to stay with her in her home in Thouars, North West France. This was good news, not least because I could order a new pannier rack from England and have it delivered to Izzy's address.

I begin making my way northwards through a series of small villages and campsites, my packing rearranged so that I can steer my badly balanced bike without it throwing me over a cliff or under a bus. It is now midsummer and the heat is making cycling less and less pleasant. I set off at 5 or 6 a.m., cycle till noon, and then spend the rest of the day lounging about.

All is going well, until I turn left when I should have turned right, and find myself in Largentière, a fairy-tale town with a fairy-tale castle, probably unchanged since the middle ages, built at the bottom of four mountains and with no way out except back up an enormous hill. I climb it and, even though exhausted, carry on until I reach the horrible town of Aubenas, where I hope to catch a train. No such luck. The station has closed and the trains replaced by buses. Buses that don't take bikes. I press on through another town, Jaujac, before finding a sweet *Camping à la Ferme* in nearby La Souche.

I begin the next day early and with an unexplained feeling of dread. Something tells me that there is a day of hell in front of me, and that something is right. Having had breakfast on a picnic site close to a river, I get on my bike, turn a corner, and my worst fears are realised: in front of me is a mountain.

There is no way round it. Literally. I check and recheck my maps with increasing fear, but cycling straight ahead and up the mountain is my only option. Until, after a short while, I realise there is another option. I can get off my bike and push.

And so I do. And continue to do for hour after agonising hour. After three hours of it, I stop to eat. Luckily, I have brought plenty of food and, more importantly, water. Having eaten, I continue pushing my bike up the increasingly narrow and increasingly steep path. After two hours after this, I turn a bend. In front of me is a metal plaque. I totter over to it. It's a diagram of the valley below. I have reached the top. My unbearable journey is over. I do an actual dance of joy, hopping up and down, shouting every swear word I can think of and directing every one of them at the mountain. Then I pick up my bike, turn another corner, and see – more mountain. I'm nowhere near the top. I'm not even halfway there.

After another hour of this, all I can do is push my bike to one side of the road, rest, and then push it to the other, crawling in agonising slowness in a zigzag pattern. As a treat, whenever I hear the sound of an approaching car, I stop and lean against the mountain wall, smoking a nonchalant cigarette, hopefully impressing gullible French children with my apparent stamina and mountain-climbing ability. 'When we grow up,' they will think, but in French, 'we too will be like that suave and sophisticated English person, cycling his heavily laden bicycle up one of the most mountainous roads in our native land while stopping every now and then for a well-earned cigarette.'

Then the car passes, I throw my cigarette to the ground, think about being sick, then carry on pushing.

It is 4.30 in the afternoon, eight hours since I started, when, dripping with sweat and aching in every part of my body, I finally make it to the actual top, totter to a patch of grass at the side of the road, fling myself to the ground and wrench open one of the cans of beer I'd saved for the end of the climb. I have two things to celebrate. It is over. And I'm not dead.

I drink my beer. I get on my bike. And then comes my reward: a long, magnificent, descending road of pure, unblemished new-laid asphalt, uncurling beneath my wheels, never ending, marred with not a single bump or crack, continuing and flowing, granting me an effortless gliding descent until, after an hour that flies by like the briefest breath of wind, I arrive at the dismal town of Langogne and the filthiest campsite I have ever seen.

'How long will you be staying?' asks the young person behind the desk, looking up with genuine astonishment when I say, 'Two days.' I feel a twinge of alarm when I register his astonishment, but don't fully appreciate the reason for it until I count the number of cockroaches in the shower. I thought the showers were grim, but that was before I saw the toilets. As I walk towards them, a pair of Hell's Angels, with piercings and tattoos covering every part of their bodies including their faces, stagger out of them, retching.

The one thing in the campsite's favour is that it is next to a railway station, where, astonishingly, I am able to take a train to the nearby town of Clermont-Ferrand. There, even more amazingly, I am able to take a train to Bourges, about a week's ride from Thouars. And it is in Thouars that I am reunited with a long-dead David Gordon.

\*

I wasn't surprised to hear David's voice when I entered Isabelle's living room. It was in David's flat that I had first met her, and her then partner, Jean-Louis. One of their habits was to keep records of their travels, and I remembered their tape recorder being produced as we sat around David's kitchen table, smoking, drinking and talking. Isabelle had dug into her collection of tapes, found one with David on it, and this was playing as I entered her house. I don't know what she expected me to say. What I did say was, 'I didn't cycle halfway across France to listen to the voice of a dead man.'

David was raised in the old school of British theatre, provincial rep and all that that entailed. Following his stint at the Arts Centre in Birmingham his career had followed a trajectory that he hadn't enjoyed, culminating in directing fading comedians in end-of-the-pier shows. 'All I had to do was watch their act then light it,' he'd complained to me. He'd decided he'd finally had enough when, entering the theatre one evening, he was told that the star was refusing to do the show until he had received an apology from the head carpenter, who had called him a c-word.

David went to reason with the carpenter. 'I know he's a c-word, you know he's a c-word, everyone agrees he's a c-word. But do me a favour and apologise to him, will you?'

'All right, David. But I'm doing it for you. Not for him. Because he's a c-word.'

The carpenter, whose name was Billy Ruck, had told David that he was thinking of abandoning his carpentry career and becoming an actor himself. Privately, David thought this not such a good idea, but tried to be supportive.

'Of course,' said the carpenter. 'I'll have to change my name. You can't be an actor with a name like Billy Ruck, can you?'

'Perhaps not,' said David. 'What were you thinking of changing it to?'

'Freddie Ruck,' said the carpenter, who was not only ambitious but had never heard of Dr Spooner.

Having retired from the theatre, David almost decided to retire from life when he returned home and found his lover had moved out and taken the furniture with him. But he carried on, subsisting on the dole and on the occasional tutoring job; at one time he devoted himself to helping the illiterate to read, which he did voluntarily, despite being flat broke himself.

David was asthmatic and a heavy smoker and became increasingly frail as he got older. I took it upon myself to get him to hospital appointments and so on. This wasn't always easy as, while he lived in London, I had moved to Brighton. I was in Brighton when I phoned him to remind him that he was due for a visit from his doctor. David told me that he 'wasn't able to get out of bed to answer the door, love.'

I rearranged the appointment and took a train to London. The doctor came, took one look at David, and told me he should be taken to hospital as quickly as possible. I was meant to collect my children, then aged four and six, from a performance of *Treasure Island* in a London theatre. Their mother agreed to drop them off at David's as we waited for the ambulance. The boys arrived in full pirate regalia. Before dumping them in front of a television in David's spare room, I asked them if they 'wanted to say hallo to David'. The six-year-old declined. The younger boy said he would, so I ushered him in.

My four-year-old son looked down at David, who was literally on his deathbed, and said, 'Well, David, I think you'll either get better or you'll die.'

'Thank you, Dr Dowie,' I said, and led him from the room.

David was barely able to speak by then, but made clear how much he enjoyed riding an ambulance in the company of two small children dressed as pirates.

I was about to leave him in the Royal Free Hospital, Hampstead, having cheerily told him, 'You never know your luck, Dave, you might get the bed Peter Cook died in.' Just before I left, a nurse came over to take a blood sample. I had been with David on many visits to the hospital, and, at every visit, somebody took yet another blood sample. I could see by the expression on David's face that he had now had enough. This was one blood sample too many. 'Time to go, David,' I thought.

The next day I went back to the hospital and learned that he had.

*

I had made myself executor of his will and now had to empty out his flat and arrange for a burial. The pitiful number of names in David's address book matched the pitiful amount of money in his bank account. The funeral, therefore, had to be cheap. It also had to be stylish. But first I had to get rid of the colossal amount of tat in David's flat. I bought about a zillion bin liners and began filling them with innumerable scraps of irritating pieces of paper, such as gas bills dating back to before I was born, with 'paid' scribbled on the bottom.

I phoned his few friends and told them what I was up to and if there was anything of Dave's that they wanted they had a couple of days in which to collect. The only one who did was Pete. Pete had his eye on some saucepans and other stuff and, having coming round to collect them, noticed David's old watch on the mantelpiece.

'You should have it,' said Pete.

I didn't want it. I didn't wear a watch and told Pete so.

'Why not?' asked Pete.

'Because if you wear a watch, people keep asking you for the time,' I said. 'It's irritating.'

'David would want you to have it,' he insisted.

'All right!' I said, 'All right! I'll take the watch.'

Anything to hurry things up.

Not wanting to wear it, I dumped the watch on my desk back in my Brighton flat. Strangely, every time I left the flat, I felt compelled to put it on. Which occasionally I did.

I wore it to David's funeral, which proved not only easy to arrange but was actually within our budget. Not knowing what to do or where to turn, I had contacted the Natural Death Centre, an organisation that offered (and still does) alternatives to the unsympathetic and expensive burials that so many of us opt for. They suggested I contact The Woodland Burial Ground in Christchurch, Dorset. I did, and learned that they would collect the body, place it in either a shroud, a wooden coffin, a wickerwork coffin or anything else that took our fancy, and then transport it to the Burial Ground; the body would be placed in the ground and there they would plant a tree.

This so very neatly dovetailed with David's only ever stated preference for a burial – 'Just stick me in a bin bag and dump me in the street, love' – that it was clearly the only choice.

Another benefit was that we could have whatever kind of ceremony we wanted. Accordingly, David's friends and I avoided both the religious and the secular form of service and made up our own.

We lowered his body into the ground ourselves. We each said a piece we'd prepared. We recited the Lord's Prayer and concluded the ceremony with the lighting of sparklers, provided by David's friend Annie, and by the singing of David's favourite song, 'The Deadwood Stage', a song that everybody loves but nobody knows the words to. Finely honed lyrics about Injun arrows and porcupine quills are dumped in favour of assorted tumpety-tums until the end of the song and the return of whips cracking merrily away (three times). Luckily, Annie had the sense to provide a lyric sheet and any graveside embarrassment was avoided. As was the sound of David's voice, booming from his grave: 'How many times do I have to tell you? Rehearse! Rehearse! Rehearse!'

I have been to quite a few funerals, many of them religious, many of them humanist, and I'm always astonished that the family and friends of the deceased hand over the job of saying goodbye to their loved one to a complete (and sometimes uncaring) stranger. Do it yourself! I want to tell them. It isn't difficult. And it will be meaningful.

A week or so after David's funeral, I was strolling along the High Street in Brighton when I spotted a sign which I hadn't noticed before, yet must have passed many times. The sign read: 'Brighton & Hove Spiritualist Church'.

Curious, I walked up the tiny alleyway in which the church lay. Something about the building piqued my curiosity, and I decided I'd attend one of their services. Not normally a fan of religious buildings, as soon as I entered the church I loved it. It was small, comfortable, furnished with flowers and, unlike many other religious buildings, possessed a tranquil, non-oppressive atmosphere. If other churches were more like this, I thought, I'd visit them more often.

I had chosen to go on an evening advertised as featuring a 'psychic reading', the kind of event in which I usually have no interest. I was sitting a few rows from the front, in an aisle seat in case I needed to make a hasty exit, when the psychic spoke to me.

'A friend of yours passed over not long ago . . . '

Which might explain why I'm sitting in a spiritualist church, I thought, while smiling benignly.

'He lost his voice before making his passing,' she continued.

How unusual. Someone not being able to speak on their deathbed, I thought, while smiling benignly.

'He'd like to thank you for all you did for him,' she said.

What a nice but meaningless sentiment, I thought, while smiling benignly.

'And he'd like to remain close to you,' she said, and then, before turning away, added, 'so would you mind wearing the watch?'

*

In Thouars, I spend a happy week with Isabelle, indulging in such luxuries as sleeping in a bed, having a roof over my head and spending hours and hours trying to fit a pannier rack to my bicycle. But after the week had passed I knew it was time to move on. The summer was pretty much over and the camping season was drawing to a close; some sites would still be open, but most would not. I decided to return home.

But I would be back, I decided. Come the spring. Marseille aside, I'd enjoyed being in France. I'd enjoyed being among the French people. I'd also enjoyed being alone. Not because I take pleasure in my own company – more because I can't stand anyone else's. I had no wish to return to old habits, such as writing, and certainly not to performing. Riding my bike and pitching my tent, that was all I looked forward to. I'd set out to find solitude, silence and scenery. I'd found all three. I liked them. And I wanted more.

# CHAPTER SIX
## Retour en France

'Show me a man who's tired of London,' said Dr Johnson, 'and I'll show you a man who's tired of drills, dogshit, litter, pollution, unbreathable air, unspeakable rudeness, unpayable rent, unaffordable housing, more drills, more dogshit, and the Northern Line.'

I'm not a fan of London, but there are times when I find London almost a pleasure to be in. Well, one time – pre-dawn; when I am cycling through empty streets on my way to Victoria Station and a train which will take me out of London, down to the coast and over to France. That's when I quite like London. The streets are empty, the buildings are impressive and often quite beautiful, and the people, and more important their cars, are nowhere to be seen.

The ferry to Dieppe leaves Newhaven at 7.30 a.m. I need to catch a train that leaves London ninety minutes earlier, so I set off in the early morning light, riding through Camden, down Mornington Crescent (named in tribute to *I'm Sorry I Haven't a Clue*, one of the greatest radio programmes ever made), along the Euston Road, past the British Museum (home of archaic British antiquities such as good manners and consideration for others), before turning into Charing Cross and onto the Mall and Buckingham Palace (the home of a family who once committed a crime so unspeakable that armed soldiers now guard every exit to make sure they can never get out and do it again) before arriving at Victoria Station, when I discover that the train to Newhaven has been delayed due to 'carelessness and inefficiency'.

I wait with a sense of rising panic for my train departure to be announced. I cannot believe that my French adventure will be ruined by a delayed train. But it is. A late departure from Victoria means I arrive at the Newhaven docks just in time to see the back of the ferry as it sets off for France. Without me. There isn't another ferry for another twelve hours, which means I have at the very least eleven hours and fifty-nine minutes to kill.

Luckily I have the whole of Newhaven to kill them in.

I manage to kill a few minutes by playing a game I've invented. I call it the Bike Game. The next time you're in a railway station with nothing to do, you might like to play it yourself. All you have to do is to wander around to wherever the bikes are kept and see if you can find two that look the same. It's not as easy as you might think. In fact, it's almost impossible.

Why is this? It's not as though bicycles are handcrafted articles, tailor-made for every customer (although some are). Most bikes are mass-produced then shipped out to bicycle shops in bulk. So what happens to make each bike so individual? Do mutations take place? Once the bike has been ridden away, does it start to become a little more like its owner? And vice versa? Are we back to the idea that part of you rubs off on your bike and a part of your bike rubs off on you until, eventually, both you and your bike are irrevocably changed and that is why all bicycle thieves must be hanged? I don't know. But it's an intriguing thought. And a great game.

I spend a further eleven hours or so cycling to Brighton, killing time in shops and snack bars, before returning to Newhaven and, at long last, boarding the ferry that will take me to France. It's only a four-hour journey, so the trip is bearable, despite the usual loutery from the drunken Brits in the bar (who, I am horrified to discover, turn out to be French). Arriving in Dieppe, late and tired, I book myself into the first hotel I see, and find myself in a nice room at €60 plus €6 for a bottle of wine.

I am paying my bill the following morning when I notice they have forgotten to charge for the wine. I point this out and am rewarded with three free croissants, thus proving that honesty is always the best policy. Unless you dislike croissants. I dislike croissants.

I leave Dieppe at 10 a.m. My plan is to cycle along the coast until I reach Mur-de-Bretagne, where I can pick up the Nantes–Brest canal, which promises flat and easy riding through pleasant countryside. My route takes me up large hills before I descend to Pourville, then on to a campsite in St Aubin sur Mer. Here I am impressed by the woman who manages the site, chasing after a departing caravan so she can say goodbye to its owners. A nice gesture, I think, until I realise that the caravan owners had left the site without paying. Or so I assume, judging by the amount of French swearing and clenched-fist waving from the campsite manager. I spend one night there, making sure to pay her before I leave, after which I take a pretty and, happily, flat route to the town of Yvetot, which is dreary but enlivened by an impressive piece of graffiti. Almost the whole of a brick wall has been whitewashed with the phrase (in English): The People of Normandy Have Not Forgotten Their Allies. I cycle on and then for the next few miles find, to my astonishment, that I am on a road going *downhill all the way*. I cannot believe it. I carry on with my descent despite two major concerns: either I am going the wrong way, or I'm going the right way but there will be massive hills to come. But no. Downhill goes the road, on and on, until I find myself crossing the large and windswept Pont de Brotonne. I'd like to stop and admire the view of the river Seine as it flows beneath the bridge, but I'm more concerned with not getting blown off it, either by the wind or the wash from enormous lorries that pass me with horrendous frequency.

I make it to the other side and find a quiet road, running parallel to the one I've just left. I have a few miles of pleasant cycling but no sign of any campsites. I find a small shop in a tiny village and buy emergency provisions before passing through the Forêt de Brotonne where, with still no campsite in sight, I book into a *chambre d'hôte*. My room is on the first floor. It is large, furnished in old-fashioned oak with open windows overlooking the garden and the hills and trees that stand above the Seine.

There is a nest of some kind in the eaves of the roof outside my window. I don't know what kind of insects live in the nest, but they're popular with the local birds, who continually fly up to feed, occasionally blundering in through my window where, panic-stricken, they literally flap about the room. '*Où est le ciel?*' they cry. '*Le ciel est allé. Je suis dans une chambre! Merde! Merde alors!*' they continue, driven mad by human beings and their insane desire to have a senseless roof over their deranged heads.

Towards evening the birds depart, I presume to their nests, and all is quiet. I sit and watch the sun set over the Seine. On the horizon, smoke issues from several factory chimneys. The smoke from the chimneys drifts between river and sky, becoming a cloudy veil behind which the sun descends, at first hidden by the smoke, then slowly revealing itself, bit by tantalising bit. I am watching a solar striptease. The sky and the smoke turn coral pink as the sun goes down with increasing speed; and then the sky darkens, turns into night, and the stripper's work is done.

Next morning I have breakfast at a shared table, which is never my idea of fun, although I have a more than satisfactory conversation with the owner.

'*Êtes-vous sportif?*'

'*Non.*'

'*Aimez-vous les oiseaux?*'

'*Oui.*'

Following breakfast I set off in the wrong direction before heading out on a road that takes me up and up under cloudy skies and spattering rain and into La Forêt. All very picturesque until I hit the main road, after which it's mostly boring scenery before I reach Pont Audemer, a pretty little town, around which I would have liked to wander, but can find nowhere safe to leave my bike.

I consult my map and see I have a choice of two routes, one of which is marked by a blue star-shaped symbol meaning 'scenic view'; or as I prefer to call it, 'bloody big hill'. I choose the non-scenic route, which takes me to the tiny village of Corneilles, where a policeman is turning away cars as they try to enter. I am in need of coffee, so cycle over to see if I can get through. As I get close to the policeman I overhear an exasperated driver saying, in what sounds like a German accent, 'Do you speak English?' to be met with a resounding, '*Non!*'

Undeterred, the German continues with a bombastic: 'I have been trying to get into this town for over a half-hour now . . . '

The cop turns away with a Gallic shrug. I point to the town and say, in French, 'I go there. Is good?' and get a friendly nod and a gesture indicating I should go ahead, which does the German driver's temper no good at all. I manage to stop myself from shouting over my shoulder, 'The people of Normandy have not forgotten their allies', as I cycle into the town and find myself bang in the middle of the Tour de France.

Hundreds of people are lining the street. More of them fill the road which winds up into the hills beyond and out of sight. I park my bike and wander over to one of the many bars. Excited waiters are leaping in and out of various doors, checking to see if there's any development on the street, before racing back inside to monitor the race on TV. I have never seen such excitement in France. Or anywhere. I manage to catch a waiter's eye and order a coffee before going out into the street and finding a vacant seat. A few minutes pass, and then, to a frenzied roar from the crowd, the Tour appears – first motorcyclists radiating importance; then cars decorated with advertising, and then, to increasing cheers and applause, the cyclists – about two hundred of them, bright sun reflected from their helmets, the glare from their Lycra-clad bodies so intense that I have to turn my head away. I look back and they have gone. The whole thing is over in less than an instant. All that is left of the parade is the gendarmerie – following the tour on motorbikes and in cars – and then the crowd begins making its way home.

I push my bike through the crowds, coincidentally following the route that the cyclists took, a complete antithesis of all that had gone before, trying to make sense of what I'd just seen. The reactions of the crowd seemed totally out of proportion to the event itself. I begin to wonder if the whole thing was genetic – some sort of acting out of a collective race memory. Does the Tour de France reawaken buried memories of medieval knights riding off to war, their colourful pennants, flashing armour and brightly decorated horses the forerunners of Lycra and crash helmets and racing bikes? Perhaps so. Probably not. But then, how else do you explain all this fuss and palaver over a bunch of blokes having a bike ride?

At the top of the hill overlooking the town I find a campsite, and wander in. The owner is English. He suggests I pitch my tent close to a lake, telling me to come back to the bar and check in later. I do as he suggests, then kill some time watching two men fishing the lake. Half an hour passes. Nothing is caught and neither of them move. Either both of these men are highly skilled in the art of Zen Fishing, or they're dead. I wander down to the reception in search of the campsite manager. He turns out to be not just English, but highly proficient in the English way of doing things, i.e., with a bad grace. Having been told I'd like to stay for two days, he works out what I owe him before telling me, 'It's hardly worth the bother.' I refrain from saying, 'Don't then.' Or, more appropriately, telling him that his is the most expensive campsite I've stayed on so far.

The next day I wander into the laundry room and check out the facilities. A notice informs me that I need to buy tokens for the machine, and that they're available at reception. As I make my way towards his office, I see the campsite manager leave it, making his way towards a nearby tractor. I walk over and tell him I'd like some laundry tokens. He sighs and rolls his eyes. Now he has to walk all the way back to his office, a distance of at least ten yards, and, as he insists on telling me, he has only just come from there. He then charges me €6, plus 50 cents for soap powder, asking me if there will 'be anything else'. 'Yes,' I want to say. 'Can you direct me to a campsite run by people with manners?'

The crowd's reaction to the Tour de France may not have made sense to me, but at least it was civil. Whole families attended, with picnics, the remnants of which they cleared up and took home with them. If only the followers of other sports behaved as well, I muse, this notion being borne home to me when, a couple of days later, I spend the night in the tiny town of Caen.

I arrive late and find a cheap hotel into which I collapse following a gruelling ride. I'd bought bread, cheese, fruit and my standard bottle of wine, but that evening one bottle of wine is not enough. I leave the hotel, staggering into the street in search of more wine, before hitting a virtually empty bar. A man at a table says something to me as I sit down, clutching my glass of vin ordinaire, but I can't work out what it is. He points to the street outside and says, '*Vous ne regardez pas?*' I smile and say '*Non*', wondering why he thinks I'd want to spend the evening looking at a street. There is something about the atmosphere in the bar that I don't like, so I finish my wine, and move to another bar. The atmosphere there is the same. Then I realise that the atmosphere pervades the whole town. It is ominous and pervasive. Something is about to happen. Something evil. Whatever it is, I don't want to be a part of it. I stagger back to my hotel, finally drunk, which is good, but also frightened, which is bad.

I fall onto the bed in my room. A noise is coming from outside, the sound of voices, becoming louder and louder still. It's only when the noise becomes more drunk, more aggressive and more violent, that I realise what's been going on. Somebody somewhere has been playing football.

And so, of course, as football is involved, it doesn't matter what kind of behaviour now takes place. It doesn't matter how many loutish voices are raised, how many bottles smashed or how many windows broken. If it's to do with football, then it's all right. Behaviour which, under any other circumstances, would have the gendarmerie up and running with truncheons at the ready is not only tolerated but smiled on.

A friend of mine once tried to explain the pleasures of football. 'When you're watching,' he said, 'you're part of a crowd of hundreds and hundreds of people all reacting in exactly the same way at exactly the same time. That's what so great about it.'

'And that,' I thought, 'is exactly why I hate it.'

I was never able to express my hatred of football. My eldest son found a way. 'I don't just hate the game,' he said. 'I don't just hate the people who play it and the people who watch it and the people who talk about it – I even hate the grass they play it on.'

But there are things in this world even more horrendous than football.

At Dol-de-Bretagne I find a campsite and a French family making life hell for everyone on it.

The daughter with the screaming baby is having a screaming row with her screaming boyfriend. This goes on for about fifteen minutes before he stalks off. 'Hooray,' thinks the campsite. 'Now the noise will stop.' But no. As he stalks off, she screams more abuse after him, so he comes back to scream more abuse at her. She screams back, he stalks off, she screams more abuse, he comes back. This goes on for another fifteen minutes before he finally decides to leave and not come back at all. The campsite breathes a sigh of relief, mistakenly thinking it's over. It's not. Now the daughter's mother emerges from her caravan. Her daughter, still carrying the still-screaming baby, re-enacts the entire row at the top of her voice, playing both parts, herself and the boyfriend. 'I said this so he said that then I said this . . . '

The mother decides to pacify the still-screaming infant by giving it a motorised toy to play with. This does not stop the baby from screaming. All it does is increase the noise. But the noise from the motorised toy, coupled with the noise from the baby, is clearly not enough. Although it's unbearable, more noise is needed. This is provided by the father, who emerges from the caravan carrying a radio playing, at full volume, French rap (with a capital C). The mother tells the father what's been going on, at the top of her voice, with interjections from the daughter, also at the top of her voice. Then the boyfriend returns, carrying a crateful of beer. He decides to lighten the mood with a series of loud and comical belches. His girlfriend starts screaming at him again. The rest of the family join in, screaming at him as he screams back. Then, still screaming, they all pile into a car, crank up the French rap (still with a capital C), and drive to the nearest town where, presumably, they will make life hell for different people in a different location until someone does the decent thing, takes out a meat-axe and kills the fucking lot of them.

The following day I reach Dinan, which, according to a guidebook, is 'Brittany's best preserved medieval town, the narrow cobblestone streets lined with half-timbered houses straight out of the Middle Ages'. True enough. What my guidebook didn't say is that not only have the half-timbered medieval houses been converted into shops selling outrageously expensive stuff to the tourists that throng the streets, but non-medieval pop music is being piped from non-medieval loudspeakers on every medieval corner. This to attract the tourists, presumably, though I'd have thought it would do the opposite.

As I leave the Tourist Office, I see a group of people standing about wearing what is obviously traditional dress. The men are in black trousers and shoes, ribboned hats, white shirts and maroon waistcoats. The women wear maroon dresses, black shawls, white blouses and lace headdresses. This can't be comfortable, as it is nearly lunchtime and the heat is close to tropical. Curious, I decide to follow them as they make their way to the village square, where someone has erected a small stage, flanked by a PA.

Three men appear, and, given that they appear from the local bar, I assume that they are musicians. I am right. Two of them pick up instruments resembling bagpipes, the third takes hold of a lute. They start to play and the men and women begin to dance, resembling schoolchildren rather than professional dancers, performing with much simpering and blushing and downcast eyes. It's totally charming and I am reminded, almost instantly, of the Bacup Nutters.

*

Bacup is a tiny village in the heart of Lancashire, to which I'd moved in the early stages of a marriage that was doomed to failure, partly because we'd moved to Bacup, a tiny village in the heart of Lancashire. We had made the classic mistake of viewing a property in the middle of summer, when everything looks lovely, then moving into it in the middle of a cold wet winter when everything turns out to be shit.

The first indication that Bacup might not be the best place to live in came when we paid a visit to the pub, which was empty except for a dog and two old men watching the fire go out. Greeting us with typical Lancastrian belligerence, one of the men asked us, 'What are you doing here?'

'We've just moved into the area,' I said, 'and thought we'd check out the local pubs.'

'If you want a really good night out in Bacup . . . ' began the man. We leaned forward expectantly.

'Yes?'

'This is it.'

I wouldn't mind, but he turned out to be right.

Nothing happened in Bacup until the following Easter. I was reading the local newspaper. The big news of the day was that there was shortly to be an appearance in Bacup of 'the Bacup Nutters'. What the Bacup Nutters do, I read, is smear black make-up on their faces, put on wooden clogs, then dance from pub to pub across the Pennines, beginning at nine in the morning, and finishing, in Bacup, at seven in the evening. This, apparently, was a traditional dance whose origins are 'lost in the mists of time'. I went along to watch them and quickly understood why. If I'd been responsible for the Bacup Nutters, I'd want their origins lost in the mists of times as well. Having begun dancing at nine in the morning, in a pub, and continued from pub to pub until seven in the evening, the Bacup Nutters were completely pissed. They could barely stand up, let alone perform anything resembling dancing. Even clog dancing. This did not bother the spectators, who were in their hundreds. Numbers, not age. Every beard-wearing, anorak-clad folkie who'd ever supped beer with twigs in it had travelled to Bacup to watch the Nutters at work. Surprisingly, not one of them appeared to be disappointed. Presumably because they had followed the Nutters from pub to pub and were just as pissed as they were.

It would be easy for me to blame Bacup for the failure of my marriage, so I will. But, in fairness to the bleak horror of that Lancashire town, the marriage was doomed from our first meeting. As I once said in my stand-up days, 'She looked at me across a crowded room, our eyes met, and she thought to herself, "One day, I'm going to divorce that man."'

It seems only fair that I should celebrate the end of our marriage with a joke, as that's more or less how the marriage began. The joke was at the expense of my future father-in-law who, deciding to pay his daughter a surprise visit, drove from Swansea to Birmingham, found me in her bed and got more of a surprise than he'd bargained for.

This was my first meeting with the man and I was impressed, mainly by his gullibility. His daughter was in her late twenties. She had spent her youth on the South Wales coast where there are beach huts. She then went to an art college in Swansea, followed by a year spent living and working in Amsterdam. And this man still believed his daughter was a virgin.

After he had left, and while I was still being funny at his expense, I noticed that I was the only one laughing. On asking what the matter was, I was told, 'It's all right for you. Sooner or later you'll be gone. But I'm stuck with him for the rest of my life.'

One of the problems with men is that they always make problems worse by trying to solve them. 'Let's get married,' I said, not realising that, with those three words, I had not only failed to solve a problem, but had created more problems than I could ever imagine.

The first one being, how to break the news to her father?

My own father had told me of the time he had asked for my mother's hand in marriage. This was not an event my father – a working-class, raggedy-arsed kid from Belfast – was looking forward to. My Victorian patriarch of a grandfather greeted him in the formality of his study and asked him, 'How much do you earn in a year?'

My dad didn't earn in a year. My dad earned in a week. But he was good at arithmetic so, after some quick calculations, was able to arrive at a figure, double it, and then tell my grandfather what he 'earned' in a 'year'.

My grandfather responded with, 'Good God, man. That's less than I earn in a month.'

My approach to my future father-in-law was similar. I didn't want to tell him I was working with a comedy-rock band called the Big Girls Blouse (his only possible reaction: 'Get out of my house.'). Instead, I told him that I was the founder and leader of a 'musical theatre group'; that I employed a manager, a stage manager, two musicians and a drummer; that we received Arts Council funding and that I had a record coming out on a respected record label. He then said, 'Well, I suppose if you get a proper job you might be able to support her.'

His daughter then made a remark along the lines of 'What makes you think I can't support myself?' Following these pleasantries, the conversation went downhill. Phrases such as 'If you think I'll be going to any weddings of yours you can think again,' were quickly followed by replies such as 'Well that's all right isn't it, because you won't be invited.' They then managed to find some common ground by screaming that neither of them had been able to stand the sight of the other one since the day she was born. Then it got personal. Following which, my future mother-in-law appeared with a tray, a bottle of sherry and four glasses, and suggested that we all 'have a nice drink to celebrate'.

I wouldn't say that I was warmly welcomed into the bosom of my new Welsh family. I was more tepidly tolerated. But I got on well with my new mother-in-law and her other daughter. I also got to know other members of the family, such as Uncle Eric.

Uncle Eric owned a barbershop in a village so small that he was virtually the only man in it, but he still had morals and values. And one of them was that he wouldn't cut any man's hair if he thought it was too long. He was also clearly gay, being, as the expression goes, camper than a row of pink tents. My father-in-law made it more than clear that he had never noticed this, didn't want to notice this, and would never notice this. Whereas the women in the family noticed it all the time. And not only noticed it but loved everything about it, shrieking with laughter at every gay word that came out of Eric's gay mouth.

On one visit, I complimented him on a diamond ring he was wearing. Eric claimed that he had won the ring, 'worth about £200', in a competition held to celebrate the diamond anniversary of Henri Wintermans Cigars. To win the diamond ring, all Eric had to do was come up with a caption for a painting: a portrait of a Regency buck presenting an eyelash-fluttering courtesan with a string of diamonds.

'And what was your caption, Eric?' I asked him.

'Thank you, Mr Winterman. I'll sew a couple on my fan.'

\*

If people ever asked me why my marriage had failed, I would always answer with questions of my own: 'Would you stay married to someone who failed to satisfy you sexually? Who belittled all your accomplishments? Who was obnoxious to the people you loved and who flirted with the people you hated? Of course you wouldn't. And neither would my wife.'

\*

I leave the dancers of Dinan and the memories of my marriage behind me, and cycle on over gruelling hills before reaching Gouarec, the beginning of the Nantes–Brest Canal, and a campsite. The charming English owner, David, offers discounts for cyclists, charging me only €10 for two nights, including €3.50 worth of washing tokens. That's more like it. The campsite is quiet and peaceful and made beautiful in the evening by small children on bicycles, who, laughing with pleasure, fly around the campsite, '*Comme,*' I find myself thinking, '*des oiseaux*'.

A long but pleasant ride along the delightfully flat canal takes me to the small town of Rohan, where I rest for two nights. Rohan, I discover, is mad. It is early on a Saturday morning as I stroll around, and the whole town appears to be drunk. I wander into a bar. A birthday party is in progress, for an adult, presumably, as no children are present, only grown-ups in fancy dress and grotesque make-up. One man, dressed as a baby in a large nappy and a pink bonnet, is sitting at the bar, staring at a puddle of beer. Suddenly, and for no apparent reason, he lifts up his head and roars (in English), 'To be or not to be – that is the question.' He then falls back into silence, staring morosely at his puddle of beer. I consider quoting the playwright Heathcote Williams and telling him, 'To be is better than not to be. That is the answer,' but the consequences are too scary to think about. Instead, I leave the bar and wander across to a car boot sale, paying a €1 entrance fee to look at a collection of the biggest load of junk I have ever seen. An old pub ashtray is advertised at €5. This is optimism beyond belief.

The town is decorated with posters of local bands, who have some of the most evocative names I have ever come across: 'Le Thugs'. 'Le Dogs'. 'Billy Bullock & The Broken Teeth'. And my particular favourite, 'Loudblast'.

The next day I reach Josselin, home of a medieval chateau. The town looks worthy of a wander round, but I am enjoying the cycling so much I carry on to Roc de St André, which was a mistake. Having set up my tent, I take a walk around the village and decide that I do not like Roc de St André. The people are unfriendly and unsmiling. The shops sell nothing except brands of beer I've never heard of and what appears to be second-hand fruit. As I walk the streets becoming increasingly depressed, I have a sudden longing for a glass of Pernod. Yes, I think. A glass of Pernod. That will cheer me up. I go to the nearest bar and ask for 'Un Ricard'. The barmaid says, 'Ricard?' I say 'Oui. Un Ricard.' She says, 'Bien,' then brings me a black coffee. Even more depressed, I crawl back to the campsite.

Terrible driving rain accompanies me the following morning. I endure it for a while, then find shelter, then move on, repeating this pattern all day until I come to a deserted campsite in St Vincent sur Oust. The rain finally stops, so I set up my tent then go into the village, where I discover a pleasant bar. Back at the campsite, two French families have taken the pitch next to mine.

They apologetically tell me, in broken English, 'We are noisy.' What that means is, they and their children like to talk. At about 8.45 I hear one of the mothers shushing the excited, chattering children, then, a little while later, the stern voice of a father doing the same. I can't bear the idea that kids on a campsite have to be quiet because of some grumpy old man from England, so I leap out from my tent and find myself facing a man with tense shoulders and a wary expression. I say, '*Pardon, Monsieur. C'est ne pas de problème pour moi si les enfants avez un conversation. C'est bon pour moi. C'est comme la musique.*'

'*Merci*,' he says, as I go back to my tent, feeling all righteous and smug. It only occurs to me later that he was probably thinking, 'It might be "*comme la musique*" for you, mate, but I've had a whole bloody day of it and now I want some peace.'

Next day, I take quiet roads towards Nantes when I come upon a quaint fishing village, Nort-sur-Erdre. But instead of sturdy, pipe-smoking fisher-folk, busying themselves with nets and the like, the whole village appears to be overrun with roadies. Huge men in T-shirts are erecting huge PA systems on every corner. Every part of the town, from bandstand to bus shelter, is being converted to a stage. In the town centre I discover the reason why. A jazz festival is just about to happen. Eagerly, I scan a poster, hoping to see the names of two jazz friends: Will Gaines, the self-styled 'Jazz Hoofer', and his accompanist, the multi-instrumentalist (and multi-talented) Charlotte Glasson. Their presence here would be a wonderful coincidence and a welcome treat. But there is no sign of either of them.

\*

I met Charlotte and Will at one of my latter Edinburgh Festivals, 1996, in which I was performing *Poems to Read to Your Parents*, a show for children. I can't remember what inspired me to go and see them, but I'm so glad that I did. Will was already on stage as I walked into the venue. He was chatting away to the audience, while dancing, as he always did, and the audience were, as always, ignoring everything he said. This was because they were mesmerised by his feet.

Will's tap-dancing skills appeared to be effortless. His feet seemed scarcely to be moving at all, but every venue he played would be filled by the rhythmic staccato sounds coming from his shoes, sounds pure and simple, enchanting and entrancing. I fell in love with Will's feet the moment I first heard them. Everybody did.

Will was born in Baltimore, Maryland, in 1928, moving with his family to Detroit where, during the Depression, he began his career, dancing on the streets 'as a way to make money'. By the early 1950s he was in New York, working in Cab Calloway's Cotton Club Show in Harlem. Since then, Will had worked with Nat King Cole, Thelonius Monk, Sammy Davis Jr, Louis Armstrong, Aretha Franklin, Dizzy Gillespie and Duke Ellington. And now it was my turn.

The piano player in Will's band was, coincidentally, a friend of mine. He said something to Charlotte, she said something to Will, and the next thing I know I was up on stage performing with them, reciting one of my poems. Will danced, tapping along to my words, while hearing them for the very first time. Taking their lead from Charlotte, the band joined in, never intruding on the words of the poem or on what Will was doing, merely complementing both, before reaching an ending so perfect that it felt as though it had been rehearsed for weeks.

It was one of the best experiences I have ever had, on stage or off it. It was also one that I wanted to have again. I started attending virtually all the shows that Will and Charlotte did, very often joining them on stage. At one gig, I decided to surprise Will with a poem I'd written.

Some men fly
Some men fall
Some men climb
Some men crawl
Some men walk about in chains
Some rejoice and some complain

But Mr Will
But Mr Will
But Mr Will Gaines

Dance on stars
Dance on drains
Dance on broken
Window panes
Dance away your ball & chain
Dance away your aches and pains
Like Mr Will
Like Mr Will
Like Mr Will Gaines

Dance for life
Dance for love
Dance for all
You're worthy of
Not for fortune not for fame
Not for glory not for gain

Ask Mr Will and he'll explain
Dance for joy and joy remains
And joy remains
And joy remains
With Mr Will
With Mr Will
With Mr Will Gaines.

Will loved it. Which meant, I soon realised, that I hadn't written a poem so much as built a rod with which to beat my own back. Over the following years, Will invited me to more of his performances, with the unspoken assumption that my 'Will Gaines poem' would always be on the bill.

One of the final shows I did with Will was in 2003, for his '75th Birthday Bash' at a club in London's Covent Garden. Among the guests were: 'bass giant' Ron Mathewson, who was born in 1944; legendary Harlem dance duo The Clark Brothers, both in their eighties; the Jiving Lindy Hoppers, an 'internationally acclaimed jazz-dance company' most of whom were in their twenties; another octogenarian, Jamaican-born saxophonist Andy Hamilton; Charlotte Glasson and me. It was a bill of mixed race, mixed sex, mixed age, and (in my case) mixed abilities. And I was prouder than I can say to be a part of it.

Reviewing the show in the *Guardian*, jazz critic John Fordham concluded his piece by writing, 'A night to savour – for music's sake, and humanity's in general'.

Will passed away in 2014. Never again will I be able to beat my own back with the rod I built for Will. This saddens me more than I can say.

\*

Disappointed at the absence of Will and Charlotte, I wheel my bike through the narrow streets of Nort-sur-Erdre, and, as I do, I pass long processions of various groups of musicians, all strolling the streets and playing as they stroll. I was toying with the idea of staying in the town for a few days and watching some of the festival, but seeing the musicians makes me think again. There are hundreds of them. And even though they're all members of different bands, they are all dressed the same (straw hats and blazers); they are all playing the same instruments (banjo, trumpet, tuba, drum); and they are all playing the same tune. After about five minutes, all I can think is 'I have to get away from this terrible jazz'. But there is no escape from this terrible jazz. Not in Nort-sur-Erdre. In Nort-sur-Erdre it is always Summertime, The Living is Always Easy, Bill Bailey Will Never Come Home and the Fucking Saints Will Go Marching In Forever.

I get back on my bike and continue towards Nantes, the sound of jazz fading behind me, to be replaced, on the outskirts of town, by the quietly pleasing peal of church bells, which are being played, weirdly, in syncopated time. The only decent music I've heard all day.

*

Nantes is large but surprisingly likeable, with its clean, wide streets, its big sky and its choice of public transport – the tram.

Somewhere in the world there is a man who thought that getting rid of the tram was a good idea. What we need to do is track this man down and hit him over the head with something large and heavy. Such as a tram. Trams are wonderful. No fumes. A timetable that can be adhered to. And lots of opportunities for fun and laughter whenever some cyclist gets stuck in a literal rut.

Despite being a large city, Nantes, the Tourist Office informs me, has only one campsite, luckily not far from the centre. The campsite, like Nantes, is big. It's also full. There is only one place left: the smallest and, clearly, the least loved pitch in the whole of Nantes. But it will do.

The campsite has a shop. It's expensive, but I'm not in the mood to go wandering around a huge city in the hope of finding a supermarket, so I shop there, stocking up on veg, fruit, tobacco and booze. For some reason I'm feeling depressed and, oddly, lonely. Solitude has been more than welcome on every stage of this journey; but there is a difference between solitude and loneliness, and loneliness is what I'm feeling now. My spirits sink lower and lower. I have alcohol, but alcohol, for once, is not the answer. Especially when the question is, 'Would you like some marijuana?' I would, but I have no idea how to get hold of any. I'm not in Holland now.

It's as I'm brooding on this, sitting at a bench overlooking the campsite while sipping on a can of beer, that an unhappy-looking young man, clutching a recently rolled cigarette, wanders over and asks me for a light. I'd bought tobacco and cigarette papers in the campsite shop, which had rewarded my custom with two free boxes of matches. I give him one. His face, appropriately, lights up. Almost as if this is the best thing that's happened to him all day.

We chat in a combination of broken English and fractured French until a friend of his makes his way towards us on a BMX bike. He's Spanish, apparently, and clearly a hustler. I watch him bum a cigarette off someone before he comes over, greets his friend, and then immediately asks me if I have any beer for them. Admiring his style, I give him twenty euros to get some cans from the nearby shop. He and his mate go off together, and I assume I'll never see them again. But they return. We chat some more as we drink our beers, then, finally, the Spanish guy mentions drugs. Do I like them? Yes, I do. Would I like some? Yes, I would. After asking how much I'd like to spend, he picks up his bike and pedals away, stopping only to shout something inaudible to some passing girls. I turn to his sad-eyed friend. 'What did he say?'

'He asked them if they would fuck him.'

I make a face.

'He does not think with his head,' says his friend. 'He thinks with his cock.'

What an idiot, I think, conveniently forgetting Debbie/Dubai.

Whatever he thinks with, the Spanish guy returns ten minutes later with the goods. I give him €40, we all start rolling up and suddenly the day becomes a whole lot better. The sad-eyed boy stops looking sad. The Spanish boy stops begging girls to fuck him. I stop feeling lonely. Finally, after a pleasant hour, I wander dreamily back to my tent and eat up every single piece of food I can lay my hands on, including some grass.

Having reached Nantes, I now have to decide where I want to go next. I pop into a cybercafé to check my emails but there is nothing of interest. I'm about to shut down the computer and leave the café when a new message appears. It's from friends of my sister. They are in France, and ask if I would like to meet. Given that they virtually saved my life when I was staying in my sister's house, I say I'd be glad to.

My sister is one of those strange, unfathomable creatures whose kitchen contains not only unopened bottles of wine but also bottles of spirits that still have spirits inside them. This made no sense to me. Or so I thought, while staying there in her absence.

Obviously, some help is required in emptying these bottles, I said to myself. I'd been engaged in this charitable work for a good couple of hours when I decided to wander out of my sister's house and into the garden. I looked at the stars for a couple of minutes, then decided to go back inside. But I couldn't. The back door was locked and I was on the wrong side of it. This was bad news. I was locked out of the house with nowhere to sleep except for a garden shed. And I was reluctant to sleep in the garden shed as it was cold and I had no underpants to put on my head. I was wondering what to do when my sister's friends appeared, on their way home from the pub. They took me to their house where they gave me a bed for the night. Next morning we returned to my sister's house and worked out how to break down the back door while avoiding any damage. We were scratching our heads over this when one of them decided to walk around to the other side of the house and check the front door. It was not only unlocked but wide open. As I'd left it.

Their email informs me that they are holidaying on the Île de Ré, which is not only quite close but also, according to my guidebook, car-free, and therefore worth a visit. All I have to do is leave Nantes, head south, and turn right. I have the usual hellish task of leaving a big city, where roads and traffic combine to make maps unreadable and escape impossible, but I finally get out. I then have a nice and easy ride to the village of Clisson, where I spend the night.

Next day I head towards a local railway station, in hope of finding a train that will take me anywhere close to the Île de Ré. The station is small and deserted, the road towards it leading directly onto the platform. Without thinking, I ride my bike onto the platform, at which point a stationmaster leaps out of his office and proceeds to give me one of the biggest bollockings I've ever had. In French. The bollocking goes on for a good five minutes before I interject with a 'Pardon, Monsieur,' at which point he stops, looks at me strangely and says, '*Anglais*?' I nod. '*Oui.*' He takes a deep breath and then gives me the exact same bollocking all over again, only this time in fluent English.

Once the bollocking is over, I am free to look at the timetable and discover that I can take a train to a town on the coast, Les Sables d'Olonne. I do so, and I'm glad that I did, for the unvarying countryside through which the train travels would have been a real bore to have cycled through. Les Sables d'Olonne turns out to be a large seaside town, so I leave it and travel to the smaller and therefore nicer town of Jard sur Mer. A night's camping there, then off through La Tranche and onto a cheap and cheerful campsite at Triaize (which charges the somewhat strange fee of €4.31). The next day I suffer a gruelling ride in gale-force winds and non-stop rain, magnified a hundredfold on the three kilometres of bridge that takes me to the Île de Ré, where I find a campsite, pitch my tent and collapse into it, exhausted.

The following day, I meet my sister's friends and generously let them buy me lunch. We have a nice long lazy time with plenty of red wine and hardly any jokes about drunken buffoons who think they have locked themselves out of their sister's house but actually haven't. Then we say our goodbyes and I stagger off to my tent, where I sleep through the rest of the afternoon and on until the following morning.

I'd planned on spending the following day exploring the car-free Île de Ré, but decide against it, mainly because it's full of cars. Instead, I head for the massive bridge and the way out. This time I have the wind behind me, which is good, because the rain is heavy, the skies are dark and the traffic is thick. I struggle into La Rochelle and on to a campsite, 'Le Bateau', expensive at €13 but opposite an estuary where boats are moored, which makes the expense worthwhile. Try mooring a lot of boats on an estuary and make them look anything less than beautiful. It can't be done.

I awake to a misty morning, clear blue skies, and a nice and easy ride alongside the river Charente, cycling along quiet roads that lead to Cognac and the birthplace of one of the most evil drinks ever devised by the pitiless minds of cruel men. Stopping in the town square to shout, 'Thanks for all the headaches, you bastards', I cycle on, spending day after enjoyable day cycling through picturesque villages before arriving at the most picturesque of them all, Baignes-Sainte-Radegonde, home to a supermarket; a café with Internet access; a shop selling English books and newspapers, plus an assortment of friendly-looking bars. 'This looks good,' I think. 'This looks like the ideal place to rest for a few days.' I follow signposts that take me to the local campsite. It's shut.

I curse a bit but I'm not surprised. It's the middle of September and although some campsites will still be open, many of them, especially les Camping Municipal, which are the cheapest and the more pleasant, are beginning to close. I decide to head for the coast, via Bordeaux, where, I hope, campsites will still be available. I can then cycle down to Spain, and Bilbao, where a ferry will take me back to England.

\*

This was my plan. It seemed like a good plan. What I didn't know was that, during the execution of this plan, I would lose a much-loved friend. And an encounter with a young female chiropractor would result in a sexual experience that I have never had before. And, I hope, will never have again.

\*

I reach a large and featureless town, Libourne. There is no sign of a campsite, so I carry on, hoping that something will turn up. Nothing does. It's getting dark. I take myself off the main road and onto a quiet country lane. There I find a field to spend the night in.

This is where I lose my much-loved friend. As I insert the pole into my little blue tent there is a loud and horrible crack – it is not, as I'd hoped, the sound of one of my limbs breaking. This is worse. This is the sound of my tent pole snapping in two. I try and remove it from the tent, hoping I can tape it together, or fix it somehow, but there is no way I can free the pole, other than cutting open the tent, and ruining it further. There is nothing I can do.

But it's a warm night. There is a full moon. Instead of climbing into the tent I wrap the tent around me and lie back. There is no light either from streetlamps or nearby houses. I look up at a sky full of stars. There is no traffic. The only sound is the sound of crickets, a sound that increases, until all I can hear is a million soulful jazz crickets, crickets wailing wild cricket riffs on tiny cricket saxophones, a wild jiving cricket requiem to my poor departed tent.

Next morning, I pack and leave the tent behind, spread across the field like a strange bird fallen from an alien sky. I don't feel guilty for leaving the tent behind, as if it were litter. It is not litter and I am not littering. Instead, I am leaving my tent behind in the hope that someone will find it, restore it, and use it, lovingly, as I did.

*

In Bordeaux, the Tourist Office directs me to the nearest camping shop. I buy a new tent then journey on to Labouheyre, a sleepy little town with no sign of a camping site and no hotels either. An old man sees me scratching my head over the Centre Ville signpost, and asks, '*Perdu?*' I reply, '*Je cherche la terraine de camping*,' and he directs me to a campsite that seems to be closed. It is deserted except for a solitary caravan. I start, dubiously, to erect my new tent, wondering if some irate official is shortly to appear and tell me (a) that the campsite is closed, and (b) to clear off. A woman wanders over from the caravan. Even though I speak to her in English, she has decided that I'm French and talks loudly, each exaggerated word accompanied by bad mime. She tells me that we can use the campsite but there is no e-lec-tri-city; and then she pretends, for some reason, to be a windmill. I thank her, finish putting up my tent, then wander into Labouheyre.

A travelling fair has come to the town but nobody has come to the fair. I am the only customer and I wander from stall to stall, feeling increasingly embarrassed on behalf of the stallholders. Even the most diligent of them is not going to waste time tempting me into having any fairground fun. I am not going to be riding the Whirling Teacups, nor the Ghost Train, nor the Dodgems. Nor am I going to be gorging myself on candyfloss and there is no way I'll be trying to win a giant fluffy toy by throwing some hoops over some ducks, as much as I'd like to. Instead, I watch a lovely happy mother who in turn is watching her lovely happy child riding a roundabout, sitting astride a miniature fire engine and, as I do, I find myself missing my kids. A fruitless task, as my sons stopped being kids a long time ago. I very much like the young men they have become and I always enjoy their company. But never again will I walk into a room and have two bundles of excitement screaming 'Daddy!' at me before leaping into my arms.

This is one of the many things I have in common with Bob Dylan. We both write songs and sing them. We both have voices that many people do not like. And we both have no one to go home to. No wives, no children. Only an empty nest and no real point in returning home at all. Perhaps this is why we are both on the road. Me on my bike; Bob on his Never Ending Tour. Perhaps we should change places, I think. Bob could borrow my bike and cycle from one campsite to another before publishing his experiences in a crowd-funded book. While I could tour the world croaking out Bob's songs while telling his rapidly dwindling audience, 'If you think I'm bad you should hear the bloke I'm replacing.'

Back at the campsite, another English couple, also in a caravan, have arrived. The female half of the pair tells me how brave I must be, travelling alone, as 'there are boys on motorbikes'.

Next day I pack, and, sitting cross-legged on the ground, check my maps and decide to move further inland. I am just about to get up and go when I notice that one of my tent pegs has not been packed away. I reach over to pull it out of the ground, thus making one of the biggest mistakes of my life.

I know how you remove a tent peg. You stand astride the tent peg, insert the hook of your hammer into it, bend the knees slightly, and then pull, taking great care not to put any tension on your spine. What you do *not* do is sit cross-legged with your back to the tent peg, turn around with the top half of your body at right angles to the bottom half, and then, using only your bare hands, try and pull the tent peg out of the ground. The reason that you don't do this is because the tent peg will stay exactly where it was, while your spine, your muscles, and every single one of your bones will immediately go into an entirely new position. This will not be a problem at first. But very soon it will be. Very soon you will be in constant and unbearable pain that will only become worse if you do something like, oh, I don't know – ride a bike.

I spend the day in increasing agony until I reach a campsite in Mugron, where I dull the pain by swigging massive amounts of alcohol. I can't swig massive amounts of alcohol the following day as I'm riding my bike. Instead I stop at every food store I come across and buy bags of frozen vegetables which I stick down the back of my trousers, earning me the kind of looks from passing French people that I can well do without.

I reach Dax, a small town I hate the sight of, and press on to nearby Peyrehorade, despite the pain in my back. There I find a Tourist Office, staffed, luckily, by a woman who speaks English. Having been told of my problem, she makes sympathetic noises before ringing a chiropractor and booking an appointment for the following day. She also directs me to the nearest campsite, where I find I can only unpack and pitch my tent by walking about bent double, doing what looks like an impression of a severely disabled Groucho Marx.

Next day I hobble along to the address given to me by the Tourist Office, where I'm horrified to discover that the chiropractor is a very attractive woman in her early twenties.

The first thing she does is to ask me to do something no attractive woman in her early twenties has ever asked me to do, before or since. 'I would like you,' she says, 'to strip down to your underpants and lie on this table.'

I do as she asks. I climb on to her table. I lie on my back and stare at the ceiling. What I have to do now, I decide, is to think of the most unerotic thing possible.

My death?

No . . .

Being operated on without an anaesthetic?

No . . .

Being tortured for information I don't have?

No . . .

Eventually, I decide on a feminist theatre group from the 1980s.

*I can't remember their name. What was their name? I can't remember. There were three of them. Three girls. I mean women. Three women.*

She leans over my prone body then asks me to turn over.

*They used to come on stage singing new words to an old tune.*

She runs her fingers down each side of my spine, stopping every now and then to prod various parts of my body and to ask, 'Is this painful?'

*The tune was Que Sera Sera and the new words were, 'You're a girl, you can't.'*

She asks me to sit up. She stands behind me, wraps her arms around me, and rocks me back and forth. Her breasts are brushing against me.

*When they were little they'd ask their parents, what could they be when they grew up? Could they be doctors or lawyers, like the boys?*

She lies me back down, takes hold of my naked feet, then places them against her chest.

*Their parents would say, 'Don't be silly. You're a girl, you can't.'*

She leans over me and says, 'I want you to push back as hard as you can.'

*Then they went to university and asked their professors the same question.*

She rolls me onto my front and begins to massage me gently, up and down my spine.

*Could they be doctors or lawyers, like the boys?*

I can feel her warm hands on my naked flesh.

*Their professors would say, 'Don't be silly. You're a girl, you can't.'*

She turns me onto my back, folds my arms across my chest, and takes hold of my shoulders.

*But now they are older and wiser.*
She rocks me from side to side.
*Now they have stopped listening to their parents and their professors . . .*
And then she says five words . . .
*They can be doctors or lawyers like the boys!*
Five words I'd been longing to hear . . .
*They can be whatever they want!*
'You can get dressed now.'
*'I'm a girl! I can!'*
I get dressed. I thank her. I pay her. I leave and go back to my tent, where I stagger around the campsite like a severely disabled Groucho Marx but for an entirely different reason.

Next day I begin packing, fully expecting a twinge followed by a spasm, followed by pain. But no. The chiropractor has done her job well. Superbly, in fact. But, then again, she's a girl, she can.

A pleasant and pain-free journey follows, as I ride along the coast and into the town of Bayonne, then on to Anglet, Biarritz and finally Hendaye, a small town that stands between France and the border of Spain. I pitch my tent for the final time. Appropriately, it is also the final night of the campsite. The following morning, as I pack away my camping gear, the campsite owners pack away theirs.

It's time for me to return home. I decide to cycle into Spain and take that ferry from Bilbao. The road to the ferry surprises me. I'd expected huge hills and I'm pleasantly surprised to find none. Instead, the road slopes gently to the ferry port, where I book myself a ticket for the following day. I then check into a hotel that costs me almost as much as the entire trip.

I have breakfast in splendid isolation before setting off to join the queue for the ferry. I am the only cyclist in a long line of lorries, cars and caravans. As we are waiting to board, a door opens and dockworkers wander out, presumably taking an early morning break. One of them shouts something and begins applauding. Others join in. I look over my shoulder. About two hundred Spanish dockworkers are applauding me. They almost certainly think that I am one of the many pilgrims who cycle, or walk, the Pilgrim's Route of Santiago de Compostela, which passes through Bilbao. They are applauding me for my commitment to a religious belief that I do not have. Or perhaps their applause is genuine, and they are clapping because I'm on a bike, rather than in a car or a caravan. Whatever the reason, applause is applause and I don't get it very often. And when I do get it, it's hardly ever from as many as two hundred people. I lift my hand in a thankful salute, heroic but modest, then I cycle onto the ferry.

In the words of the man who inspired the pilgrimage of Santiago de Compostela, 'It is finished.'

Until the next time.

# CHAPTER SEVEN
## Dad

It was 2008 and Dartmoor was calling. The place, not the prison. The website 'Visit Dartmoor' promised, 'winding country lanes . . . little or no traffic . . . ancient villages . . . rivers and streams', all of which sounded good to me. 'There are 368 square miles of spectacular scenery,' the website continued, 'mile upon mile of quiet wilderness and welcoming pubs. So what are you waiting for?' Nothing, I thought, and booked a train to Exeter, cycling twenty-five miles to Okehampton, a town situated on the northern edge of Dartmoor and the start of my proposed journey. There I had a phone call from my mother. My dad had fallen over, bashed his head on a radiator, and was now in hospital. My mother had rung to tell me there was nothing to worry about, which meant there was something to worry about.

Research the backstory of almost any successful comedian and you will invariably find an absent father. But there are many ways in which a father can help his son achieve comedy success. Cruelty, emotional coldness and tyranny will always work. It certainly did for Vivian Stanshall, leader of the Bonzo Dog Doo-Dah Band, and a wonderfully funny man. 'I'm still terrified of him now,' said an adult Stanshall. 'And he's been dead for two years.'

Robin Williams also referred to his father as 'frightening'. Steve Martin's dad brought out the comedy in his son by beating him with a belt. But most comedians' fathers don't need to go so far. All they need to do is abandon their son at an early age, either by leaving them or by dying.

I might have been more successful in my comedy career if my dad had had the decency to behave like any of the fathers listed above. Instead, he worked tirelessly and unceasingly, day in, day out, earning enough money to raise his children in a loving and supportive environment. The selfish bastard.

He was repaid by his eldest son, i.e. me, with sarcasm and mockery. I once gave my dad – born in Belfast – a piece of paper on which was written:

'How do you keep an Irishman busy for over an hour? PTO.'

On the other side was written:

'How do you keep an Irishman busy for over an hour? PTO.'

My dad turned the paper over three times. Then gave it back to me with a look so sorrowful it very nearly broke my heart.

I decided to abandon my trip to Dartmoor and went to see my dad.

*

Following his brief period of hospitalisation Dad quickly acquired a taste for falling, and began indulging in it fairly frequently. But falling wasn't his main problem. His main problem was being unable to breathe.

After retiring, my parents had moved to Southport, a seaside town on the north-west coast of England, where my dad took up golf. My dad's attitude to playing any form of sport was exactly the same as almost every other man: it wasn't the taking part that counted, it was the winning. And if he thought he couldn't win, he didn't play. As soon as my dad felt that he was not on top of whatever game he was playing, that game was abandoned. So the football he played in his youth gave way to darts; the darts gave way to snooker; and failing eyesight, and a less accurate aim, meant that snooker gave way to golf.

Southport's Municipal Golf Links, at which my dad played, has a course of just over 6,000 yards, a course my dad was increasingly unable to complete. 'Haven't got the puff,' was his clinical diagnosis. Through the months that followed, slowly but surely, more and more puff was taken from him until, eventually, my dad would not have any puff at all.

Having visited him in hospital, it was obvious that my dad's condition was not going to get any better; it was also obvious that someone had to be with him. My mother could not be expected to cope, alone, with the increasing frailty of a man she had loved and lived with for over half a century. My three siblings were all working. I wasn't. It was clearly up to me to be there for him. And there was another reason for me to be there. A good one, too. At some point I might return to stand-up comedy.

There is now a generation of comedians who, rather than do the decent thing and tell us a string of silly jokes, instead burden us with their opinions and their musings on life. Consequently, we are now seeing a comparatively recent trend: the Three Stages of Stand-Up.

Stage 1: The comedian is aged about twenty to thirty and he/she can't get a girl/boyfriend.

Stage 2: The comedian is aged about thirty-five to forty and he/she now has a girl/boyfriend. And kids.

Stage 3: The comedian is aged about fifty and he/she has had a parent die on them. Usually a father.

The good thing about being a comedian and having a father die on you is that you can express your grief on stage, get reviews that speak approvingly of your sensitivity and humanity, and also make a decent whack of money out of it. Which is not an option available to, let us say, a greengrocer. When a greengrocer's father dies, there's no money to be made at all. It's more likely that money will be lost, given that the only thing greengrocers can do is to place a card in their window saying, 'Closed Due to Death In The Family'. A card I have also seen in the windows of tobacconists and pubs but never, oddly, in the window of an undertaker's.

There are, I would imagine, further Stages of Stand-Up that the current generation of comedians has so far failed to reach. But if one day you're leafing through the programme for the Edinburgh Festival Fringe and come across a show with a title such as 'My Colostomy Bag and Me', you'll know that one of them has got there. My money's on Stewart Lee.

So, given that I might return to stand-up, spending time with my dad before his imminent death seemed to be not just the decent thing to do, it might even be tax-deductible. So I was with him for his increasingly frequent trips to the hospital and for his somewhat amusing excursions into hallucination and (slight) dementia. I was with him as his world became smaller and smaller, as every journey became more and more difficult, as the illness that began with him unable to complete a round of golf became one in which he could not get out of his own bed.

At one point he had sat on the side of that bed, as I waited to help him to the bathroom, wheezing and fighting to gain a breath and also to bring up the mucus that was choking him. 'I . . . am . . . sick . . . to . . . death . . . of . . . this . . . ' he said, and I, compassionately, thought, 'If only that were true.'

On another occasion, he had decided to make the long and impossible journey from his bedroom to the tiny garden where, in earlier days, he would sit and smoke and gaze at the flowers and the sky. My parents lived in a ground-floor flat, so there were no stairs involved, but it was still a long and difficult journey, beginning in his bedroom, then taking him through the living room, up two steps into a corridor, through the kitchen, then out through a back door into the garden.

The journey was not only long and impossible, but my dad had decided to make it at something like two o'clock in the morning. I thought we should at least give it a try. I had bought him a walking frame, and he hauled himself out of his bed, pulled himself up onto it, and then began shuffling from his bedroom into the living room, with me holding onto his arm. Halfway across the living room, his legs buckled beneath him. I managed to stop him from falling but there was no way he could carry on. There was also no way he could walk back to his bed. Somehow I managed to get myself both behind and underneath him, and half-fell, half-dragged him back to the bed, falling down onto it, with him, farcically, on top of me. I managed to roll him off me, pulled his legs up onto the bed, and then tried to prise the walking frame free of his fingers. He would not let go; he was still determined to continue his journey, still determined to get to his garden.

'If you won't let go of a walking frame,' I remember thinking, 'No wonder you won't let go of your life.'

But he did.

Usually, when the house was quiet and settled, I would get out a bottle of wine and drink before going to sleep. On one particular night, I didn't. I didn't even consider it. Instead, I climbed into bed and drifted off to sleep, waking just before dawn.

Normally, on waking early, I would check the time, faff about with the pillows and then try and get back to sleep. On this occasion, I simply lay quietly in bed, as if I were waiting for something to happen. It was then that I heard the voice of my dad, crying out, a single shout coming from somewhere above my head. And, as I heard his cry, the room I was in seemed to slide around me, at an angle, and I felt as though I was sliding too, slipping between this world and another reality altogether.

My heartbeat increased and, for a few seconds, I felt a sense of panic. Then normality returned and I turned over and went back to sleep, as though nothing had happened.

The next morning my mother woke me and told me that my dad was dead.

*

Derren Brown, a performer who uses 'magic, suggestion, psychology, misdirection and showmanship', is easily, in my pompous opinion, one of the finest performers to have ever set foot on a stage. A part of his performance (some might say too large a part) consists of him replicating and debunking the effects and trickery used by pseudo-psychics, most particularly those who claim to have contact with the dead. To which I say: hooray. Fraudulent psychics who prey on the bereaved are not just putrid low-life bottom-feeding scum. I'll go further. They are worse than bicycle thieves.

However, the fact that Derren Brown is able to expose psychic fraud does not mean that genuine psychics do not exist. After all, some people have been known to fake orgasms. But if there are genuine psychics out there they will not, I believe, be found on television or in huge concert halls and other venues normally reserved for comedians. They certainly won't be earning any money. True psychics will, I suspect, be quietly working somewhere else, without publicity. Possibly in a church hall somewhere. One that is nicely decorated and furnished with flowers.

Derren Brown is an atheist, and, like many other atheists, can't stop talking about God. Some atheists, not so long ago, were so full of the desire to communicate their belief that there is no God that they had a message to that effect printed on the side of a London bus. Why they couldn't make do with a felt-tip pen and a toilet wall is beyond me. Why, I wondered, had they arranged for that message (and a badly worded message at that) to be printed on the side of a bus? Presumably they thought that committed Christians, or the holders of any kind of faith, would read their message and instantly reappraise their belief systems. How typical of atheists that is. One might almost think that atheists have no respect for other people's intelligence. But, then, one might think that atheists have no respect for intelligence at all.

I once wrote a clumsy poem I was proud of. In it, I described an ant, running in 'panic-stricken state' after my hand, 'immense and monstrous brushed it from a picnic plate'. The ant's panic-stricken behaviour was, I suggested, an intelligent reaction to a possible threat.

If we can see intelligence at work in a figure as small as an ant, is it so difficult to postulate an intelligence that might be even bigger? Perhaps as big as a universe?

The atheist has no time for this notion. As far as the atheist is concerned, the best that intelligence can do is to grow to about six feet in height, have a big moustache and mad hair and come up with a theory to explain relativity. And that's about it. That's as far as intelligence can go.

There is a scene in *The Silver Chair*, a book by C. S. Lewis, in which an evil witch is trying to persuade two children and a creature called Puddleglum the Marshwiggle that the reality in which they believe does not exist. The only real world, she tells them, is the underground cave they are trapped in. Puddleglum counters her argument, first by extinguishing her magical fire with his bare foot, then by limping over and telling her that perhaps she is right – perhaps he and the children have invented things such as trees and grass and the sun and the moon and stars. Perhaps this black pit of a kingdom of hers is the only world. But if it is, he tells her, he doesn't think much of it. So much so, says Puddleglum, that he would rather live in his imaginary world than in her real world any day. Puddleglum, he informs the witch, is on the side of Aslan, his god, even if there isn't an Aslan. He is going to live like a Narnian, even if there isn't a Narnia.

The voice I heard above my head was, I believe, the voice of my father's soul, crying out as it left his body, as a baby will cry out as it enters into life. I also believe that Derren Brown (whom I admire) and his atheist friends (whom I don't) could happily offer me plenty of other explanations. But I do not listen to atheists, thank God. Instead, I listen to Puddleglum the Marshwiggle. And, like him, I'd rather live in my imaginary world than in the atheist's world any day. Perhaps because, in the atheist's world, my loving and lovable dad is dead and gone for ever. But in my world he is still around, still playing games involving balls, only now he has plenty of puff with which to play them.

Or perhaps my dad is sitting somewhere ethereal, puzzling over a piece of paper with the same message written on both sides: How Do You Keep An Irishman Busy for All Eternity? PTO.

# CHAPTER EIGHT
## Not Quite Land's End to Nowhere near John O'Groats

Following my father's funeral, I returned home to London, knowing that more change was imminent.

I'd expected various outcomes from my camping trips – a bad back, pneumonia, the invasion of my body by deadly campsite parasites. None of these happened. What did happen was that I developed an increasing love of solitude, silence and scenery. Silence especially. Back in London, I found myself growing increasingly weary of the endless chatter of voices – one voice in particular: my own.

That voice had been babbling away for at least forty-five years, its motivation always to draw attention to the person doing the talking, and almost always by making them laugh. Now I was wondering why. Why this constant desire to make people laugh? Was it some form of comic validation? Was this the best I could do with my life? I decided enough was enough. I no longer wanted to hear that voice. In order to turn it off, I decided to take it far away from everyone it knew. The property market at that time had become, in the terminology of estate agents, 'mad'. I sold my London flat for more than three times the price I'd paid for it, which meant I could buy a static and dilapidated houseboat on the Norfolk Broads and still have enough money to live on.

Once I'd made the move I quickly discovered the truth of the saying 'A boat is just a big hole that you throw money into.'

Even a boat that doesn't move. Various things needed doing to it, including replacing a roof, so while builders busied themselves with that I decided to cycle the clichéd Land's End to John O'Groats route. 'I won't commit myself to doing the entire thing,' I'd told myself. 'I'll simply start at the bottom and see how I get on.' After all, it's a long way.

The first thing I do is to miss my train. Arriving in Penzance four hours later than I'd planned, I decide not to faff about consulting guidebooks (partly because I didn't have any guidebooks), but simply book myself into the first hotel I see. This turns out to be a mistake. The first hotel I see is staffed by a burly, bearded bloke. His method of checking me in consists of surly requests for my details, which I give. He then tells me that my bill will be 'Forty pounds. In advance.' No 'please'; no 'thank you'; and all this accompanied by the unspoken accusation that I am the sort of person who would do a moonlit flit without paying the bill. I sign in with as good a grace as I can manage. I cannot believe that this oafish man is actually as rude as he appears to be. Surely this is some kind of Cornish comedy act, I tell myself. After all, this is a hotel he's working in, part of a service industry. Nobody, while dealing with a respectable adult cyclist with a credit card, would be as seriously ill-mannered as this, surely?

But he is. Having watched me wheel my bike into a storeroom, where I strip it of its four bags of luggage, he tells me there is no lift available, as 'this is a listed building'. He then steers his considerable belly into the listed bar, leaving me to struggle up three flights of stairs to my listed room. By the time I get there, I am gasping for breath and have horrendous pains in my chest. I throw my luggage on to the floor and myself onto the bed, wheezing and fighting for breath until, slowly, it returns to normal.

A wiser man than I might have spent some time thinking about these effects – the shortness of breath, the wheezing, the pains in the chest. I, being less than wise, was more concerned about getting (a) myself out of the hotel and (b) beer and tobacco into me. Which was a pity. A minute or two's contemplation then might have saved me a mountain of grief later.

I wander off to enjoy the streets and the pubs of Penzance. It's not long after eleven o'clock when I return to the hotel and find both doors, front and back, locked. The key I have been given fits neither. I am scratching my head and wondering what to do when a second customer appears, in the same predicament. Both of us are hoping that the other has a mobile phone with which to ring the hotel. Neither of us has. Also, the hotel has decided that a modern-day appliance such as a doorbell would not suit its listed appearance. With no other choice we bang on the front door.

Eventually, the burly bearded bloke appears and proceeds to moan at length about us getting him out of his bed. I lose my temper. If he wants the luxury of going to bed while hotel guests can't get to theirs, I tell him, then why not try issuing guests with front-door keys? The burly bearded bloke's reaction is to suggest, at the top of his voice, that I am 'always very welcome to stay somewhere else, SIR', the SIR being pronounced in such a way that it's quite clear that what he actually means is SCUM.

I say nothing. Instead I climb the many stairs that lead to my bedroom, while wondering what the purpose was of his belligerent remark. It's hardly likely that I would say, 'Thank you. On reflection, I will take advantage of your kind offer and stay elsewhere', then go upstairs, repack all my stuff, come back down, dig out my bike, get my money back, then go off at what is now past midnight in search of another hotel, so why on earth did he say it? Oh, I know why. IT'S BECAUSE HE'S A DICK.

The following morning I decide against having breakfast in a bar, which, apart from smelling of stale beer, has a radio playing pop music at full volume. I ask the burly bearded bloke if I can collect my bike and he responds with 'Oh yes, fetching a bike is one of the few things we somehow manage to get right.' Sarcasm for breakfast, I think. How lovely. Another row begins as I wheel my bike outside and pack my luggage on to it, with him following me and throwing insolent remarks in my direction.

'Last night,' he says, 'you treated me like poo.'

'This is what happens,' I say, 'when you behave like shit.'

This does not endear me to him. More insults are thrown my way: 'What kind of a hotel is this?' I say. 'You wouldn't even offer to help carry my luggage.' To which he replies, his face an angry purple, practically spitting the words in my face, 'Why should I?'

'Because you work in a HOTEL, you idiot,' I reply, unable to believe what he has just said to me. 'Welcome to Cornwall,' I add, before I cycle to the nearest Tourist Office where I register an ineffective complaint. (Ineffective because, despite telling them I was cycling from the bottom of Britain to the top, I heard nothing until I returned home months later and found a letter asking me if I wanted to 'carry on with' my complaint. I did. But by then it was too late.)

The day is improved by a pleasant ride along the coastal path that runs from Penzance to the intriguingly named Mousehole, my journey only slightly marred by the fact that, as I leave Penzance, I pass hotel after hotel, any one of which would easily have made a better alternative to the one I chose.

The bags on my bike have been badly packed, probably because they were packed in anger, and the weight is not distributed well. This is made clear when, as a favour to a car behind me, I turn aside on a narrow road to let it pass. Thrown off balance, my bike rears up in the air. For one giddy moment I am my childhood hero, Clayton Moore aka the Lone Ranger, astride his 'fiery horse with the speed of light, a cloud of dust and a hearty "Hi Yo Silver"'. The next, I am just some twat falling off his bike. And cursing himself for giving way to a car.

I pick myself up, repack my luggage, then press on to Mousehole before branching off across country and reaching Sennen, a small village about half a mile from Land's End. I consider cycling the half-mile to the Land's actual End, and then cycling the half-mile back, but decide that this would be the action of an idiot. Instead, I begin a long haul to St Just, which not only has a lovely square but also a lovely pub selling lovely pints. I have two of them before reaching the campsite, which is small, attractive, staffed by a friendly owner and one of the few campsites in Cornwall that does not have strange and conflicting rules about who is welcome to stay on their campsites and who is not. As I will discover later.

I am finding the Cornish hills a struggle, especially as they are cunningly arranged so that no sooner have you got to the bottom of one than you are almost immediately toiling up another. After an agonising fifteen miles of sweating, groaning and swearing I arrive in Hayle, which has a railway station, the sight of which I greet with sobs of relief. The hill to the station is so steep that I cannot get myself, my bike and my luggage up it. Instead I strip the bike, lock it, leave it, climb the hill with my bags, return, unlock the bike, push the bike up the hill, repack it, wait for a train, and then, a short while later, get off the train and cycle along narrow country lanes that lead to a huge but deserted campsite. The reception is closed but there is a doorbell, which I ring. A window opens above me and a woman's head pokes out. 'Are you on your own?'

I say, 'Yes.'

She comes downstairs and opens the reception door.

'Only if you were with another man I wouldn't let you in,' she says. 'Don't get me wrong,' she adds, 'I've got nothing against gays. I just won't have same-sex couples staying here.'

Her husband appears. 'A lot of campsites won't,' he tells me. 'They drink a load of lager then smash up the toilets.'

I cannot believe that we are still talking about gay men. Drinking a load of lager and smashing up toilets is not the behaviour of any of the gay men I know. Drinking a load of Chardonnay and redecorating the toilets? That I could understand.

I spend the night alone on the deserted campsite. Next day, I take a Sustrans route to Newquay where I find a campsite and a sign that reads: 'Couples only. No single men.' Why? I roll my exasperated eyes then cycle on until I find a campsite that is prepared to admit people who would simply like to camp, rather than people who are camp, or people who may or may not be camp, but are on their own.

The campsite is pleasant enough, as there is next to nobody there. To counter the solitude, pop music is being broadcast in the toilets. The broadcast comes courtesy of Cornwall's 'Pirate

Radio FM' and it pleases me that, unbeknownst to the idiot DJs who prattle gaily and irritatingly away, their merry banter only exists to cover the sound of constipated caravanners straining at their stools.

In Newquay I wander into a pub. I am the only customer there and the barmaid knows this but has decided, rather than serving me, to spend her time collecting glasses and emptying ashtrays. Finally, after a good ten minutes, she makes her gum-chewing way to the bar and says, 'What can I get you?' to which I say, 'Extremely annoyed.'

I sit outside with a pint and a cigarette. I enjoy the pint but I'm not enjoying the cigarette. Perhaps because, as the hills have got bigger, my breath has grown shorter and more and more painful. I sit and smoke and picture my lungs as two old men with broken teeth and yellow faces, reminiscing about the things they were able to do when younger: Play football. Run about. Breathe. I decide I have got to give up smoking. I resolve to stop first thing tomorrow morning. After the first fag of the day. The vital one.

Next morning, I have my first and vital cigarette of the day, then, a few minutes later the less vital one, and, finally, the least vital of all. But I still have it. Then I take my precious collection of smoker's stuff: my tobacco, my papers, my filter tips, my lighters, carry them over to the campsite bin, open the lid and throw them inside. They lie forlornly at the bottom of the bin, staring up at me, former friends, hurt and rejected. But I do not care. I feel better already. Healthier. Clean. I have made a decision that I will feel good about for the rest of my life. In fact, I'm already feeling good. Five minutes later I stop feeling good and feel like a cigarette.

I take Sustrans Route 32 to Padstow, cycling across country to the village of St Columb Major, which is small and pretty but nothing to write home about (although given that I send a postcard to my mother, I actually do). Twenty or so miles later I am on a hill overlooking picturesque fishing boats moored in an even more picturesque harbour. This is Padstow, famously the home of one of Britain's many celebrity chefs. The celebrity chef in question is one Rick Stein, who, like the rest of Britain's celebrity chefs, became famous by cooking food on television, then sitting back as thousands of viewers poured into his restaurants, eager to see if it tasted as bad as it looked.

Having booked myself into a nearby campsite, I stroll into Padstow and amuse myself by counting the number of buildings that have Rick Stein's name attached. I can find only four: a restaurant, a bistro, a café and a chip shop. 'Come on, Rick,' I think. 'Make an effort.'

I wander along the harbour wall overlooking the estuary and come across the Padstow Tourist Office. Inside, I pick up a leaflet, produced by local shopkeepers, that gives a short history of the town as well as details of its pubs, shops and restaurants. Nowhere is there any mention of Rick Stein. The thousands of tourists who pour into Padstow to eat his celebrated food may love Rick Stein. The locals clearly don't.

I put the leaflet back in the rack.

I have now run out of things to do in Padstow.

I sit on a bench. I drum my fingers on the woodwork. I stare out at the picturesque sea. In the old days, I think, when I was a smoker and time was hanging heavily on my hands, I would fill both the hours and my hands with something useful. Like a cigarette. But now, of course, I don't smoke.

Having started to think about smoking, I soon can't think of anything else.

The good thing about being a smoker, I've always thought, is that you always have something to look forward to. When you're having a meal, you think, 'I can have a cigarette after this.' When you're having sex you think, 'I can have a cigarette after this.' When you're having a cigarette, you think, 'I can have a cigarette after this.'

This is also true of drinking. If you enjoy drinking, then the phrase 'Let's have a drink' covers almost any possible event. What shall we do when we're happy? Have a drink. What shall we do when we're sad? Have a drink. What shall we do while we're waiting for our drinks? Have a drink.

Having had this thought process, I now want a beer. But there's a problem. When Mr Alcohol comes along, his good friend Mr Tobacco usually comes with him. I can't have one without the other. I sit and ponder my predicament for a minute. Then I hit on the only sensible solution – giving up on giving up. I march into the local supermarket, re-equip myself with smoker's stuff (old friends, so happy to see me again), go to the nearest pub, buy a pint, take it to a bench outside, have a sip of beer, then draw a massive lungful of cigarette smoke into my smoke-starved body.

God. It feels great.

In a perfect world, I would now hear a voice coming from the sky, and that voice would be saying, 'Enjoy it while it lasts. Your smoking days are very nearly over.' But the world is not perfect and I don't hear that voice. But I will.

The next day is cold, wet and windy. I decide to have breakfast at the famous Rick Stein café. I order Rick Stein's toasted sourdough bread with homemade marmalade and coffee. When the toast comes it is cold and underdone. The coffee is served in a cup, rather than a pot. The homemade marmalade never arrives. Presumably, it's still at home.

I now have nowhere to go and nothing to do and only rotten weather to do it in. So I take shelter in the nearby Metropole Hotel, where Padstow suddenly becomes an enjoyable place to be. I sit and read, happily undisturbed, for a good few hours. I have a comfortable armchair to sit in. There is no piped music. The staff leave me alone. And all for the price of one pot of Earl Grey and, a little while later, one pot of coffee. (In a POT, Rick Stein. An actual pot.)

Next morning, the weather improves, so I leave Padstow and set off along the Camel Trail, another former railway line, which runs through Wadebridge and Bodmin before ending at Wetfordbridge, approximately eighteen miles away. It is there that I see a wooden plaque that reads:

*The clatter of trains has long since passed*
*And the babble of the Camel can be heard at last.*

But, depressingly, the Camel Trail has come to an end. I cycle to Camelford itself, then on, through increasingly filthy weather, towards Launceston. The seemingly endless number of lorries, speeding past me through the driving rain, does not help the horribleness of the journey. Or my mood.

It's not much of a life being a lorry driver on your way to Launceston. The road is dull. The view is dull. But, luckily, Launceston has found a way to make the lives of lorry drivers so much more enjoyable. First, Launceston makes sure there is only one way for anyone to reach the town, which is by using a huge main road. Launceston then fills that road with huge holes. Having done that, Launceston sits back and waits for torrential rain to come. This doesn't take long. Once the torrential rain appears, Launceston then invites every lorry driver in the entire world to 'come along to rain-soaked Launceston and enjoy a merry game of Splash The Cyclist'. They all come.

Baffled by the absence of a sign that reads: 'Welcome to Launceston. Drive How You Like', I leave the horrid town and its horrid road, and, some twenty miles later, find a campsite in the tiny, and mercifully quiet, village of Bridgestow. Only £6 a night, plus it has a laundry. I do mine, washing all the clothes I have while I stand, naked, underneath waterproof jacket and trousers, feeling both strange and a little erotic. No. Not erotic. Not erotic at all.

Next day, a few miles north of Bridgestow, I experience authentic déjà vu as I cycle into Okehampton, where not long ago my proposed ride around Dartmoor came to a halt, thanks to my dad becoming selfishly ill and dying.

I then have a beautiful ride along another former railway line, this one forming part of Devon's Tarka trail. According to an information board at the ride's beginning, there are 180 miles of the Tarka Trail. The section I am riding runs for thirty miles between the towns of Braunton and Meeth and, happily for me, runs downhill. All I need do is sit in the saddle and watch the scenery fly by. No cycling required. I sit and freewheel all the way from Great Torrington to the town of Bideford, riding not only through tunnels of towering trees, from which I can hear the song of bird after bird, but also beside a river, which jumps and gurgles its way over rocks and stones and dappled sunlight. How perfect it all is: the trees, the birds, the sunlight, the water. This is some of the most beautiful scenery that I have ever seen.

But beautiful scenery is not enough. Someone has decided to improve it. By adding some Art.

First, there's a statue of a man alone upon a bench. Then, a little further on, a statue of a woman alone upon a bench. Then a bench on which the man and the woman are sitting together. Then a bench with the man alone. Then a bench with the woman also alone. So, no matter in which direction you are travelling, the couple are apart, they come together, and then they're apart again.

Which is all very well, and the best of luck to the artist who produced it. My only problem is, what's it doing here? Are the sky and the trees and the river and the sunlight and the bird song not enough? Do they need to be enhanced?

In more civilised parts of the world, art is kept in museums and galleries where it won't get out and bother the rest of us. But not here. Here, someone has decided to put art in the open air despite the fact that the open air might be better off without it. It's the same mentality that thinks we must have music playing everywhere we go. It doesn't matter where – bookshops, restaurants, dentists' waiting rooms. It's as though nothing could be worse than being in a room somewhere with 'nothing to occupy our minds'. We must be distracted at all times. I used to think this notion was nonsense and a bad idea. But then I rode on a London tube train and had to think again.

It wasn't a long journey, but that didn't stop me from berating myself for not having something to 'occupy my mind' – a book, a newspaper, a magazine, anything. I sat there, fuming and frustrated. Then a bunch of schoolchildren got on. They weren't worried about having nothing to occupy their minds. Their minds were happily occupied, thank you very much. They were having the time of their lives. Every single part of their journey was of interest to them, from the view out of the window to the tube train itself.

'Look at these children,' I said to myself. 'Are they berating themselves? No. Do they need to be distracted? No. Why? Because *they are enjoying the journey*.'

Struck by the contrast between my behaviour and the children's, and, more important, deeply impressed by my own insight, I fell into a deep and brooding introspective state which only ended when I realised I was sitting in a tube train with no lights on. In a terminus. That was shut. And the first thought that came to my mind was, 'If it wasn't for those bloody kids . . . '

I have what might be described as an artless ride to Barnstaple, before staying at another expensive campsite. £11. Clearly I'm heading further into tourist territory. The next day brings a long hard climb to Exmoor. It is cold, windy and raining. I arrive at Dulverton – a nice little village but with nowhere to stay, so I press on to the only campsite within reach – arriving exhausted, after twelve hours' cycling, to be charged a staggering £14. I compensate for this unwanted expense by throwing myself into a really bad mood and spending more money in a nearby pub.

Next day I cycle to Taunton, through Minehead, then on to Burnham-on-Sea, a town so boring it's twinned with itself. Here, the Tourist Office tells me, there are only two campsites. One is immense and expensive. The other is small but a long way away. I cycle around in baffled despair, then chance upon a small sleazy campsite in a small sleazy pub garden. The toilets and showers are filthy, but at only four pounds a night I am not complaining. Or having a shower. Or going to the toilet.

I cycle into Glastonbury via the strangely named village of Street, while vaguely wondering if somewhere in Street there's a street named Village. Which, I would imagine, is what everybody does. I'm setting up my tent when a young woman comes over and starts chatting. She is touring with her boyfriend. They are also camping but travelling by motorbike. What she'd rather be doing, she says wistfully, is travelling on a bicycle, slowly and happily, rather than quickly and unhappily on the back of a motorbike, making a lot of noise, gobbling up the miles and robbing her of any chance to enjoy the scenery.

Later, I watch her reaction as her motorcycling boyfriend talks to a pair of cyclists. They are heading for the same destination as him. 'But,' he says happily, 'I'll be there before you.' His girlfriend turns away. She looks as though she's about to be sick.

This relationship, I think to myself, is not going to last. The thing the man is most proud of is the same thing that makes the woman want to vomit. As usual.

The next day I decide to walk to the top of Glastonbury Tor. This decision would make a lot more sense if I didn't suffer from vertigo. Glastonbury Tor is 525 feet high, which doesn't sound a lot, but it is, especially when you're halfway up it. That's when the whole of Glastonbury Tor starts spinning around your head, your legs turn to jelly and your testicles turn to water. You'd like to stop but you can't. There's a queue of people behind you, it's a very narrow path, so you have to keep going. You do this while mentally chanting 'Don't look down, don't look down', which only serves to remind you that there is a down which you then look at it. You keep your eyes fixed on the impossibly distant top, which, miraculously, you eventually reach, with heavy breathing and an aching chest. Then you sit and wait for your panting to stop before you look at the view and think, 'Yes. Very pretty. Very nice. But I could have bought a postcard.' You then face the horror of going down. This is much harder than going up and made harder by the fact that now you have to look down. All the way.

It is while making my shaky descent that I pass another vertiginous fool who has chosen to climb Glastonbury Tor. She is sitting on a bench, visibly shaking and moaning to herself, over and over again, 'Oh my. Oh my.' She's either halfway up and can't go down or halfway down and can't go up. My heart goes out to her. But not my hand. Instead, I continue my selfish descent, 'Oh my. Oh my' receding into the distance, until I reach the bottom, leaving her behind me, still sitting on her bench, and sitting on it, probably, for the rest of her life.

\*

I leave Glastonbury and battle against the wind to Wells then on to Radstock, where I take a traffic-free route along the canal to Bath. Here, I find an Internet café and search online for a nearby campsite, choosing one which is, according to the dirty lying dogs who own it, 'Very Close To City Centre'. After thirty minutes of cycling and still no sign of it I ring them to ask for directions. The owner tells me he has no idea how I get to his campsite as 'I only took it over three months ago'.

A blanket of fine mist, wet but not cold, is all around me the next day, as I cycle along the canal path to Bristol, again without a map. My plan is to buy maps in Bristol, but when I arrive I can't face the effort of locking my bike then trudging around looking for shops that sell maps. Instead, I have an arduous slog following Sustrans signposts through the hills of Bristol before I reach the Severn Bridge and the road that leads to Chepstow.

My plan was to cycle from Chepstow to Monmouth and then find the grave of the late Jake Thackray, which I would anoint with a bottle of Newcastle Brown Ale.

Jake Thackray is considered by many, myself included, to be one of the finest singer/songwriters this country has produced. Unfortunately, as with so many artists, alcohol got the better of him. He spent his final days in Monmouth, gaining both weight and an aversion to performance. He died of a heart attack on Christmas Day.

Jake Thackray had been kind to me, when I was a young man. I'd supported him at a gig at Manchester University. He not only watched my act and afterwards gave me some welcome advice, but he also had two bottles of Newcastle Brown Ale waiting for me when I came off. A lovely gesture, and partly the reason for my plan to visit his grave and anoint it with a bottle of the stuff. (Well, I wouldn't want to drink it.) But after cycling the hills of Bristol, I was exhausted. The hills that led out of Chepstow looked a lot worse. I took one look at them, thought, 'Sorry about this, Jake, but sod it', and headed for the station and a train to Reading.

The train is fairly full to begin with, and picks up more and more passengers as we make our way east. I cannot understand why it is so busy and why it's full of people with rucksacks and tents and crates of beer until we reach Reading and I realise that there's a festival on. Nobody tells me anything.

It's close to nine o'clock as I begin cycling around the town, hoping to find a hotel or a B&B, which I do. In fact, I find hundreds of them. And all of them are full. I'm about to give in, return to the station, and either find a train to somewhere else or a back alley to sleep in, when I see a sign in a café window offering accommodation. The owner is locking up for the night, but he books me into a room, not only cheap and serviceable, but also containing an ashtray. I have been fighting the urge to smoke all day but an ashtray in a hotel bedroom is such a rare event that I decide that it would be churlish not to use it, go out, buy some cigarettes, bring them back and smoke them. How wonderful it is to be able to use any fatuous excuse to carry on killing yourself.

I have a quick ride around the town the next morning before I find the Sustrans Route that runs alongside the river and into the picturesque countryside that leads to Henley. As I enter the hill that stands above Henley I find myself cycling beside a huge, wooden fence that runs parallel with the road and wonder if I'm cycling past the house of the former Beatle, and the regrettably late, George Harrison.

I am and it is.

George was the only Beatle, as far as I know, to have written a song with a bike in it. 'Pisces Fish' is a song on his final album, in which he describes a bicycle ride along the part of the river Thames that runs through Henley. The ride begins badly for George due to a problem involving his chain and a crank, but he solves the problem (which is more than I could do) and continues his journey, the same journey that I make as I cycle alongside the Thames, seeing the same sights he mentions in his song: a brewery, geese, a temple on an island, and, as I do, I wish there was someone around to ask me if I ever knew George Harrison. 'Know him?' I would say. 'For God's sake – we used to go on bike rides together.'

From Henley I cycle to Banbury and then enjoy a sunny ride to Stratford-on-Avon, to which I often used to cycle from Birmingham, before I gave my bike away to a rag-and-bone man. (Let it go, John. Let it go.) I remember Stratford as being small and pretty. Now it's large and ugly. I spend the night in a hotel, then next morning visit a 'riverside bistro' for breakfast. I ask the Brummie waitress if she has Earl Grey tea. No, she tells me. Only 'normal' tea. They don't do toast, she tells me, so I ask for a croissant. The waitress shouts to someone in the kitchen, 'One Cross Ant.' She then pours boiling water into a minuscule cup, takes a teabag out of a box, lays it next to my cup and charges me a penny less than five quid. The room is full of the sound of pop music coming from a tinny radio so I take my tray outside, fondly imagining that I will enjoy my croissant and my tea by the side of the river. Minutes pass as I wait for the croissant. The croissant does not appear and my tea is getting cold. After five minutes I take a sip of tea, which more or less empties the cup. I sit as yet another five minutes go by, during which I wonder how picking up a piece of pastry, putting it on a plate and taking it outside could take over ten minutes. After another five minutes I give up and go. As I'm leaving, the waitress finally appears and calls out, 'What about your Cross Ant?' I turn and answer, 'What about your cross customer?' A bewildered look crosses her uncomprehending face and, for a moment, I feel sorry for her. But only for a moment.

I have an enjoyable ride through the West Midlands ending in a mostly off-road route alongside the River Rea to Birmingham, the journey ending in Cannon Hill Park, home of the Midlands Art Centre, where my showbiz life more or less began.

I decide to wander into the Arts Centre and wallow in nostalgia.

Except there is no nostalgia in which to wallow. The building has been rebuilt, refurbished, refashioned and renamed. MAC is its current title, presumably because the people of Birmingham can't cope with long, complicated words such as Midlands, Centre and Arts. Nowhere can I find a trace of a memory of the time I spent there. Everything I remember about the Midlands Arts Centre has gone.

This is typical of Birmingham. Decide to take a stroll down Memory Lane in Birmingham and you'll find it's been knocked down. I don't know what it is about Birmingham architects and Birmingham city planners, but after a couple of years they look at various bits of Birmingham and get itchy fingers and a voice inside their head saying, 'Knock it down! Rebuild! Rebuild!' They did this to my childhood home (not that I blame them), and all the buildings around it, the comic book shop, the sweet shops, the cinemas. But there are a few places that, mercifully, they have left alone.

One of them is the Fighting Cocks pub, about half a mile from the Arts Centre, in nearby Moseley Village. Another is the Bull's Head, also a pub and also in Moseley Village. The Fighting Cocks used to be where the hippies drank. The Bull's Head was home to the junkies. The people who drink in the Fighting Cocks now, I discover, are smart urban professionals. The hippies have migrated to the Bull's Head. They're older hippies, obviously; hair gone, stomachs protruding. I don't know which pub the junkies use. Presumably none. Presumably the junkies are dead.

I can't decide which of the two pubs to have a nostalgic drink in, so, employing the wisdom gained from years of alcohol use, I decide on both. I begin with the Fighting Cocks, where I sit at a table and listen to a man extolling, to everyone in earshot, the virtues of the newly acquired dog which lies panting at his feet.

WOMAN: What's his name?

MAN: Dudley.

WOMAN (*Incredulous*): Why'd you call him that?

MAN: I didn't. The rescue centre did. Anyway, what's wrong with Dudley?

WOMAN (*Laughing*): Nothing. Unless you live there.

MAN: I do.

Having exhausted the charms of the Fighting Cocks clientele and their dogs, I move on to the Bull's Head and there, to my astonishment, is Pete the Feet.

Years ago, Pete the Feet was a Fighting Cocks regular. Nicknamed Pete the Feet because he thought the wearing of shoes was the act of an eccentric person, he had, at that time, long hair, a wispy moustache and wore faded blue jeans and a T-shirt. Now, thirty years later, he has no hair, a wispy moustache, and is wearing faded blue jeans and a T-shirt. I look down at his feet. They are bare. I am pleased to see that no sign of recidivism can be laid at the foot of Pete the Feet.

My fondest memory of Pete the Feet is of the time he entered a Fancy Dress competition, held one Christmas in the Fighting Cocks. Pete the Feet was dressed as a barefoot policeman. He came second. The first prize went to his girlfriend. She came dressed as Pete the Feet.

After a happy chat with Pete the Feet I wander off to take a look at my old school, Park Hill Primary. I am wheeling my bike towards it when I pass two Brummies having a jokey, good-natured argument. They're of the same age, probably grew up together, and both have the same thick Brummie accent. One of them is white. The other is a Sikh. Seeing them, I am reminded of an old joke:

Q. How can you tell if he's a real Brummie?

A. He wears a shamrock in his turban.

It gives me a pang of pompous pleasure to see that a slightly racist joke has become an extremely pleasant reality.

I stand outside the gates of my old school, another building still miraculously intact, and remember the early Fifties, when I first went there, and when the first wave of immigrants came to Birmingham. In particular, I remember Paul, the first, and, at that time, the only black child to attend my school. I have no idea how it felt to be the only black child in an all-white school. How could I? I can only hope that he encountered curiosity rather than hostility. And I can only wonder if his progress in our all-white school society was made easier by the fact that he was shit-hot at football. He was also shit-hot at other sports and everything to do with education. I met him, a few years later, when we were both in different secondary schools. His was one of the top schools in the country. Mine was one step above a Borstal.

Our meeting happened because, in my secondary school, the lunchtime custom was for all pupils to be herded into the playground while the school doors were locked behind us. Not much caring for this, some classmates and I formed a school rugby team, meaning we could spend our lunchtimes indoors practising our non-existent rugby skills. There was one unforeseen consequence to this brilliant plan: sometimes we had to play rugby. One game was against King Edward's Grammar School and it was during that game that Paul and his teammates ran embarrassing rings around us. Paul was easily recognisable. Not just because of his sporting skills, but because he was still the only black-faced child in an all-white school.

It's while I'm remembering all this that a door of my old school opens and a teacher leads a line of children from the main part of the school to the playground at the rear. As they pass, I see children of virtually every skin colour and ethnicity available, from Asia to Zimbabwe. I see a rainbow of children.

I cycle on to the city centre, through once-familiar streets, now changed beyond all recognition. On Broad Street, once the home of a few dismal shoe shops and a pub, there is now an explosion of nightclubs, theatres and cocktail bars. The canals, that once offered nothing but abandoned prams and drowned cats, are now crowded with brightly lit bars and designer-clad couples walking hand-in-hand. Everywhere I look I see the expansion and growth of a vibrant and confident city. It makes me sick. It's as though Birmingham is screaming to the world, 'Bigger and Better than London! More Canals than Venice!'

'But still a joke,' I want to shout back.

'We know!' says Birmingham. 'Why is that?'

'Because of your accent, mate.'

Perhaps Birmingham's principal achievements are its nightclubs and its theatres and its art galleries and, as it's constantly saying, its having more canals than Venice. Or perhaps its true achievement might be that, after years of integration begun by courageous souls such as Paul, children can now attend a school without any concern whatsoever about the colour of their skin.

And that anyone, regardless of race, colour or creed, is entitled to call themselves a Brummie. And to be just as obstinate, cloth-eared and stupid as the rest of them.

The next day I take a train from Birmingham to Cheltenham, where I buy maps, then cycle through winding country lanes and tiny villages to Tewkesbury, followed by Worcester, then Stourport-on-Severn. There, I come across the 'Goodnight Sweetheart', a 1940s-themed tearoom, into which I pop for a 1940s pot of tea and a pre-war crumpet. An old-fashioned record player is playing Bing Crosby and the Andrew Sisters as I wander about checking out the memorabilia, which includes not only items from my childhood but also, on stairs hidden from the rest of the café, a framed photograph of the Beatles, autographed by all four of them, *and only lightly screwed to the wall*. This has nothing to do with the 1940s, but now is not the time to quibble over the authenticity of artefacts and time periods. Now is the time to drink my tea and eat my crumpet before coming back later with a small screwdriver and a large coat.

Then it's off to the canal that leads to Ironbridge. It's still raining heavily as I cycle the long and straight towpath, peering through rain-spattered spectacles at an increasingly strange sight ahead. It appears to be a group of alien beings with bulges erupting from the tops of their heads. I wonder, with rising excitement, if I've blundered into Narnia and am about to run into either Dufflepods, or, more thrillingly, Marshwiggles. But then I get closer and they turn out to be neither. They turn out to be nothing but fishermen sitting underneath big bloody umbrellas and ruining my day.

Disappointed, I cycle on and find myself in the tiny village of Hampton Loade, where I come across an old-fashioned railway station. The station, a sign informs me, is one of many restored to use by the historic Severn Valley Railway. I stop to enjoy the view, not only of the steam trains, but also the many men who are loving being there, and the women and children who are wishing they were somewhere else. One man simply stands and stares at the trains, a look of total pleasure filling his face. I'm with him on this one. Like him, and everybody else who grew up in the days of the old-fashioned steam trains, the sight of one fills me with pleasure. And not just because of the nostalgia they invoke, but because, like a bicycle, a steam train is a work of art. The only mistake you can make is to go for a ride in one. You think you're in for a treat. You're not. The real treat is to watch one go chuffing past, not to sit inside, looking out at all the people looking in.

There is also something of an irony here. In my childhood, the big thrill was not to watch old-fashioned steam engines but to wait for the rare, awe-inspiring electric monsters that roared their terrifying way from Birmingham through Olton Station and on to London.

'It'll be very fast and very loud,' I had warned my brother as we stood with our grandmother, waiting for just such a train. 'But don't worry. It'll soon be over.'

The train came screaming through the station and was, as I predicted, very fast and very loud and very soon over. What I'd failed to predict was that my brother would grip my grandmother's arm so hard that it would be bruised for weeks. And that I would wet my terrified pants.

I cycle from Ironbridge to Telford where I plan to take a train to Shrewsbury. The rain will not stop, the wind is constantly in my face, and my temper is not improving. The cycle path ends at the large, impersonal and (as they always are) hideous Telford Green Shopping Centre. 'Over 160 retail outfits', boasts a sign, as though this were something to be proud of. But there's more to Telford Green Shopping Centre than 160 retail outfits. There's also an eighteen-year-old man clutching a bible. He too has something to sell. It is God and, unfortunately for him, he has chosen to sell God to me.

'Excuse me,' he says, 'Have you ever heard of the name Jesus Christ?'

I stop and stare at him.

'What?'

He starts to repeat himself. I interrupt him. 'I heard what you said.'

He looks at me fearfully.

Then I say, 'How old do you think I am?'

This is tricky for him. Get it wrong and I might turn cross. Get it right and I might turn cross.

'Um . . . ' he says. 'Well . . . er . . . I suppose . . . '

I interrupt him again. 'Never mind how old I am,' I say.

He blinks. 'OK.'

'Do you think,' I say, 'that I have been living in this country – a Christian country – for never mind how many years, and yet I've still managed to have never heard of Jesus Christ?'

'Well, I suppose . . . '

'Because that would make me an idiot, wouldn't it?'

He clears his throat and looks away.

'So,' I say. 'Do I look like an idiot to you?'

His nervous eyes flicker as he looks me up and down. I catch sight of my reflection in a shop window: my rain-covered spectacles are halfway down my nose; mud covers my shorts, my legs and my socks; what is left of my hair is sticking out of my head in a style that can only be described as 'mad professor'.

'Don't answer that,' I tell him, then I stalk off, pushing my bike into the station, while he, presumably, gives up on selling God, pushes his bible into a bin, then goes and sits, shaking in a pub, wondering why, of all the mad people shuffling around Telford Green Shopping Centre, he had to pick the maddest of them all.

The train to Shrewsbury takes about five minutes. Finding the tourist office, thanks to signposts that disappear then reappear then disappear again, takes me half an hour. I persevere, get there and get a list of nearby campsites and B&Bs. I then cycle on to nearby Wem, where there are several campsites. I decide to choose the smallest, even though it's a few miles out of my way, reasoning that it should be the cheapest. When I get there, they charge me fifteen quid.

Next day I pack and set off, heading from Wem towards Chester via Whitchurch. I'm cycling happily along when I become aware of a strange clunking noise coming from my back wheel. At first, I think I've picked up a twig that has caught in a mudguard and will shortly slip loose, but no. The clunking continues. I dismount and have a look. A lump has appeared on the rim of my back wheel. I have no idea what it is or what to do about it. I get back on my bike. A couple of turns of the pedals and my bike comes to a stop. The wheel has jammed. I get off my bike and look down in horror as the rim slowly peels away from the wheel before dangling uselessly from it. The bike cannot be moved. I am in the middle of nowhere. There is nothing I can do.

It is fortunate for any cyclist stranded on the road that runs between Wem and Whitchurch that this is the home of a Mr P Foster. What Mr P Foster likes to do is hang around outside his garden gate and keep an eye open for any cyclists having any kind of trouble. He then attracts their attention and motions them over. The cyclist then picks up his bike, staggers up to Mr P Foster's garden gate, and puts his bike down. This is when one of the lenses in the cyclist's spectacles decides to fall out, hitting the ground but luckily not breaking. Mr P Foster is prepared for this. Mr P Foster says, 'Wait a second,' before disappearing into his house and returning, moments later, with a spectacle-fixing kit. He then picks up the spectacle lens from the pavement (you are unable to find the spectacle lens yourself because you need your spectacle lens to find your spectacle lens), mends your spectacles, has a chat about what's wrong with your bicycle, goes back into his house, makes a phone call and a short while later Ernest & Mary Ashton arrive in their spacious van. They load your bike into it and drive you to the nearest bike shop. There the kindly bike shop owner replaces your wheel. You then cycle back to Mr P Foster's house and collect your luggage from his garage (where it has been stored to make your journey to and from the bike shop less difficult). Mrs Anne Foster then offers you a bed for the night, taking charity and compassion to heights undreamed of. You thank her, but politely decline, before asking the Fosters for their name and address. Mr P Foster hands you his business card. You take it, thank them both again, then cycle off, promising yourself that you will send Mr and Mrs P Foster a thank-you present as soon as you possibly can. And do you do that? No. Of course you don't.

I find a campsite in nearby Chester, at £5 per night. It is a weekend and the site is filling quickly. Not with motorhomes, which are banned here despite being unobtrusive and quiet; but with cars, which are very obtrusive and certainly not quiet.

It never ceases to amaze me that motor manufacturers can brag about all the electronic devices with which they equip their cars, from sat-nav systems to neck-massaging headrests, but making a door that will shut quietly is beyond them.

A car arrives on the campsite. The husband parks it, gets out of it, slams the door. His wife opens her door, gets out of the car, slams the door. The kids in the back of the car open their doors and get out. But they don't slam their doors. No. They can't be bothered, and leave them wide open. This is not a problem, as their parents simply slam their doors for them. Then the husband realises he has left his cigarettes in the car. He goes to his car, opens the door, gets his cigarettes, slams the door. His wife, meanwhile, opens the boot to get out the stuff they brought for the trip. She takes out a couple of suitcases, puts them down, slams the boot. Meanwhile, her husband realises he has forgotten his lighter. He goes back to the car, opens the door, gets the lighter, slams the door. Then he walks round to the boot, opens it, takes out the crate of beer that was too heavy for his wife, puts it down, slams the boot. His wife carrier her suitcases to the door of their caravan. But where is the key to the caravan? It is in the car. She opens the car door, gets the key, slams the door. She takes her suitcases into the caravan. The husband takes his crate of beer into the caravan. For a short while there is silence. Then the family leave their caravan and return to their car. Four doors open. Four doors slam. The engine starts. The radio is turned on. The engine is running. But then the wife or the husband or one of the kids remembers they have left something in the caravan, open their door, slam the door, go into the caravan, get whatever it is that they've forgotten, come back to the car, open the door, get in, slam the door, and the car drives off.

Then more cars arrive. They all have doors.

From Chester I ride to Runcorn, then take an off-road cycle path to Widnes, which takes me to the outskirts of Liverpool. My plan is to take a train from Liverpool to Southport, spend some time with my mother, and then continue further north through Preston and on to the Scottish borders, before Scotland itself. But then again, I think, is that what I really want to do? Haven't I had as much of England as I can take? As I cycle through the sea of litter that surrounds Liverpool airport, I begin to wonder.

*

Some years ago, David Icke, a football player turned sports pundit, experienced some sort of mystical event which converted him from a pundit to a prophet. He then began touring Great Britain, lecturing on his cosmic conspiracy theories. I went to see him. At one point he said that following 'extensive research' he had come to the startling conclusion that the 'so-called Virgin Birth may never have actually happened', and I thought to myself: 'This is what happens when a footballer reads a book.'

David Icke's theories developed over the years into the belief that members of the British royal family belong to a worldwide elite of shape-shifting, blood-drinking extraterrestrial reptilians. I have no problems in believing this. The only problem I have is believing that a worldwide elite of shape-shifting, blood-drinking extraterrestrial reptilians would spend their time rattling around a freezing cold, draught-ridden palace, spending hour after hour awarding honours to C-list show-business personalities who have all done so much for charity. If I were a shape-shifting, blood-drinking extraterrestrial reptilian, I think I could find better things to do with my time.

If you're going to posit a conspiracy theory of any kind, posit one that bears out the facts as we know them. It seems to me that there *is* a conspiracy afoot, possibly global, but undeniably at work in England. I believe this conspiracy is organised by a group that originate from either another planet or another dimension.

I don't know exactly where they come from, but it is obviously a place that is ugly and vile and their mission is to make our world exactly like theirs.

I call this group the Ugluminati.

Why does every town in England look the same as all the others? Why does every high street have the same ugly shops selling the same ugly goods while from the same ugly speakers comes the same ugly music? And what about the 'people' who fill these ugly streets? Unable to chew gum with their mouths shut, or to eat while sitting down, they walk about constantly filling their faces with the ugliest food they can lay their hands on; food that is labelled 'fast food' because, when you see what it looks like, you think, 'I'd rather go on a fast.' Unable to take a step without carrying cardboard cups of cardboard coffee, forever talking into little black boxes to remind themselves of who and where they are, 'It's me. I'm on the train.' Walking about with wires coming out of their ears, listening to instructions being beamed into their alien heads: 'First the left foot, then the right . . . '

Are these creatures actually human? I find that hard to believe . . .

Take litter. Please don't expect me to believe that human beings would deliberately foul and besmirch the very place in which they live. Surely it is only an alien mentality that thinks a planet can be improved by covering it with cigarette packets, cigarette butts, pop bottles, beer cans, crisp packets, discarded fast food wrappings, and, on more occasions than I care to remember, used nappies?

The 1951 movie *The Thing from Another World* ends with the exhortation, 'Keep watching the skies!' I used to think that phrase prophetic. Now I don't. Now I believe that our planet is being attacked not from without but from within; and that reality is a lot less like *The Thing from Another World* and a lot more like *The Invasion of the Body Snatchers*, a film in which alien seedpods gradually replace the whole of humanity.

Rather than watch the skies, perhaps we should be watching ourselves. Which would be easier if we weren't so ugly.

\*

I decide to visit my mother and then go home. I could travel further north but, I ask myself, why? It will only be more of the same. I'd like to cycle in Scotland, but I'd prefer to treat Scotland as a foreign country, and not an extension of England. (Unlike a nameless award-winning comedian who once told an Edinburgh audience, 'I've just come back from a tour of Australia. It's so nice to be performing in England again,' before wondering why the rest of his act was received in grim silence.)

I remembered the time I was about to leave for Europe on my first cycling trip and my mother had said, half joking, 'Europe? Why Europe? What's wrong with your own country?'

I'm now in a position to tell her.

# CHAPTER NINE
## Norfolk/Ungood

I return to my houseboat and spend the autumn cycling around Norfolk, making many visits to the path that runs along the North Norfolk coast, enjoying the tourist-attractive Wells-next-the-Sea, as well as the equally charming Cley, also next-the-sea but, for some reason, not so prepared to show off about it. The coastal town of Cromer is a 1950s delight, unlike Great Yarmouth, not only further down the coast but also further down the food chain. If you're the kind of holidaymaker who thinks that Blackpool is vulgar and brash, try a visit to Great Yarmouth and see what vulgar and brash looks like when people really make an effort.

I also make several trips to nearby Diss, in a futile attempt to find the graveyard I once slept in; partly for reasons of nostalgia and partly because I left a pair of pants there.

I'm enjoying the tranquillity of houseboat life, the silence broken only by the quacking of ducks and geese and, at one time, the thrilling sight of a seal diving from the bank into the river. All is going well until one night when, sitting at home alone, I find myself unable to breath.

I stagger outside, stub out the cigarette I'd been smoking, then sit on the river bank, desperately gasping for breath. Eventually it comes. I sit, the panic subsiding as my breathing gradually returns to normal. Then I go back inside and try to work out what happened to me. While smoking another cigarette.

It gets worse. The hill that leads from my houseboat to the high street is, for some reason, becoming increasingly steep. I can only walk up it if I stop and rest every few paces. My breathing is laboured, I have pains in my chest, and I am coughing up great globs of phlegm every ten minutes.

But I still continue to smoke.

I try to stop. I buy tobacco, smoke some of it, then throw the rest away, swearing I will never smoke again. Then, an hour or so later, I am toiling back up the hill to buy more tobacco. This carries on for several weeks until I decide that what I need to do is 'clear out my pipes' with some hard exercise. Cycling is all very well, but it's a gentle activity. If I take up running, I reason, I'll get my lungs working, I'll bring up all the phlegm, I'll be able to breathe properly, and then I'll be able to smoke some more. Good plan.

Being a costume-wearing-compulsive, I spend unnecessary cash on running shoes, running trousers and a running sweatband to fit around my soon to be sweating head, and then I set off. Three minutes later, I have collapsed, bent double, tears streaming from my eyes, fighting for breath, coughing, retching and spitting, with a pounding pulse and palpitating heart. Running, I decide, is not the answer.

But what is? According to the tobacco industry, the only way to successfully wean myself from a nicotine habit is by indulging in more nicotine: nicotine patches, nicotine chewing gum, nicotine nasal sprays, nicotine inhalers, and, more recently, nicotine inhaled as vapour. All of which makes no sense. Nobody says to somebody on a diet, 'Eat more cake!' And, anyway, why should stopping be so hard? I manage it for eight hours every night when I'm asleep. I'm not waking up every fifteen minutes and having a smoke. Nor am I struggling out of bed, into my clothes, and then out into the streets looking for an all-night garage because I'm running low on cigarettes. This does happen. But only when I'm awake.

And what stupid behaviour that is, I think, before I remember other examples of smoking-related stupidity. Such as the time when I had no money and was wandering the streets, picking up discarded dog-ends, taking them home, emptying them out then rolling up and smoking something that felt as though it was ripping my lungs out.

Why did I put myself through such miserable degrading behaviour? Is it something I wanted to do? No, I think to myself, before using the world's feeblest defence: 'I was only obeying orders.'

Orders given to me by a plant.

For virtually the whole of my adult life, I realise, a plant has been ordering me about: telling me what to do (smoke) and when to do it (all the time). Well, I decide, not any more. A mantra comes to my mind, resonating with increasing viability and power: I WILL NOT BE DICTATED TO BY A PLANT.

I will stop smoking. I will not be using nicotine substitutes that only keep you addicted to the thing you're supposed to be giving up. I will simply repeat the same phrase, over and over: I WILL NOT BE DICTATED TO BY A PLANT.

I do this. And not only does it work, but it works almost immediately. In a very short time, I throw away my tobacco, my papers, and my collection of lighters. Finally and for ever, I am a smoke-free man.

Until that evening, when I take myself down to the pub. No sooner have I sat down with my pint of beer than a voice is whispering in my inner ear. 'Wouldn't a cigarette go nicely with that alcohol you're drinking . . . ?'

I've had enough of this.

'It doesn't have to be a cigarette,' says the voice.

I begin to bristle.

'What about a cigar?' says the voice.

I start to seethe.

'You don't inhale when you smoke a cigar,' the voice continues.

I've just about reached breaking point . . .

'A cigar wouldn't hurt.'

And then I snap. The voice becomes a living thing, a cigarette, six foot tall with a face and a neck, around which I have both my hands. 'Let's see how you like it,' I say, and then I begin to choke this Cigarette Monster, choke it to its death, all the while reciting my mantra, 'I WILL NOT BE DICTATED TO BY A PLANT.'

The cigarette monster runs away. The desire to smoke has gone – and it never returns.

Neither does my breath. I still can't climb the hill to the high street without stopping to rest. Even worse, I'm no longer able to ride my bike. If walking up the hill from my houseboat is hard work, pushing a bike up it is even harder. And when, after much effort, I manage to get my bike to the top of the hill and onto the road, even the smallest of hills proves impossible for me to cycle. And I'm talking about the hills of Norfolk.

It seems I have no choice. I have four stages to go through: (1) See a doctor. (2) Be diagnosed with cancer. (3) Go into hospital. (4) Die.

*

You'd think, with your death imminent, that the person in charge of telling you so would get his or her skates on and tell you fairly quickly. No such luck. Every two weeks, I toil up the hill to my doctor's surgery to get my cancer diagnosis. But does my doctor give me my cancer diagnosis? No, he does not. Instead, my doctor prefers to play some sort of cat-and-mouse game.

First, he takes a blood sample and sends it away. I wait for two weeks. The doctor rings me. I toil up the hill. The tests are negative. My doctor takes another blood sample and sends it away. I wait for two weeks. The doctor rings me. I toil up the hill. The second sample is also negative. My doctor decides that an X-ray of my chest may shed some light on the state of my lungs. He books me into a hospital. I go to the hospital. My chest is X-rayed. I return home. Two weeks later, the doctor rings me. I toil up the hill. My lungs are cancer-free. My doctor then suggests he takes another blood sample and, in two weeks – and then I lose my temper. I've been toiling up the hill to his surgery for nearly two months, I tell him. Can't things be done any quicker? My doctor is offended. And indignant. 'We can't work miracles,' he tells me. I tell him that I don't want a miracle. What I want is a diagnosis followed by some treatment. Miffed, my doctor makes an appointment for me to see the Practice Nurse. *On the following day.*

I toil up the hill and see the Practice Nurse. She asks me to blow into a tube. I do. She then gives me my diagnosis, proving yet again how much more efficient the world would be if it was run by middle-aged women, preferably ones who've had children.

'It's COPD,' she says.

Somewhere, in the back of my mind, a faint bell is rung. I look at her blankly.

'Chronic Obstructive Pulmonary Disease,' she explains. She then tells me what it is and what I can do about it.

COPD is a disease in which the airways and air sacs of the lungs have been irreversibly damaged by smoking, in my case by about 50 per cent. And what I can do about it is nothing. It's incurable. However, stopping smoking is good. If I had carried on smoking the disease would have got worse, my life would have become a lot shorter, and then I would have died.

It's then I remember where I had seen the letters COPD before: on my dad's death certificate.

You'd think that COPD, which can be fatal, would be a little better known. But no. Perhaps because it lacks a snappy and memorable name. Or perhaps because publicity-hungry, headline-grabbing cancer gets all the attention instead.

It's as if cancer is the only disease going. Every time you walk to the shops you're faced with charity collectors and their cancer buckets. Every workspace has people signing up other people to sponsor cancer-based fun-runs or cancer-based bike-rides. Every time you open a newspaper there's another story about some celebrity and how they've either won their 'brave battle' against cancer, or, if they've died, how they 'lost their brave battle' against cancer. And the only thing this constant talk of cancer accomplishes is a morbid fear that you've caught it yourself. Any minor ailment, twinge or ache triggers the automatic response, 'It's cancer.' Which doesn't help much, given that one of the things that causes cancer is worrying that you might have cancer. All this would annoy me less if the chances of getting COPD weren't much higher. If you're sixty and you smoke, your chances of getting cancer are about 10 per cent. If you smoke at any age, your chances of getting COPD are one in four. And if you're wondering whether you've got it or not, if you cough in the morning then you have. It's not proof that your really healthy lungs are expelling all those poisons, as I used to think. No. What I was expelling was the mucus produced by my lungs to cope with the effects of COPD.

Perhaps one of the reasons why COPD is less well known is that any smoker suffering with shortened breath, chest pains and a hacking cough assumes they've probably got the famous cancer, and, rather than do anything about it, think 'I'll take my chances', and reach for the cigarettes. I know I did. And so did my dad.

Having given me my long-awaited diagnosis, the Practice Nurse prescribes pills to cope with the mucus and inhalers to help with the breathing. My life is now easier. But riding a bicycle is still beyond me.

Which means I have to give my bicycle away.

I don't want to repeat the mistakes of my past and give my bicycle to a rag-and-bone man. Neither do I want to sell it to a stranger. But it has to go to someone. It's a bike. It's not meant to be locked up somewhere and left to rust. It's meant to be ridden.

Browsing the Web, I come across the non-profit organisation, *Bikes to Africa*. Reading further, I discover that I can take my bike to a drop-off point in nearby Ipswich. From there my bike, along with hundreds of others, will be shipped to Africa where it will be used either by a child riding to a school; by a nurse to visit the sick; by someone needing to collect vital supplies, such as water or firewood; or to reduce the times of journeys, often vital journeys, from hours to minutes.

My bike will be going to a good home. One of the best homes a bicycle can go to. Knowing this does a lot to lessen the imminent pain of separation. For both of us.

We take a train to Ipswich, intending to cycle to the drop-off point. This will be our last ride together. But then I discover, on leaving the station, that the front tyre has been punctured. With no other choice, we walk together to the drop-off point, a distance of just over a mile.

All too soon, we arrive. I remind my bicycle of the good it will be doing in Africa, of how happy it will make its new owner, and how enjoyable its new life will be. My bicycle agrees with everything I've said. We both know that our parting is for the best. But we are both still sad.

One last look, one last pat of the saddle, and then I walk away, leaving my bicycle behind me. We are parted for ever. I walk back to the railway station in Ipswich and then I travel home. Alone.

# CHAPTER TEN
## Putting the Ire in Ireland

'Jesus,' said the tipsy Irishman, supping from his roadside can of beer, 'You look like something out of *The Terminator*.'

And so I did. Though I preferred to think of myself as looking like something out of *Batman*. As I kept on saying to myself, and to anyone who would listen: 'If Batman rode a bicycle, this is the bicycle Batman would ride.'

The bicycle that Batman would ride is black, naturally. It can be folded, allegedly, and, more importantly, it is electric. This means that I can not only go on bike rides again, but on rides in a world that is completely flat and which has God's hand on my back, pushing me along like some benevolent dad. Buying this bike is one of the best decisions I've ever made. The only drawback to riding an electric bike is meeting people who are forever asking me if I'm riding an electric bike.

'Yes,' I reply. At which point, every single one of them asks the same question: 'And does it charge itself as you ride it?'

And then I say, 'No,' refraining from adding, 'Because that would make this a perpetual motion machine, which hasn't been invented yet because they're impossible.'

The second drawback is the occasional self-righteous cyclist who accuses me of 'cheating'. I could point out that you could make the same accusation of people who use gears, or tyres, or even pedals, these all being additions to the original design, but I don't. Instead, I wait until they're halfway up a particularly steep hill, then I cycle past them. Smugly.

There are also people who think that an electric bike is something you just sit on, switch on, and sail off into the sunset on. 'No,' I have to tell them. 'That's a lawnmower.' An electric bike is exactly the same as an ordinary bike: if you don't turn the pedals, it doesn't go. There is no other difference, which is disappointing, as I'd hoped that buying a new bike meant buying new clothes. Which meant more shopping. But no. My old clothes will be fine. I am able to do *some* shopping, though. My new bike has a luggage rack, but I can't attach any luggage to it. Its only use is to carry the battery that powers the engine. What I can do, is buy the Carry Freedom trailer, which is towed behind my bike, and is not only easy to assemble and easy to fit, but just as easy to take apart. Having bought a trailer, I now need to buy something to contain the things I'm going to be trailing, which means I get to buy a stylish (and waterproof) Big Red Bag.

Previously, all I had worn on my head, while cycling, was a baseball cap. The brim not only kept the sun out of my eyes, but could be swivelled around to stop the same sun from burning my neck (riding a bike is the only way you can wear a baseball cap back-to-front and not look like a tit). But given I'd never ridden an electric bike before, I decide to buy a helmet, which means I have to work out what my brains are worth.

I could buy the average chain-store helmet, which means I value my brains at approximately thirty-five quid. Or I could take my brains more seriously and protect them with an electronic airbag, made by a Swedish company, Hövding, and priced at £250. I decide that my brains are worth about sixty-five quid and buy a helmet for roughly that amount. Not wanting to look like some sort of human fly, I reject the standard helmet and buy something closer to what Arnold Schwarzenegger would wear. It's while wearing that, and cycling along on my new electric bike with my Big Red Bag on top of the trailer behind me, that my squiffy Irish friend compares me to a Terminator. The only time anyone has ever compared me to anything cool. Which is surprising. After all, I'm a bald, bespectacled cyclist who doesn't have a girlfriend.

\*

My previous camping trips had all been based on unfulfilled hopes and broken dreams. I'd imagined warm nights beneath starry skies, acoustic guitars strummed around campfires, dusky-eyed young women gazing dreamily at the slightly older but still fascinating cyclist sitting thrillingly close. In reality, there were no campfires, only municipal campsites, and the only people I ever saw were grey-faced Germans trundling chemical toilets towards the shower block. Now, as I ride through Southern Ireland, my dreams are similarly romantic: misty morning loughs, ceilidhs in whitewashed stone-walled pubs, dusky-eyed colleens gazing dreamily at the slightly older but still fascinating cyclist sitting thrillingly close. These dreams also remain unfulfilled. I'm not saying that any of the above isn't available in Ireland. I'm just saying it was never available to me.

\*

My journey starts with a train to Holyhead. The train company, according to its website, will carry bikes (providing you pre-book), but, they proudly announce, they don't carry trailers. So at Euston station I take the trailer off the bike, take the Big Red Bag off the trailer, take the wheels off the trailer, place the wheels and the rest of the trailer in a large laundry bag brought with me for that purpose, hoist the laundry bag over one shoulder, hang the weighty Big Red Bag from the other and, steering my bike with my free hand, lumber my way towards the waiting train. The only problem I have is with the metal bar that attaches the trailer to the bike, which pokes out of the laundry bag and bangs the top of my head with infuriating regularity. Thank God I'm wearing a helmet. I stagger to the train, stow away my bike, find my carriage, find my seat, stow away my luggage, then sit back, breathless and exhausted. Two hours later I arrive in Chester, where I have to change trains. This means I have to collect my luggage, collect my bike, get off the train, load up my bike, wheel my bike to a lift, take the lift up to the concourse, wheel my bike to another lift, take that lift down to the platform where I find the Holyhead train, stow away my bike, stow away my luggage, find my carriage, find my seat and collapse into the seat, while all the while the metal bar that attaches my trailer to my bike bangs the top of my head with infuriating regularity.

Things aren't helped by a placard in my carriage which reads, 'Let the train take the strain.'

At Holyhead I reassemble the trailer, fit it to the bike and set off in search of the B&B I'd booked earlier. This takes longer than I'd expected, as Holyhead council have decided that equipping their streets with signs telling you what the streets are called would make life too easy and much less of a challenge for any Holyhead visitors. A taxi driver gives me directions and I find the tiny back street in which I'm staying. The owner has left a note on the door: 'Can't Hear The Doorbell So Please Ring'. The telephone number is written underneath. I ring it. No answer. The owner must be out. Perhaps that's why he can't hear the doorbell. However, he's left a message on his phone saying that the front-door key has been left underneath a plant pot on the front step. How wise, I think. No one would dream of looking for it there.

I'm happy to share the owner's belief that the thieves of Holyhead don't have the wit to read notes on doors, make phone calls, listen to messages, pick up plant pots, take keys and then help themselves to the contents of a house. But I'm not going to make life easy for them and leave my bike outside. Instead, I take it into the house and park it in the hall. My room, as always, is on the top floor. I haul my luggage up to the room, and then spend a happy fifteen minutes lying on the bed trying to get my breath back. Not long afterwards the owner knocks on my door and tells me 'not to worry about my bike as it will be fine in the hall'. This is good news. If he'd asked me to move it I would have had to kill him.

The next day is a Friday, and also the thirteenth, but I fearlessly board the ferry anyway. The company's website promises a 'stress free' journey to Dun Laoghaire, which is a few miles south of

Dublin, but I swiftly feel stressed as there is nowhere on board to escape the TV; television sets are everywhere. In Dun Laoghaire I disembark, and, impatient to start my journey, decide against exploring the town and set off. My plan is to cycle along the coast towards Cork, and, as usual, simply see what happens. In other words, my plan is not to have a plan. Again. I am becoming used to my electric bike, and find the best thing to do is to cycle at the lowest setting, which keeps the power consumption low, meaning the battery lasts longer. The wind is in my face, which doesn't help, but I persevere over large hills into Bray, then have a nice long descent into the seaside town of Greystones. There is nowhere to camp, but I find a B&B at €50. I shower, then mooch around the town.

The next day is cold and windy, the wind once more in my face, as I cycle to Wicklow. I find a campsite close to the sea and take a solitary stroll along the deserted beach, which, as always, reminds me of the Acker Bilk tune, 'Stranger on the Shore', while I, as always, wish that it didn't.

'Stranger on the Shore' is the only instrumental featuring a clarinet to go to Number 1 in the charts. In 1969, the Apollo astronauts took a copy with them on their journey to the moon. Which isn't far enough. Acker Bilk referred to the tune as his 'old age pension', which is fine. I just wish his old age pension wasn't stuck in my head for the whole of the following day and the day after that and the day after that.

The wind is in my face the next day as I cycle on to Arklow, a dreary town full of dreary shops and no campsites. I find a B&B at €35, close to the town centre, and have a pint of Guinness in a nearby pub.

The received wisdom used to be that you haven't tasted Guinness until you've tasted it in Ireland. Perhaps that was true some years ago, but it isn't true now. There is a difference between the Guinness in Ireland and the Guinness in England: it's about 50p. And not in Ireland's favour.

I travel from Arklow through Courtown, the wind in my face, then on to a campsite in Kilmuchridge. €8 plus another €2 for electricity, but, I am told, showers are 'free for cyclists'. I jokingly say, 'Because we need them more,' and get the serious reply, 'And it's harder for you to get here.'

Then a gruelling ride up the many hills of Wexford, with – guess what – the wind in my face. This wind-in-the-face thing is getting on my nerves and, literally, up my nose. Plus, the roads of Ireland are easily the worst I have ever cycled on, cracked and broken, with enormous potholes strategically placed at the bottom of every enormous hill.

I reach a campsite in Wexford and realise, when I wake in the night on cold, hard ground, that my mattress has been punctured. I can only repair it by locating the puncture, which means immersing my mattress in a bath full of water and, given that finding a bath full of water on a campsite is impossible, I decide to replace it, so stroll into Wexford. I'd thought that a stroll around the town while shopping for a new mattress would be a pleasant way to spend the morning. I was wrong.

I find a camping shop and greet its owner with a cheerful 'Good morning'. He responds with a grunt. I ignore his grunt and ask, 'Do you sell Thermarest mattresses?'

'Eh?'

'I'm looking for a Thermarest mattress.'

'What is that?' he asks, belligerently.

'It's a self-inflating mattress made by a company called Thermarest,' I say.

'Here,' he says, reaching under the counter and producing something bigger than the trailer I hope to carry it on. 'This is a self-inflating mattress.'

'Thanks,' I say, 'But it's not the kind I'm looking for.' As I reach the door he suddenly snarls, 'You won't find any in this town.'

He seems pleased at the prospect. He's also wrong. I find a branch of Argos which sells self-inflating mattresses similar in size and shape to a Thermarest. The assistant asks me if I want a bag to carry it away in. When I say that I do, she charges me an additional 22 cents. When I comment on the unusual amount and light-heartedly say, 'Why not twenty cents? Or twenty-five?'

she snaps, 'Tax. You may not have to pay tax in England but in Ireland you do.'

I then visit the library, where I ask the librarian if, and how, I can access the Internet. Without looking up, she responds, 'Come back in an hour.'

I cannot understand why everybody is being so rude. Then I pick up a local newspaper and discover why. The Queen of England is making a visit to Ireland. It will cost the country about a million euros. And it's obviously all my fault. Clearly, the Queen of England wouldn't have dreamt of visiting Ireland if I hadn't rung the Palace and invited her personally.

'But where will I stay?' she'd asked.

'There's plenty of campsites,' I tell her. 'And if you come on a bike the showers are free.'

I had experienced rudeness and belligerence in Ireland before, during the late Seventies, when I toured there, supporting a band. The band in question was Alberto y Lost Trios Paranoias, and when the lead singer wasn't having objects hurled into his face by members of the crowd, attractive colleens were beguiling the backstage security staff before helping themselves to the contents of our dressing rooms.

Alberto y Lost Trios Paranoias, or the Berts as they were known, were yet another comedy-rock band, this time from Manchester. At that time I was living in the bleakness of nearby Bacup, home of the famous Nutters, and finding like-minded people such as the Berts was a lifesaver. Most of the band members were ordinary working musicians with, as was usual in a comedy-rock band, virtually no sense of humour. An exception was, as it invariably is, the drummer, Bruce Mitchell, a man around whom legends have accrued like gaffer tape to the jeans of a roadie.

Most of the people who took mind-expanding psychedelic drugs during the nineteen sixties decided to keep a low profile while doing so. Bruce wasn't one of them. It was about two in the morning when Bruce, having expanded his mind, was happily walking along London's Wardour Street with his feet stuffed into two dustbin lids. A passing policeman asked him, 'What the fuck do you think you're doing?' Bruce replied, 'I'm walking on the surface of the moon.'

Being asked 'What the fuck do you think you're doing?' happened to Bruce a lot. During our tour of Ireland, Bruce decided he'd like to take a look at the Giant's Causeway, a series of immense basalt columns formed about fifty to sixty million years ago by intense volcanic activity. Most tourists who decide to take a look at this ancient wonder do so by parking their cars in the nearby Visitor's Centre then walking to it. Bruce decided to drive. There was a safety barrier in the car park, designed to stop drivers from doing just that, but that didn't bother Bruce. He simply lifted it aside, drove down to the Giant's Causeway, decided he didn't think much of it, then reversed the van back up and out through the exit. This time it was the turn of an angry security attendant to bang on the side of the van and ask Bruce 'what the fuck he thought he was doing?' Bruce rolled down his window and told him, 'It's all right. We're in a band.'

As well as working with the Berts, I became involved in Manchester's music scene, performing at various punk venues, including one venue, the Russell Club, where, as was usual for the time, the audience expressed their dislike of the acts on stage by spitting on them. You might wonder how the audience expressed their approval of the acts on stage. They did this by spitting on them. What I didn't realise was that being spat on by the youth of Manchester would indirectly lead, years later, to my very nearly becoming a cool dad.

## INTERLUDE: A COOL DAD

My younger son came home from school one day and said, 'Dad, is it true you used to tour with Joy Division?'

It was true. I had. I'd almost forgotten about it. It was nearly twenty-five years before, after all. What I'd also forgotten was that during those years the cult of Joy Division had grown, and now kids of my son's age, about sixteen, were listening to them. The band was considered cool and so was anyone associated with them. Even me.

Apart from sharing the same initials, Joy Division and I shared the same record label.

Factory Records, formed in the late 1970s was the brainchild, principally, of Tony Wilson, a television presenter and unlikely music fan. I had got to know him, partly due to his attending the clubs at which I had become the target of spittle-crazed youth. He enjoyed my act and told me that he intended putting out a record. He had three bands signed to the project, needed a fourth, and wondered if I had any songs that he could use. Unluckily for him, I had.

The record, *A Factory Sampler*, was released in January of 1979. A series of gigs was organised. Other Factory bands on the bill included A Certain Ratio, Orchestral Manoeuvres in the Dark and, of course, Joy Division. 'This will be a democratic gig,' Tony Wilson had announced. 'We will change the running order every night. No single band will be top of the bill.' And so it very nearly was. Every night there was a different running order. And every night Joy Division was at the top of it.

Which suited me fine. Having them finish the evening meant (a) I didn't have to follow them and (b) I didn't have to sit through their doom-laden music and could sit in the pub instead.

I didn't get to know any members of the band. I don't even recall speaking to any of them. Strangely, though, I do remember exchanging a nod and smile with Ian Curtis, the lyricist and singer, at almost every gig we did together; as if to acknowledge that we both came from very different worlds and it was probably best to keep it that way.

Ian Curtis took his own life in May of 1980, a tragedy that seems to become even more tragic as the years go by. Tony Wilson died of a heart attack in 2007. An enthusiastic proselytiser of all things Northern, Tony was often referred to as 'Mr Manchester'. On the news of his death, the flag that flew above Manchester Town Hall was lowered to half-mast. Deservedly so.

RIP both men. And thank you, Tony Wilson, for helping me to become (very nearly) a cool dad.

*

In Ireland, I leave Wexford and set off, not only with wind in my face, but also sleet. The sleet becomes bored with its sleety existence and swiftly turns into the far more manly driving rain. Enjoying its transformation, it stays like this all day; a day that becomes, as days often will, one in which everything goes wrong.

My Big Red Bag has been sliding about on top of the trailer and is now rubbing against one of the wheels. The wheel begins grinding against the waterproof coating on the Big Red Bag, creating a high-pitched whining noise, which I decide to ignore. I then take a wrong turn and cycle up a steep hill that turns into a dirt track and then stops altogether. I am on the edge of a forest with nowhere to go. This gives me the chance to find out what has been causing all the high-pitched whining. When I see the state of my Big Red Bag I am horrified. I get off the bike to fix the bag. The bike falls over. I swear, pick up the bike, reposition the Big Red Bag, then cycle back down the hill to the main road, where I realise that I'm now lost. I have no idea which stretch of the road I'm on, where the road is going, or where it has come from. All I know is that the road is full of cars and they are all driving as fast as they possibly can, probably because their owners want to get out of the rain and go home. As do I.

I decide to get away from the constant stream of cars, so I leave the main road and cycle down a series of back roads, hoping to spot a signpost. There are no signposts but there are potholes. I am soon seriously lost, but at least I have the driving rain to keep me company. Also, all the fun of avoiding the potholes. After several hours of this, I turn a corner and find myself back on the same stretch of road I'd left earlier, which is still full of cars all driving as fast as they possibly can. Having no other choice, I stay on the road and try to cope with the non-stop driving rain and the non-stop driving drivers. Finally I come across a signpost, which informs me, I am relieved to find, that I'm at least going in the right direction. I press on and reach the tiny village of Arthurstown, close to the Waterford Harbour estuary, which I hope will have a B&B. It does. It is called Arthur's Rest, but Arthur does not answer his doorbell. Presumably he's resting. I take a ferry over the estuary and onto the road that leads to Waterford, hoping to find a B&B on the way. After twenty minutes, there is no sign of any B&Bs and my electric battery is running low. I am not far from Waterford though, I reason, where accommodation should be both plentiful and easy to find. Then I spot another of Southern Ireland's rare, but welcome, signposts. But this signpost is not so welcome. Apparently I made yet another wrong turn and I'm now cycling in the exact opposite direction to Waterford. And it's too late to turn back now. My battery is on its last legs and so am I. My big fear is that I will run out of power then find myself at the bottom of a hill. If that happens, I am doomed. On the plus side, the countryside looks nice. Or it does until the sun begins to go down, taking the light with it. This is all I need. Now my big fear is that I'll not only be stuck at the bottom of a hill without any means of getting up it, but I'll be stuck there in the dark. But then, miraculously, I find myself descending a long, long hill into Dunmore East, a tiny seaside village where there's an inn, which is not only open but has accommodation. I grab a beer from the bar, crawl up the stairs and get into my room and outside my beer. A dreadful day has come to a welcome end. And not just a welcome end, but also a quite beautiful one. My room overlooks the bay and later, as I eat food ordered from the bar, I watch the moon appear in a cloudless sky and do its lunatic dance upon the waves below my window. Ah.

The next morning I pack, leave, and spend the day struggling up large hills before finding a campsite, which is in the charge of the Vaguest Man in Ireland. I give him a €50 note. He gives me change for €20. It takes about an hour to sort this out. I then try to buy a token for the shower. He charges me €1 but fails to give me the token. Following the €50 debacle, I can't face going through it all again, and all for the sake of €1, so simply don't have the shower I just paid for.

The next day the winds are in my face – of course they are – but the sun is shining and the rain has stopped, which means I have an unusually pleasant journey to Dungarvan, where I find a campsite charging €10 to camp, but nothing for charging my battery, which is good. What isn't good is that the campsite is overrun with hens. As I make myself an evening meal of bread, cheese and tomatoes, various hens run up and run off with my food. One hen is particularly persistent. I assume this to be the Alpha hen. It grabs a large piece of cheese and runs off with it. I decide to teach this hen a lesson as to who's who in the pecking order. I chase after it. The hen runs behind my tent. I run after the hen. The hen ducks under a guy rope, doubles back, and makes off with a bit of my bread. I can't believe it. I have been outwitted by a hen – the stupidest creature in the farmyard. First, the geese in Holland. Now, an Irish hen. Will these bird wars never end?

The chain on my bicycle has started to rattle for no apparent reason. This worries me, so I cycle into Dungarvan the following morning, where the Tourist Office directs me to a bike shop. I meet the owner and explain the problem. He says, 'Come back in an hour.' I leave my bike with him and stroll about for sixty minutes before returning. The job has not been done, because, the owner tells me, he 'had to go out'.

I leave him to it for a second time and wander off to have a late breakfast in the Shamrock Café, where dynamic and efficient women provide me with not only a huge basket of toast and marmalade but also a pot of delicious coffee. I then go back to the bike shop. The job is still not done, but I am now accustomed to the Irish way of doing things and simply stand over the owner until he does it. As he solves the chain-rattling problem, and inflates my tyres without being asked, I tell him that I'm not having a great trip so far. He tells me that he's not surprised. I ask his advice for a good place to go. He thinks for a while before finally suggesting Killarney. Killarney is 150 kilometres away.

I leave Dungarvan and spend another day with the wind in my face, as well as rain, before I reach Youghal, a town named after an Irishman with a phlegm problem. I book myself into a B&B, then stroll around the town before calling into the local pub. The barman greets me by ignoring my presence and continuing to read his newspaper. He can't be doing this because I'm English. I haven't spoken, so my accent hasn't given me away. Neither am I wearing a sign on my chest that reads, 'Hallo. I am English. Please Treat Me Like Shit.' Eventually, he looks up and I'm finally, and grudgingly, served. As I sip my beer I wander around the pub, which is scattered with memorabilia. I am pleasantly surprised to discover that John Huston and Gregory Peck stayed here while filming the classic *Moby Dick*. There is a letter from Huston, displayed on a wall, in which he says how delightful the people and the town of Youghal are, and how well they have treated his crew and himself. What a pity, then, that the current barman is a miserable, unhelpful and surly little tit. Not much Moby but plenty of Dick.

A long, slow and monotonous ride on the N25 takes me towards Blarney. I pass a pub and decide to stop, hoping for a pot of tea. The pub is tiny. It's also empty. The owner appears from a kitchen behind the bar and looks at me blankly. I say, 'A pot of tea?'

He looks at me even more blankly. He then says, 'Potato?'

'No,' I say. 'Tea. A pot of tea.'

'No, no, no,' he says. 'We don't do nothing like that.'

'No coffee?'

'No. There's a place down the road a mile back . . . '

He names the place. I remember seeing it and it's actually about five miles back. I feel like saying, 'Thank you so much for being too sodding mean to put a kettle on the stove, shove a teabag into a cup, and charge me two quid for it you unhelpful Irish sod.' Instead, I say, 'All right. Just give my potato and I'll go.'

I arrive in Blarney, home of the famous Stone, the kissing of which is meant to give you 'the gift of the gab'. I find this claim doubtful, but then again, clearly, it worked at least once. Why else would hordes of American tourists fork out good money to snog a lump of rock?

I find a campsite. It's a Friday, and, feeling I could do with a rest, I decide to book myself in for three days. I change my mind when the person in the campsite office asks me if I need to use electricity. I tell her I do, but only to charge my bike's battery. 'It takes about four hours,' I tell her, 'And costs about half a euro.'

She smiles sweetly, then charges me an extra €10 'for the electricity'. At which point I reach the conclusion, 'Sod this' and decide to leave the next day. My intention is to head north before turning west and on to Killarney. The next day I reach the Killarney road and a blustering wind, backed by hard, driving rain, hits me, once again, full in the face. I have now, finally and for ever, had as much Ireland as I can take. If the wind is so insistent on blowing me eastward, I decide, then eastward I will go.

On the other side of the Irish Channel is the coast of Wales and the home of a woman who was once my wife. I send her a text telling her I'm thinking of heading in her direction. She responds with an invitation to visit her. This seems like a plan. Why continue making myself miserable in Ireland, I think, when I could be making life miserable for an ex-wife in Wales? I turn my bike towards the coast and, with the wind and the rain finally behind me, I begin, at last, to enjoy my visit to Ireland. By leaving it.

# CHAPTER ELEVEN
## *Wales*

As the Rosslare ferry enters the port of Fishguard, my thoughts turn with some anticipation towards the woman who is waiting – a woman I have seen only once since our marriage ended, over twenty years ago. A chance encounter had led to us spending a chaste evening together in my London flat. My fear had been that the evening would consist of stilted conversation followed by the return of old resentments before ending with a screaming row. Instead, we'd got on well. Very well. This had been a surprise to me, until I realised we were like two old men, meeting for the first time, thinking they had nothing in common before realising that they'd both fought in the same terrible war. But on opposite sides.

Now we are about to meet for the second time and, as I wait for the ferry gates to open, I find myself wondering if there might still be a spark of attraction between us. If so, it's a spark I intend to fan into an ember, then a flame, then finally, if not an actual bonfire, at least something I can warm my hands on. Then I wheel my bike off the ferry and find her dressed from head to foot in asbestos; two fire-fighters stand either side of her, both breathing through gasmasks and clutching an axe. They are with us through the rest of the day; they are with us when we go to the pub for supper, they are with us when we walk back to her house, and they are most definitely with us when we retire to our separate bedrooms, vigilantly standing either side of her bedroom door.

The next day is something of an improvement. The fire-fighters are nowhere to be seen as she drives us to a nearby place that I've always wanted to visit: Portmeirion.

Portmeirion is, famously, the village designed by the architect Clough Williams-Ellis, in which was filmed *The Prisoner*, a 1960s TV series starring Patrick McGoohan. McGoohan played an unnamed former secret agent who is trapped in the mysterious Village. Each week McGoohan (Number Six) has to battle his captor (Number Two) while trying to discover who is running the mysterious Village (Number One). At the end of the series Number One turns out to be Number Six, which caused something of a furore at the time, despite the programme beginning each week with the same piece of dialogue:

NUMBER SIX: Who is Number One?

NUMBER TWO: You are Number Six.

*The Prisoner* was, perhaps, ahead of its time, in that it began as a standard secret agent-type thriller but quickly became more surreal and more fanciful as the series progressed and the writers and producers realised that they had no idea how to end it, or even what was going on. In this way, the programme became something of a trailblazer for other ideas that began well but descended into tosh, such as the TV series *Lost* and the British Labour Party.

While my former wife wastes her time admiring the Portmeirion architecture, the gardens, and the extensive range of exotic plants, I engage in more worthwhile activities, i.e. running around pretending to be Patrick McGoohan. Then we return to her car and she drives me back to Fishguard, where I plan to cycle along the Pembrokeshire coast to Swansea, before taking a train home. I unfold my bike, reassemble my trailer, and we bid each other goodbye, my fond hope being that once she feels my strong, manly arms around her the spark of attraction that she may or may not feel for me will burst into passionate flame. Instead, I find myself hugging her from the waist up only. The fire-fighters are back. I mount my bike and cycle away, rejected by the same woman for the second, and, I would imagine, the final time.

Say what you like about me, but when I get dumped and divorced I stay dumped and divorced.

*

I cycle around Fishguard until I find signposts for the Sustrans route which will take me along the coast to Swansea. The route from Fishguard runs alongside a busy road. It's also uphill, and the Welsh wind has decided to mimic the behaviour of its Irish friend and is blowing full into my face. I push on until I reach a campsite on the coast, close to the city of St Davids. St Davids is small, picturesque and popular with tourists, so the campsite is correspondingly big and impersonal. It's also full. The receptionist is doubtful that they have room for me, despite my owning one of the smallest tents known to man. I ask her why the town is so busy. 'Is there anything special happening in St Davids?' I ask. 'Yes,' she replies. 'August.'

Eventually she finds me a spot tucked away in the corner of a field. Having set up my tent, I wander into town. Every bar and every restaurant is heaving. I'd hoped to find myself in a quiet, quaint fishing village with quaint fishermen's cottages and quaint fishermen quaffing pints of wallop while entertaining customers with quaint fishermen's tales. Instead, I'm surrounded by the whole of north London. My immediate reaction is to get out of St Davids as quickly as possible.

I leave the next day, cycling along quiet lanes before reaching a large and steep hill which, I am pleased to see, has defeated a party of slim, young cyclists who, according to their T-shirts, are doing something charitable for cancer. Or, more accurately, the victims of cancer. We form an orderly queue, halfway up the hill, pushing our respective bikes to the top, at which point they mount up and disappear, and I have the road to myself. A long descent takes me to Newgale Sands then an off-road section leading through sand dunes to a spot high above the seaside town of Broad Haven. From this vantage point I can see nothing except houses, houses and more houses. I had thought of stopping there, but, with no campsites in sight, I carry on to the nearby town of Haverfordwest and soon wish I hadn't. Haverfordwest had attracted me, with its name so evocative of a nineteenth-century private detective in a deerstalker hat, but there is nothing attractive about its huge roads, its non-stop stream of traffic and its complete absence of cycling lanes. I decide to get out of the town as quickly as possible, and follow signs to the railway station, where I take a train to the next stop along, Johnston. There I pick up a traffic-free route, enjoying a lovely downhill ride to Pembroke Harbour then, a short while later, Pembroke itself. Having cycled more miles than I meant to, I am too tired to find a campsite, let alone pitch my tent and then find food. Luckily, I spot a hotel. Unluckily, it turns out to be full. The manager recommends another hotel close by, but I don't like the look of it and, despite my tiredness, continue pushing my bike along the High Street, hoping for something better. I am rewarded by finding The Woodbine, a fine B&B with a lovely room and a welcoming landlady, who obligingly helps me store my bike and trailer in her garage. I then have a welcome shower, supper in a pub and a pleasant surprise when I return to my room – an unnoticed DVD player and a pile of DVDs to go with it. I decide on the movie *School of Rock*, watching it for about the hundred and twenty-seventh time while, as usual, awash with tears.

Next morning I load up my bike and get back on the road to Swansea. It's cold and raining. After more than an hour of this, I become increasingly fed up, then suddenly overwhelmed by the desire for a cup of tea. Yes, I think. A cup of tea. I'd like that. As the rain continues and the cold worsens, the desire for tea becomes more and more urgent and is soon joined by thoughts of toasted teacakes, firelight glinting on brassware and buxom waitresses in crisp white blouses and full-length black pleated skirts. A few miles later I reach the village of Lamphey, where not a single teashop can be seen. But then I spot a sign advertising a hotel. I will not name the hotel but it's located in the Western part of the world and it considers itself to be Best. This hotel, the sign informs me, serves 'teas, coffees, bar snacks and lunches'. There's no mention of buxom waitresses in crisp white blouses and full-length black pleated skirts, but I don't care. Tea will do. A helpful arrow points me in the direction I need to go and half a mile later, I pull into the courtyard of a hotel full of Hasidic Jews. They give me curious looks as I make my way through them and into the reception, where the receptionist informs me that the hotel is closed for a private function and that a cup of tea is not possible. I am not happy about this and make that clear in a fashion I can only describe as biblical. 'Why don't you put up a sign saying so?' I say, before leaving the hotel, returning to my bike and unlocking it. I am just about to cycle off when the hotel manager appears, presumably to apologise for his misleading sign and to offer me a complimentary cup of tea. Instead the following conversation takes place:

'Don't you think you're overreacting?'

'What?'

'I said, don't you think you're overreacting?'

'What do you mean, "overreacting"? There's a sign in the village saying you sell tea. When I get here, you don't sell tea. In what way am I overreacting?'

'Nobody else has complained.'

'Nobody else cycled half a mile to get here. Why don't you put up a sign saying the hotel is closed?'

'Don't be ridiculous.'

'What's ridiculous about it? If you can't be bothered to change the sign, hang an old blanket over it. This is a hotel. Surely you can get hold of an old blanket. Ask your wife.'

'I don't care for your attitude.'

'Do something about the sign and I'll change it.'

'I wouldn't serve you anyway.'

'You're threatening to refuse me a service that you wouldn't provide in the first place?'

'Leave the premises.'

'What?'

'I said, leave my hotel.'

'I'm trying to! If you hadn't come over I'd be gone by now.'

And then I leave. Ten minutes later, the rain stops and the sun comes out, which only goes to show whose side God is on. The sun lifts my mood, and fifteen minutes later my mood is lifted further when I enter the village of St Florence and find a pub that, despite having a sign outside their door saying that they serve tea, actually does.

My thirst for tea finally satisfied, I cycle on to the seaside village of Saundersfoot, followed soon after by another seaside town, Tenby. Both are small, both are a little shabby and run down, and both are full of tourists. I move on. The cycle path takes me along the coast, and, following some demanding hills, I find myself more and more tired. About fifteen miles from Tenby I come across a pub that offers accommodation. At least, it has a sign outside it saying it offers accommodation. The pub itself is closed. I cycle on, disappointed and with a worsening temper. Luckily, there is a campsite a few yards up the road. It's small and looks a bit rough around the edges, but it will do for one night. Plus I can, presumably, get something to eat in the pub.

Having pitched my tent, I wander down to the pub and wait for it to open. It does and I wish it hadn't. It's dingy and deserted and the only beers available are nasty-looking lagers, most of which I haven't heard of. I decide on a pint of Guinness. The landlady asks me if I want it 'with a swoosh'. I have no idea what she's talking about. It turns out that she doesn't have Guinness on draught, only in cans, but she can 'swoosh' it with some form of pressurised liquid.

I say I'll give it a go. The landlady does her swooshing thing and hands me my drink. 'It's very popular,' says the landlady.

It isn't popular with me. It's one of the most disgusting things I've ever tasted – and I've drunk lager out of cans that students have used as ashtrays. I then ask her, 'Are you doing food tonight?' 'Yes,' she says, then disappears. I presume to fetch a menu. I am wrong. Fifteen minutes pass in which I am left alone. I've now had enough of the pub but still no supper. She returns, stands at the bar and continues to ignore me. I buy crisps, peanuts and chocolate and head back to the tent.

At 4 a.m., I'm woken by the sound of rain. It's coming down

hard and after a while I become more and more concerned about my bike. The manufacturers of my bike are not fools. They know that their bikes will be ridden in the rain and their bikes are designed so that this won't be a problem. But the rain is torrential. After half an hour of worrying, I get out of my sleeping bag, struggle into my waterproofs, unlock the bike, wheel it up a short hill and into the shower block, where it will at least be dry until morning. I then go back down the hill, get out of my waterproofs, get into my sleeping bag and spend the rest of the night alternating between sleep and worry.

Next morning, I wake early. The rain has stopped and my first thought is to check my bike. I do and, as I feared, the bike refuses to start. I am stranded in the middle of rural Wales with a dead bike and a load of luggage. I ring the shop that sold me the bike, speaking to a helpful engineer. He advises me to wait a few hours for the bike to 'dry out'. He is confident that the problem isn't permanent. I check on the bike every thirty minutes. After three hours, it still won't start. I now have to decide whether to spend another day on the campsite, or find another option. I do some map-reading and decide my best bet is to call a taxi to take me to the nearest railway station. The taxi arrives, and, £45 later, I arrive at Carmarthen and buy a ticket to Paddington, via Swansea. I wheel my bike and trailer onto the platform, disassemble my trailer, fold my bike, wait for the train, load the bike and my luggage onto the train, arrive in Swansea, load the bike and luggage onto the London train, arrive in Paddington three hours later, reassemble my trailer, unfold my bike and wheel it out of the station. I am now faced with wheeling my bike across London from Paddington to Liverpool Street and a train to take me back to Norfolk. Unless . . .

I switch on my bike. It starts. There is a God.

As the train to Norfolk leaves Liverpool Street, I sit back in my seat and reflect on my journey. Ireland had been a bad choice. I hadn't enjoyed my time there at all. But then, I wondered, can I condemn an entire country after only one small trip to only one small part of it? Then I remembered the appalling weather, the appalling state of the roads and the appalling manners of the people and I think: Yes. I can.

The trip to Wales, though, had been a better idea. I'll go back, I decide. I liked the time I spent there, the countryside and the people. Well, most of them. There's a hotel manager who has to die.

My thoughts turn to my former wife. I'd enjoyed seeing her again, even though our parting had made me sad. But nowhere near as sad, I reflect, as the first time we'd parted. Then I had experienced gut-wrenching sadness of a kind I'd never known before. And not just because my heart had been broken and my marriage was over. But because I had no gigs.

# CHAPTER TWELVE
## London – Edinburgh – Brighton – Israel

It's 1980 and I'm having a drink with Bruce Mitchell, drummer with the Berts and now the purveyor of unwanted but incisive advice. 'You're very funny in the van,' says Bruce. 'Why can't you be as funny on stage?'

Those words cut deep. Over the past year my performances had gone from bad to worse to fucking awful. Since I'd turned (for want of a better word) professional in 1971, I'd been working in isolation. I didn't know one other person who did stand-up comedy. Later on in life, I wouldn't know anyone who didn't, but in those days I was on my own. And it was becoming more and more difficult. When I wasn't supporting a band such as the Berts (or an even lovelier Mancunian band, the Smirks), I was playing in dingy pubs or music clubs around the North West. The venues were noisy and the audience's attention span was short. I'd given up on stand-up comedy. Instead, I was using backing tapes for songs I'd written, relying on lighting changes to make an impact, and throwing in a lot of swearing. Any funny stuff was saved for friends in the pub or the back of a van; hence Bruce's perceptive remark.

The more gigs I did, the more jaded I became. Glugging from a bottle appealed to me more than gigging for a living. My marriage, meanwhile, rumbled down the rocky road that led to separation. When we finally decided to part, I knew it was time to move on.

And not just from Bacup. I needed to get away from the kind of gigs I'd been doing. I'd had enough of performing to audiences that spat on you if they liked you and spat on you if they didn't. I decided to get back to the world of fringe theatre where nobody in the audience spat on you; mainly because there was nobody in the audience.

A move to London seemed the best option. It had to be. I had no others. I also had no future, no marriage, no money, no home, no gigs and no act to do in the gigs I hadn't got.

I remembered a review published in the *Birmingham Post* only a few years before. Written by one Robert Low, it spoke of my 'leaping on and off stage in a seemingly endless series of incredible costumes . . . his imagination seems inexhaustible'. Well, not anymore, Robert Low. My imagination is not just exhausted; it's stumbling round the kitchen at three o'clock in the afternoon, with a terrible hangover, wishing it was back in bed.

Some showbiz careers go up like a rocket. Mine had come down like the stick. Now I had to find a way to begin again. Burned-out rockets didn't get a second chance. Maybe burned-out comedians did.

\*

'You know cleaning?' said the sceptical old lady, standing on the doorstep of her house in Golders Green.

'Yes,' I told her, somewhat irritated. 'I know cleaning.' Then I went into the backyard with the broom she gave me, began sweeping, and broke the handle.

Friends in London had provided spare beds, floors and couches as I found ways to make money for the deposit I needed to rent a flat. An actor who did domestic cleaning 'while resting' told me about an agency he used. The agency took only a small percentage of the fees he earned, he told me, and, enticingly, there was very little cleaning involved. All that the clients wanted, according to my actor friend, was someone with whom they could share lonely afternoons and large glasses of gin. This, I thought, was the job for me. I signed up and was quickly introduced to a series of clients who had no interest at all in sharing large glasses of gin. The only thing that interested them was getting their houses cleaned. Preferably without my breaking their best broom.

One client was an overweight man in the fashion business who had clearly decided that this year's must-have accessory was a cardiac arrest. 'I sell high-end haute couture,' I overheard him shout down an ivory-coloured telephone inlaid with gold leaf as veins throbbed in his neck and sweat ran down his face. 'And what you've sent me is a load of . . . a load of . . . ' he paused, his mouth chewing angrily, his brain working overtime in search of the most damning phrase he could come up with, before landing on: 'FROCKS.'

His bathroom made his phone look like a monument to good taste. The en suite purple bath with the gold taps in the shape of swans was almost forgivable. What wasn't forgivable was the en suite lavatory, placed in the exact centre of a doorless frame in plain view of a king-sized bed. What message was he sending to the world? 'Happy to take a dump in front of my girlfriend'?

After a few months of cleaning, I'd scraped together enough money to move into a bedsit flat. Then began the weary work of finding gigs. I needed sixty minutes of material to do shows in Arts Centres, fringe theatres and the like. I had about ten. But I worked away, writing a new act and pursuing contacts I'd made through the years. One such contact was Neil Titley, an actor, poet, beatnik, bootleg record producer and entrepreneur. Neil was taking a collection of one-man shows to that year's Edinburgh festival. He was appearing as Oscar Wilde. He'd also acquired an actor playing the poet Dylan Thomas, another actor playing the writer Frank Harris and a third playing the artist James Whistler. Would the comedian John Dowie, he asked me, be interested in taking part? Thinking that his collection might benefit from having someone in it who was still alive, I said I would.

The venue Neil had booked formed part of the Edinburgh University Students' Association. It was a reasonably-sized hall with a bar attached. Having a bar attached to our venue was considered an asset. It certainly became an asset in my case when into it walked the actor Freddie Jones.

Freddie Jones is considered by many, me included, to be one of the finest actors of his, or anyone's, generation. He created the part of Sir in the original production of *The Dresser* by Ronald Harwood, appeared in several David Lynch films, and eased into old age by accepting a role in the TV soap *Emmerdale*. But it is for his work in the theatre that he is best known and most admired. Having spotted Freddie Jones in our bar, examining the various posters adorning the wall, I was determined to speak with him. I made my way over, introduced myself, told Freddie that I was part of a bunch of people up in Edinburgh doing shows, and that it would be a privilege to buy him a drink and to share his company.

Freddie said he'd be glad to, came over to our table, introduced himself to the rest of us and then, before sitting down, glanced up at the string of dusty bulbs that ran above our heads. 'Just getting into my light,' he said, before beginning the first of a series of showbiz anecdotes. All was going well until an eighteen-year-old lad, helping us out as a menial and a gofer, joined us. Under the impression that we were just a bunch of blokes sitting round a table and chatting, he did a terrible thing: he started joining in. None of us knew how to tell this boy to shut up and Freddie wasn't about to do so. Luckily, Freddie's wife then arrived, at which point Freddie became the envy of every heterosexual male sitting at the table. And not just because Freddie's wife was one of the most arrestingly beautiful women we had ever seen – but because she knew how to treat an actor. The eighteen-year-old lad made yet another interruption. Freddie's wife leaned over, slapped him on the wrist and said, 'Shush! Freddie's talking.'

Several pints later, Freddie was ready to leave. Discovering that I was doing a show that evening, he promised to come and see it. I told him I'd be delighted if he did. I didn't expect him to turn up. He did.

With Freddie Jones in the audience, there was no way I was going to do a bad show. I ad-libbed my way through the bits that didn't work (and there were lots of those). I improvised new material. I did the best show I could. Afterwards, Freddie came backstage and offered me his criticisms, criticisms that were perceptive and valuable. He also offered praise. I was flattered and pleased. But, more important, I was also on the road to comic recovery. Thanks to Freddie Jones, I now had the beginnings of an act.

Back in London, I resumed the tedious process of finding work. I got to know the management of the Finborough Theatre Club, a tiny room above an Earls Court pub, and began performing there, booking myself in for two-week runs, hoping that reviews and word of mouth would help build an audience. No. At one particular performance, my audience consisted of seven people. Five were from Sweden and the other two didn't know each other. My act was going badly. You could smoke indoors in those days and a Swedish woman decided to do so, lighting a cigarette then whispering something to her friend. I stopped whatever it was I was doing and said something like, 'No whispering while I'm on stage, thank you very much. If you've got something to say then please share it with the rest of us.' Seven people now thought: 'Not only is this man not funny but now he's taking it out on us.' The Swedish woman looked at me apologetically then said, 'I am sorry. I am just saying to my friend – this is the first cigarette I smoke in eight years.'

I worked wherever I could, touring around the country on an irregular, haphazard basis, writing, rewriting, then rewriting again, until I had an act that was as good as I could make it. In 1982, I took myself back to Edinburgh, booking myself a space in a newly opened – and some say prestigious venue – the Assembly Rooms.

*

In the earlier days of Edinburgh, the average theatregoer had to rush from venue to venue, battling pouring rain, freezing winds and mountainous hills, in order to see a show that might be good, bad or bleeding awful. Then, in 1981, along came a man called

William Burdett-Coutts, who quickly put a stop to all that. What William Burdett-Coutts did was to hire the Assembly Rooms, a huge building in the centre of Edinburgh, then fill it with shows on all floors and at all times of the day and night. Now all that the average theatregoer had to do was visit one single venue in order to see a show that might be good, bad or bleeding awful.

The Assembly Rooms had performance spaces of varying size from the Music Hall, seating over 700, to the Wildman Room, a big cupboard with some chairs in it. I played the big cupboard, doing a midnight show for every one of the entire three and a half weeks of the festival, managing to be drunk on stage only once.

Of the many visits I have made to Edinburgh, that year remains a golden one. On one particular afternoon, I was seated among a circle of people in the Assembly Rooms bar. In that circle were actors, musicians and performers, some of whom had been heroes of mine for many years. In years to come, they would still be heroes. Some of them would also become friends.

Roger McGough and Brian Patten were there, two of the Liverpool Poets who came to prominence in the Sixties, their work still inspiring and seminal. Another poet, Adrian Mitchell, called a waitress over and, in an act of astonishing generosity, unnoticed by almost everyone else, quietly asked her to take orders for the entire party. If the bill came to anything less than fifty quid I'd be very surprised. Robin Williamson, founder member of the Incredible String Band, spoke to me. 'I understand your work is quite acerbic,' he said, his lilting Scottish brogue making the word 'acerbic' sound both lyrical and demeaning. A small man with large spectacles, holding court to anyone who'd listen, had seen my show and introduced himself. 'I'm Dennis Main Wilson,' he said, and my jaw dropped, my mind flashing back to the countless comedies, on radio and television, which Dennis had produced, enhancing my life through my teenage years; comedies featuring such heroes as Tony Hancock, Eric Sykes and, of course, Spike Milligan.

It was a golden afternoon in a golden Edinburgh in which every day was filled with sunshine, every night was filled with laughter, everybody got a good review and nobody ever had a hangover. And I was the only comedian in town. But this wouldn't last much longer. Soon there would be hundreds of the fuckers.

First there was Alexei from Liverpool, bursting onto the stage like bile from a boil, slagging off social workers and people from Stoke Newington. Next there was Tony from Ladbroke Grove, a lofty bloke with a lofty tone, ranting on about the police and marijuana. Then there was Ben, a know-it-all from university, banging on about Margaret Thatcher and not much else. Then another comedian came. Then another. Then more and more and more. 'We're Alternatives,' they said. 'Yes,' sneered the Old Guard, 'Alternatives to comedy.' But soon the Old Guard, with their jokes about Pakis and mothers-in-law, were gone. In their place came the New Guard, with their jokes about Conservatives and menstruation. Then the New Guard disappeared, lured away by big money in advertising and small parts in films. Taking their place came drama students, out-of-work actors and social workers from Stoke Newington. Unable to perform sets longer than twenty minutes, they travelled, like condoms, in packets of three, taking their sixty-minute shows from the burgeoning clubs of London up to Edinburgh, where the Festival Fringe lay on its back with its legs in the air and was happily tickled all over. Perrier, bottlers of fizzy water, whose fatuous Comedy Award was previously given to whichever Oxbridge university performed the smuggest revue, widened its self-aggrandising net. Soon comedians were unashamedly taking the Perrier franc and posing for the cameras with bottles of the stuff – the only time comedians in Edinburgh have ever touched water. Television companies, waving chequebooks and waiving talent, were all over the Fringe like rats on raw meat. Badly written and badly produced sitcoms came. Badly written and badly produced sitcoms went. Talking Head shows followed. Talking Heads were axed. Panel shows popped up like pustules. Scriptwriters were put on suicide watch. Comedians proliferated in plague-like proportions, their audience proliferating with them. Fresh-faced comedy kings, who once would have been grateful for seven people in a room above a pub, now stood centre stage in giant arenas as praise, applause and riches rained down upon them like showers of golden piss.

Or, to put it another way, a lot of people found a new way to make friends and earn a living.

And my life got a whole lot easier. Not only were there gigs; there were also people to get the gigs for you. As comedians poured out of the woodwork, so the agents and promoters – the 'suits' – followed suit.

Addison Cresswell was barely into his twenties when we met, but already he was making his mark on the world. He began his career booking acts for Brighton Polytechnic, before becoming an agent, working for himself, finding acts and promoting them. During one particular Edinburgh Festival, he hired a room in a pub, normally the home of hardened Scottish drinkers, and used it to showcase his rapidly increasing portfolio of comedians. Later on, that portfolio would expand to include names such as Michael McIntyre and Jonathan Ross, but in those early days his list of clients was small and less prestigious. I was one of them. Another was Julian Clary.

If I was a documentary film maker I could have made a small fortune by simply filming the faces of the hardened Scottish drinkers in that pub, as Julian, dressed in heavy make-up, leather boots and a PVC corset from which dangled bondage accessories, made his way through their bar and towards his stage. I marvelled at Julian's courage and feared for his safety. Which was a complete waste of my time. In a very short while, Julian had charmed and befriended every one of them.

Addison called his venue the Comedy Boom and boom was what comedy did. As part of Addison's rapidly expanding list of clients, I was soon touring the country, doing a seemingly endless series of gigs, booked either by Addison or his associate, Joe Norris. One of the gigs they booked me into was The Band in The Wall, a club in the heart of Manchester. Many Mancunian buddies came along to the gig, including my old friend Bruce Mitchell. I saw him after the show. 'So, Bruce,' I said. 'What do you think? Am I as funny now as I was in the van?'

'What van?' said Bruce.

Addison died at the shockingly early age of fifty-three. I was more than saddened by the news. I had liked Addison and always enjoyed his occasionally eccentric company. One of the shows I directed, during the latter days of my career, was a stage version of *Whale Nation* by the poet/playwright Heathcote Williams. *Whale Nation*, an elegiac tribute to the largest mammal on Earth, has been described as 'the most moving poem in English since *The Waste Land*'. Addison came to see the show, and afterwards, his eyes still red from weeping, said to me, 'Brilliant, John, brilliant. You should get Kleenex to sponsor the tour.'

The last phone call I had from Addison changed my life. The 1980s were coming to an end. I was in my bedsit flat, feeling quietly depressed, when Addison rang. One of his acts was ill. There was a gig that needed doing. Was I available? The last thing I felt like doing that night was going out and being funny. I didn't want the gig but I did want the fee. So out into the London night I went, arriving at the usual room above a pub, this time a pub in Bethnal Green. The act I had to follow consisted of disabled members of a community youth theatre doing a sixty-minute play about child abuse. Not an easy act to follow. After they finished, I took the stage to an audience that, as Lenny Bruce once put it, 'was either sobbing uncontrollably or reaching for digitalis'. Under those circumstances, a comedy gig can go one of two ways; and one of them is not a good way. Luckily, mine went the other way. I got laughs. And more. After I'd finished, a woman put her head round the dressing room door and asked if her friend could buy me a drink. I said, 'Tell your friend I'd like a large vodka and tonic.' Expecting the drink to be carried into the dressing room by some male comedy geek, I was surprised to see a woman swaggering through the door, carrying a large vodka and tonic, and changing my life for ever.

## INTERLUDE: MY DAD'S BOOK

As the oldest member of the family, it was my job to tell my dad that he wasn't going to appear on *Wogan*, a television chat show hosted by the avuncular, twinkling Irishman who hardly ever got on people's tits. On his retirement, my dad had wondered what he was going to do to fill the time hanging heavily on his hands. 'Why not write your biography?' someone suggested. My dad thought this was a great idea. He sat down with a pen and paper. A few days later it was finished. All he had to do now was go through the formality of getting it published and then he'd be on *Wogan*. It was all perfectly straightforward. My dad was no fool. He had seen people appearing on *Wogan* because they had written books. My dad had written a book. Therefore, my dad reasoned, he would be appearing on *Wogan*.

Having given my dad the heartbreaking news of, 'No *Wogan* for you, mate,' his interest in being an author waned. However, I typed up his reminiscences, had them bound and copied, and gave them to the family as a celebration of his seventy-fifth birthday. While typing the manuscript I came across the story of how my dad first met my mother.

*After work, my main hobby was dancing. We used to go quite often. Always had a few drinks just to get up courage. On one of these occasions my friend (Lofty) and I had a few jars and arrived at a dance in the Tower Ballroom. As we went in there were two girls standing together, not dancing. Plucking up courage we asked for a dance and they accepted.*

*That girl has been leading me a dance up to now.*

Well, I thought, rolling up my metaphorical sleeves, here we go. I turned the page and read:

*After the usual courtship, we got married.*

I turned back the page. Surely I had missed something? But no. There was no mention of the wooing, the first date, the proposal, none of it. Later, I asked my dad why. He gave me an old-fashioned look and said, 'There are some things you don't talk about.'

\*

After the usual courtship, we shacked up together.

I'm not using names in these stories, if I can avoid them. Not because of fear of litigation or, more likely, violent reprisals, but because I figure that other people's names are their own business. If I had to choose a name to describe the woman who changed my life, I'd probably take a leaf out of John Mortimer's *Rumpole of the Bailey* and refer to her as She Who Bends All Others To Her Will.

She was also the answer to an age-old scientific riddle.

Q: What happens when an irresistible force meets an immovable object?

A: They live together.

We had been living together for only a short while when she decided to bend my will to hers and enhance our relationship with the input of a third party, i.e., a baby.

Here's how a comedian responds to the idea of having a baby:

'You put a baby in a room full of adults and immediately that baby becomes the centre of everyone else's attention. And that's my job! And I have to work for that attention. I have to tell jokes, dominate the conversation, ignore everybody else ... All a baby has to do is lie on its back, dribble and throw up ... I can do that. After half past eleven most nights I usually do.

'You get a baby – bald, no teeth, incontinent – and everybody loves it. You get an adult – bald, no teeth, incontinent – and they put you in a home. And who puts you in that home? Your old baby.'

\*

The woman who wanted me to impregnate her with my seed was, despite that wish, easily one of the most intelligent people I have ever met. Nevertheless, I was still convinced that I could outwit her – even though, as I later proved, I lack the intelligence to outwit a hen. Rather than argue with her over her wanting a baby, I decided on a more tactical approach. I would host a party and invite every person I knew who had a child of any age – from newborn babe to surly teenager. Once she sees how children behave, I reasoned, any desire to have one of her own will vanish. I held the party. Every child that came behaved with sickening impeccability. Nine months later, to the very day, our first son was born. So much for tactics. Two years after that, we had our second son. By which time, the idea of living in London had become intolerable. How many people would want to raise their children in a smelly, smoky, squalid, car-filled, dogshit-ridden city? Millions is the answer. But I wasn't one of them. And neither was their mother. Although we both needed to be in London for work purposes, we didn't need to be there all the time. We could easily live somewhere else. But where?

Our decision was helped by the fact that I once played the part of James Bond. Not, obviously, in one of the many movies that have made the franchise a byword in sexist bollocks, but in a comedy version. *James Bond – The Panto* was a show written and produced by Cliffhanger, a theatre group with whom I had made friends following mutual appearances at Edinburgh and elsewhere. Having been cast in the title role, I then spent a more than happy three weeks rehearsing in their hometown of Brighton.

Let me insert some advice here: if you're going to have a job, try and have one in which, out of eight hours of work, at least four of those hours are spent laughing. That's the kind of job I had with Cliffhanger. That is why I happily made the fifty-minute train journey from London to Brighton every day, and then strode with determined feet to the rehearsal room, knowing that from the moment I arrived there I would spend most of the rest of the day in a state of helpless giggling.

One line of dialogue, which didn't even make it to the performance was: 'Q has invented a fountain pen that squirts ink in your face when you sign a peace treaty.'

Brighton has long been known as 'London-by-the-sea'. It has changed since the time I lived there, having become a lot more London and a lot less Sea, but before it did its combination of theatre and music people, its art students, its gay community and its occasional whiff of ozone made it a lovely place in which to live, and, more importantly, a much nicer place, certainly when compared to London, in which to raise children.

And so we moved there, finding a house in a Brighton suburb, where we watched our children grow and I enjoyed some of the happiest days of my life.

From time to time I see new parents with their children, usually in parks or in playgrounds, and, as the children play, the parents busy themselves with their phones or their newspapers or their iPads. 'Go on,' I think. 'Enjoy your distractions. After all, those tiny lives will be with you for ever. But that phone call can't wait.'

Grandparents rarely make the same mistake. You rarely see a grandparent yakking on a mobile when there's a grandchild around. Grandparents know that life is fleeting, that children grow too quickly, that soon they are gone for ever and that every single second must be savoured. (Grandparents also inspired the world's only amusing car sticker: 'I love my grandchildren. I wish I'd had them first.')

Apart from enjoying the company of my children, I was enjoying an experience I'd never had before. Having a local and being one of the regulars.

The local was called the Park View. The regulars were a bunch of middle-aged men. And some of them were men with the cruellest sense of humour.

Chris the Pill (a pharmaceutical salesman) had remembered to buy his eggs and his bacon but had forgotten the bread. After some swearing, he left the bacon and eggs on the bar and went back up the hill to the bakery. This gave Nick the Nurse (a nurse) plenty of time to take the eggs into the pub's kitchen, hard-boil them, put them back in their box, back on the bar, then stand around with the rest of us. Chris the Pill came back, finished his pint then went home to cook his breakfast. No one said anything. Fifteen minutes later, Chris the Pill came back to the pub and said quite a lot.

Roger the Alcoholic (an alcoholic) came in one day, sporting a black eye.

'How'd you get the black eye, Roger?'

'I fell asleep in a bottle bank and somebody put one in.'

Roger discovered that another regular, George the Jeweller, a wheeler and dealer in antiques and such, was having an affair with his wife. Deciding to confront him, a drunken Roger knocked at George's door at three o'clock in the morning, waving a Second World War pistol. 'That's a very nice firearm, Roger,' said George, taking it from him. 'How much would you want for that?'

Barry the Bore had two hobbies: one was building a model of Brighton Pier in his living room using unopened boxes of A4 paper. The other was talking about it. Discovering that the pub was giving away six 'free' whisky glasses to anyone who drank twenty pints of a particular brand of beer, Barry decided that this was an offer he could not refuse. Having drunk the twenty pints he needed, in one session, Barry was given his six glasses, tucked them under his arm, staggered out of the pub, had a confused altercation with a bus shelter, fell over and smashed the lot.

Through it all, standing like a pipe-smoking rock, was Norman. Norman had turned eighty more than a few years ago and his house was at the top of a long and steep hill. Nevertheless, every day he'd insist on walking home, despite our urging him to take a taxi. 'It's less than the price of a pint, Norman,' I'd say. 'I know,' said Norman, 'but all the old biddies who live on that hill all know where I've been. And the disapproving looks on their faces as I walk past their twitching curtains is the only thing that keeps me going.'

Every time Norman left the pub, someone would say, 'I hope I'm like Norman when I'm his age.' And every time they did I would say, 'I just wish I was like that *now*.'

\*

Spending time with my growing children was having one obvious influence on my thought processes – thinking about fatherhood.

At one time my parents came to stay. I was changing a nappy and looked up to see my dad staring at me as if I were some sort of Martian. I indicated the nappy I'd just changed. 'You've never done this, have you?' I said. My dad, with more than a touch of regret said, 'In my day you didn't even push the pram.'

This and other events led me, by one turn or another, to thinking of Joseph, the earthly father of Jesus. I began to picture him as the first New Man, standing happily in the background, letting his child take all the glory and his wife take all the credit. At that time I was directing actors and performers in one-man shows. It occurred to me that there might be a play in this idea, and, one afternoon in the Park View, I started trying out jokes on one of the hapless regulars. Jokes such as:

MAN: I hear your house is really big.

JOSEPH: No, not particularly, why?

MAN: Oh that son of yours. He's always saying 'in my father's house there are many mansions'.

All well and good, until I sat down to begin writing and thought, 'Hang on. There's a crucifixion at the end of this. How do I joke my way around that?'

The answer, I discovered, is that you don't.

Eventually, I completed *Jesus My Boy*, a play that has been performed in theatres around the world, thanks, in good part, to a production in London's West End starring the actor Tom Conti.

Originally, I had performed the play myself. Not because I thought I was perfect casting for the role, but because there's nothing like having to perform your own words on stage to make you realise what a heap of puerile drivel you've written and demand a rewrite. After a fortnight's worth of performances the script was as good as I could make it. I knew it was time to hand it over to someone else. But who? Who could I persuade to perform it? And where would the performance take place?

I am a strong believer in the idea that a voice inside your head might possibly come from an outside source. I am aware that this may be a definition of madness. I also think that ignoring that voice might be another definition of madness. Be that as it may, I was at home, looking through the television schedules, when I came across a listing for a show featuring the actor Simon Callow – a one-man performance of a Charles Dickens story. I turned the page. Not my cup of tea. Then a voice inside my head suggested that I watch it. I said I didn't want to. The voice insisted. I protested. The voice said, 'I really think it would benefit you to watch that particular programme.' I gave in.

I found the first ten minutes extremely difficult to watch, but slowly and surely Simon Callow's performance (and Charles Dickens's writing) worked their magic upon me. By the finish, tears were streaming down my face and my body was racked with sobs. However, I am a professional. Blinded by tears I may have been, but that doesn't mean I can't scribble down the name of the producer and have an unsolicited package on his desk by first thing the following day.

Except that all the way to the post box I had another voice inside my head – the voice that should definitely be ignored: the voice that says, 'Why bother?' Even at the exact moment I was putting my package into the post box, the voice would not stop its pessimistic nagging. 'Nothing will come of it. They'll have had hundreds of scripts like yours. Forget about it. You're wasting your time,' until, finally, I lost my temper and said, 'I'm only posting a parcel! If I don't post it, nothing will happen. If I do post it, something might.'

Into the box went my parcel. Out of my head went the voice. The next day, the producer rang. His name was Tom Kinnimont. He liked the script. He had some ideas. We arranged to meet and, six months later, in December of 1998, Tom Conti was performing *Jesus My Boy* at the Apollo Theatre, Shaftesbury Avenue.

Not everything about the production was to my liking. I didn't care for the unnecessary and expensive set. I thought the comedy sometimes outweighed the humanity. Nor did I like the lighting cues that sometimes took the place of the storytelling. To which I say: 'So what?' Tom Conti was the man on stage, not me. Any choices he made were his right and his prerogative. Also, the fact that I hold an opinion doesn't make that opinion right. Other people's opinions, even if contrary to mine, are just as valid. My eldest son's, for example: 'I thought he was much better than you, Dad.'

A few days before *Jesus My Boy* opened, I was being driven somewhere by a member of the production company in his Bentley. I remember him saying, 'If that play of yours goes well, you'll soon be driving one of these.' Which worried me. Not just because I can't drive but because earning enough money to buy a Bentley was never my motivation for writing the play in the first place.

My mind went back to the Birmingham Rep, where my performance of the play had taken place in its studio theatre. After one performance, the stage door keeper came to my dressing room to tell me, thrillingly, and for the first and only time in my life, that there were 'two women at the stage door who wanted to see me'.

'Finally,' I thought. 'All of my sexual birds have come home to roost.'

Needless to say, the women at the stage door were not there for that. They were there to tell me they'd enjoyed my play. Especially, they said, as they'd just returned from Israel, where they were involved with peace work. I was touched at their taking the trouble to come and speak to me. Having chatted briefly, we said our goodbyes. As they left, I placed a hand, lightly, upon each of their shoulders.

*

When I was nine years old, I was playing alone in the unused attic of our house in Birmingham. I noticed that there was no bulb in the light-bulb socket that dangled from the ceiling. Looking closer, I was intrigued to see there were two brass buttons in the middle of the socket. Standing on a chair, I wondered what would happen if I pressed one of the buttons.

I soon found out. The electrical shock sent me flying from the chair. As I hit the floor, two thoughts came to mind: the first, as an avid comic-book reader, was to wonder if I could now fly. I couldn't. The second was that I would never touch the buttons in a light-bulb socket ever again. I haven't. Neither have I experienced another shock like it. Not until that night, at the stage door of the Birmingham Rep, when I placed my hands upon the shoulders of two women who had been working for peace in Israel. The shock I felt then was just as real, just as electric, as the one I'd experienced in an attic in Birmingham forty years before.

About a year after Tom Conti's performance I surprised myself by deciding I wanted to perform the play again. Easter was approaching, which seemed an appropriate time for the play to be staged. My friends Gavin Hackett and Steve Ullathorne produced the show, staging it in a tiny basement in London's Fitzrovia. I gave a total of five performances. After one of them, a shy young man put his head around my dressing room door and asked me if I was Jewish. 'Not yet,' was my answer. He told me that he was a comedian from Israel and would like to translate and perform my play. I said I'd be delighted. Normally, I would ask him to get the rights by going through my agent, but that didn't seem right. Instead, we shook hands.

Not long after that, I was on a plane to Israel, on my way to watch Gil Kopatch, one of Israel's premier comedians, perform his translation of my play.

The last thing I wanted, as I found a seat in Tel Aviv's Habima Theatre, was for any attention to come in my direction. All I wanted was to sit in happy anonymity at the back of the room, and watch the audience watching the play. I was about to do exactly that when a man spoke to me in Hebrew. I replied in English. He looked concerned. Did I realise, he asked, what I was about to watch? A play performed in Hebrew? Reluctantly, I told him I'd written it. His face lit up. 'You must come and sit with my wife,' he told me. 'She is the senior drama critic for the *Jerusalem Post*.'

I had no idea what to expect of the performance. I didn't much care whether it was good, bad or indifferent. The fact that it was taking place was good enough for me. Neither did I know the exact meaning of the words Gil used in his translation. But I do know how he said them. Dressed in white, accompanied by a musician playing a guitar, he spoke and danced and sang his way through the performance. I loved every second of it.

During the time I was there, Gil and his sister took me on trips to different parts of their country: the Dead Sea, Masada and Jerusalem. We also visited the Church of the Beatitudes, which is situated on a hill near Capernaum.

The church has been built to commemorate the spot where Jesus is supposed to have given the Sermon on the Mount. The church is 'Byzantine in style with a marble veneer casing the lower walls and gold mosaic in the dome'. In other words: kitsch. It's also in the wrong place.

If I've learned only one thing after years of performing stand-up and directing dozens of one-man shows, then it's what centre stage is. And where.

Centre stage is the very best position for any solo performer – a comedian, for example, or a long-awaited Jewish prophet – to stand. From centre stage the performer commands the attention of the entire audience. And where centre stage was, this church wasn't.

I grabbed hold of Gil by the arm. 'It's not centre stage,' I said. 'What?' said Gil, but I was gone by then, walking away from the church and further down the hill, towards a flat piece of land that overlooked the valley below. A fence and a board with 'Keep Out', written in several languages, barred our way. Ignoring the sign, Gil hopped over the fence. 'It's your country,' I thought, taking Gil's action as permission, then followed him over the fence. Gil stood to one side as I walked to the spot where, over two thousand years ago, a man may or may not have given a speech that would resonate through the centuries. I looked at the land below me, imagining the upturned faces of the crowd, all eyes focused on this exact spot. Then I stood aside and Gil took my place. He stood for a moment in silence then stretched out his arms, lifted his face to the sky and danced in a small but perfect circle.

On the hill above us stood a church, a mighty structure of marble and gold, standing in a space that could only have been, at best, the dressing room to which Christ and his supporters would have retired, to drink wine, discuss the performance, and ignore the notes given by an uncredited director. Below the church, on the humble patch of land where Jesus may actually have spoken, where I stood and where my good friend Gil Kopatch danced, there stands another commemorative structure. It is a tree. A solitary tree.

*

I had enjoyed my time in Israel and returned to England a happy man. Also, a vindicated one. It's doubtful that I'd have written *Jesus My Boy* if I were still performing stand-up. And yet, when I decided to stop, many well-meaning friends and colleagues had tried to make me change my mind. Even today, over twenty years later, I'm still sometimes asked if I'll 'ever go back to stand-up'. I always answer, 'No.' Very few people ask my why.

*

In 1992 I'd been booked to perform my comedy act in yet another smoke-filled room above a pub. I was about to leave when my four-year-old son asked me where I was going.

'I'm going to work.'

'Can I come?'

'No.'

I looked at my son's disappointed face. What kind of work am I doing, I asked myself, that I can't take my own child to?

It was then that I made him a promise. Having explained, as best I could, why he couldn't come with me, I said, 'But one day I'll do a show that you *can* come and see.'

It took a further two years for that promise to come true – and two years is a long time in the life of a four-year-old. But I'd made him a promise and I kept it. It was the best promise I have ever made. And it killed my comedy career stone dead.

# CHAPTER THIRTEEN
## Dogman

Where Dogman came from is beyond me. I knew he would be a creature that was half-man, half-dog. I knew that he had to befriend a young boy living with a bad-tempered father. And I knew that he had to make friends with, and be adopted by, an elderly couple who lived in a lighthouse. But that was all I knew.

One of the first lessons I learned from Dogman is this: it is better to play with somebody else than it is to play alone. Having spent day after futile day trying to write the script on my own, I did the sensible thing and called Tony Haase, a former member of Cliffhanger and one of my Brighton friends.

Tony is a giant in stature and has a giant-sized imagination to match. I had spent hours failing to write a conversation for Mr Lighthouse Keeper to have with his wife, a conversation to not only set the tone for the play but to establish them both as characters. I got nowhere. Tony came into the writing room, thought for a second, and then this happened:

MR LIGHTHOUSE KEEPER: Good morning Mrs Lighthouse Keeper! I've oiled the cogs, trimmed the wick and polished the reflectors!
MRS LIGHTHOUSE KEEPER: What a lot you know about lighthouses, darling.
MR LIGHTHOUSE KEEPER: That's why I'm a lighthouse keeper, darling. I love being the Lighthouse Keeper. It's so comforting to have a lighthouse, isn't it dear?

MRS LIGHTHOUSE KEEPER: Yes, dear. If nothing else, it helps take our minds off our childless marriage.

With the script under way, my next task was to make a phone call to a genius: Neil Innes, not only a founder member of the Bonzo Dog Doo-Dah Band, the musical contributor to Monty Python, the creator of the Rutles (a Beatles parody so accurate that Rutles songs have turned up on Beatles bootlegs), but also a hero of mine who had become, thrillingly, a friend.

I didn't want to exploit our friendship by asking Neil to write songs for the show. On the other hand, I wanted to exploit our friendship by asking Neil to write songs for the show. After the usual small talk, I started into my hard sell. 'Neil,' I began. 'I'm working on a show for children . . . '

'Great,' said Neil. 'Who's writing the music?'

Another friend on board.

Next I needed to find a director. I had already bagged the role of Dogman for myself. I had no intention of directing as well. But I had no idea who would be the right choice. However, God moves in mysterious ways and very often does so in the form of Barry Cryer.

In the world of British comedy, Barry stands alone. (And if Barry had written that sentence he would have added something along the lines of 'a deodorant might help'.) Like many post-war comedians, Barry made his comedy debut at London's Windmill Theatre. Unlike them, he progressed to writing and performing in London nightclubs; was spotted by David Frost; became part of the satire boom of the 1960s; wrote for comedians ranging from Jack Benny to Morecambe & Wise; is an honorary member of Monty Python's Flying Circus and is perhaps best known for his appearances on BBC radio's *I'm Sorry I Haven't a Clue*, which he's only been doing since shortly before the First World War.

But it's not just his CV that elevates Barry among the ranks of other comedians: it's the interest and the support he gives to newer and younger performers. Most comedians with Barry's CV wouldn't bother to go out and watch one of their contemporaries, let alone some fresh-faced youth. Barry does. Speak to any of the younger comedians who know Barry and they will all tell you the same thing: Barry's approval and friendship means far more to them than any showbiz award ever could. Unless there's a cheque involved, obviously.

I had got to know Barry over the years, even making an appearance, thrillingly, in his autobiography. In the paperback version of his book, I appear on page 195. After reading it, I sent Barry a postcard thanking him for mentioning me and writing beneath my signature, 'P195!'. Barry's wife, Terry, happened to see it and said, 'It's nice of him to send us a postcard. But why has he written PIGS! on the bottom?'

I was puzzling over who would direct *Dogman*, when Barry coincidentally rang. 'I'm in Brighton at the weekend,' he said. 'And there's someone I'd like you to meet.' A couple of days later, in the bar of a seafront hotel, Barry introduced me to Victor Spinetti.

I couldn't believe my eyes. As a stone-cold Beatles fan, Victor's face was more than familiar to me, as it is to literally thousands, if not millions, of other stone-cold Beatles fans. Victor appeared in all of the Beatles movies, partly because, according to George Harrison, 'My mam fancies you'. Victor also co-wrote a play with John Lennon, went with him to India where he administered medical advice (and Beecham's Powders) to Keith Richards (he snorted them), and had a theatrical career that encompassed people as varied as Joan Littlewood, Richard Burton, Elizabeth Taylor, Franco Zeffirelli and the rock star known as Prince. And that is only scratching the surface of Victor's career.

Needless to say, Victor had one or two stories to tell. As had Barry. As the champagne-fuelled afternoon sped by, and as I sat between the master joke teller that is Barry Cryer and the sublime raconteur that was Victor Spinetti, I had one of the few intelligent thoughts of my life: 'I think I'll keep my mouth shut.' How right I was. In terms of joke telling or theatrical anecdotes, I wasn't just out of my league, I was in another country, couldn't speak the language and I'd lost my passport.

I can't remember which of them told the story of Sir John Gielgud directing a play meant for the West End, but I will never forget the story. That has been burned into my memory for ever.

At a certain point during rehearsals, one of the actors decided to take a pause. Sir John, watching from the stalls, leapt to his feet. 'What are you doing?'

'I thought I'd pause there, Sir John,' said the actor.

'No!' cried Sir John Gielgud. 'Never pause in the West End! Never! I once paused in the West End and I heard a man in the front row say, "You beast. You've come all over my umbrella."'

The afternoon came to a close, but only because Barry had a show to do that evening. As he staggered off to his hotel bed to sober up before his gig, Victor and I stood at the bar having one for the road. Then two for the road. Then three, then four . . .

'This is karma, love,' said Victor. 'We must do something together.'

'Well,' I began, 'as it happens . . . '

*

'I've read the script,' said Victor, a fortnight later. 'And I love Dogman.' At which point I knew I had made the perfect choice. As a potential director, Victor had said exactly the right thing. Not, 'I love the script', but 'I love Dogman'. On the first day of rehearsal, the wisdom of my choice was made even clearer. Victor rolled his trousers up to his knees, becoming again a nine-year old boy, and that's how the rehearsals began.

*Dogman* premiered a month later, at the Riverside Studios in Hammersmith.

The theatre world is awash with insincerity and phoney compliments, as epitomised by 'Darling you were wonderful.' But there was nothing phoney or insincere about the words my sons said when they came backstage following the first performance. 'Daddy. We loved it.'

The only compliment I have ever wanted. Job done.

Except it wasn't. The script would need cuts and rewrites. Plus there were offstage dramas to get through, not least when the actor Phil Nice, who played the part of Dogman's schoolboy chum, Emerson Fisher, was rushed to hospital following a medical emergency of a kind I can only describe as 'selfish'. Phil, I was told, would be out of action for at least a week. There was nothing we could do. The show would have to be cancelled. Having been given the news I relayed it to Vic, beginning with the phrase 'We have a problem.'

'It's not a problem,' said Vic. 'We just don't have a show.'

I put the phone down. An hour or so later, Victor rang back. He had a solution.

\*

The world of variety has seen some strange successes. During the 1940s, Peter Brough, a ventriloquist, performed to a weekly audience of fifteen million – on the radio. In my youth, a particular favourite of mine, a man called Bob Blackman, made numerous television appearances hitting himself over the head with a tin tray while singing the cowboy song 'Mule Train'; he died from a brain haemorrhage in the early Nineties. But perhaps the strangest story of all was that of a stuffed fox.

*The Basil Brush Show* ran from 1968 to 1980, attracted millions of viewers, and hardly any envy whatsoever from the thousands of human performers who never even got to appear on Basil's show, much less have a show of their own. To rub salt into this open showbiz wound, Basil Brush was supported in his unstoppable career by several patronised human beings. From 1973 to 1976, one of them was an actor by the name of Roy North. Roy was a friend of Victor. He was also performing in a play at the nearby Lyric Theatre. The timing of his play and the timing of the *Dogman* show meant that he could, theoretically, do both. Providing he was able to learn the script overnight. Was Roy prepared to do that? Yes, he was.

Early next day, the cast came in to rehearse and guide Roy through the show. After rehearsals finished, there was a thirty-minute break before the curtains opened and the show began.

It was like a scene from some 1950s *A Star Is Born*-type musical. When he wasn't on stage, Roy was in the wings having a whispered rehearsal before cast members took him back on for his next scene. He did not make one mistake. His performance was perfect.

Afterwards, the communal dressing room was full of backslapping admiration for Roy and his achievement. The show's pianist, Simon Wallace, put his head round the door.

'Knock knock,' said Simon.

'Who's there?' we asked.

'Phil.'

'Phil who?'

'That's showbiz.'

*

*Dogman* was performed at the Pleasance Theatre in Edinburgh, during the 1994 Festival fringe. Dogman masks were on sale in the foyer before the show, which was a joy in that, whenever Dogman was on stage, he could look out and see smaller Dogmen looking back at him. When the show was over I would take off my Dogman suit and sit in the Pleasance Theatre courtyard and watch little children, still in their Dogman masks, playing and pretending to be him. The secret identity I had wanted since I read my first Batman comic was finally mine.

Victor came with us for the first week of the Edinburgh run and, as usual, was a hard taskmaster. Any member of the cast who thought that performing a show for children meant that they were in for an easy time was made to think again. Victor insisted on the absolute best from every one of us, at all times.

On one occasion, a stagehand could be seen, moving a piece of scenery, while Dogman made an entrance. I, in my Dogman costume, did what I assumed an actor ought to do and pretended that the stagehand wasn't there. Victor was furious. 'Dogman is friends with everybody,' he told me. 'When he sees somebody else on stage, he doesn't ignore them. He goes up to them and says hallo.'

The stagehand was a large and genial young man whose name, happily for the show, was Moose. Following Victor's instructions, Dogman entered, saw Moose and said, 'Hallo, Moose.'

'Hallo, Dogman,' said Moose.

Dogman then led Moose to centre stage.

'Boys and girls, ladies and gentlemen,' said Dogman, 'this is my friend Moose. Moose is one of the many people who help make the *Dogman* show. There are lots of people who help to make the *Dogman* show. There are people like Moose, who move the scenery. There are people who work the lights. There are people who make the costumes. There are people who sell the tickets and people who help you to your seats and people who clean the dressing rooms and people who sweep the stage. And do you know what's really sad? None of these people ever get a clap.'

Perhaps you'd care to imagine what the audience did next.

*

You can't persuade someone like Victor Spinetti to work on a show like *Dogman* for money. Love of the character is the only thing that will work. Victor, who wouldn't have wanted it any other way, was paid exactly the same as the rest of us, a fee that, as he put it, 'doesn't even pay the champagne bill, darling'. But Dogman rewards his friends in other ways.

Victor was due to fly to the USA to give a talk to some 8,000 fans at a Beatles convention, something that he did quite often. We were chatting when I happened to ask him what his exit line was. 'Oh, I don't have an exit line, love,' said Vic. 'I just tell my stories then I clear off.'

I found it hard to believe that an artist with Victor's experience left the stage without an exit line.

The conversation turned, not unnaturally, to the Beatles, and I found myself drunkenly saying, 'You know something, Vic, I've always thought that the whole Beatles thing would have been just as worthwhile if the Beatles had only ever written one song – "All You Need Is Love".'

Victor gave me a strange look, then told me, 'That's more or less what John Lennon said.'

On his return from the Beatles convention, I asked Victor how it had gone.

Victor gave me an embarrassed look. 'At the end of my talk,' said Vic, 'I said to them, I'm finishing now, but before I go I want to tell you one more story. John Lennon once said to me, Victor, I've written a lot of lyrics for a lot of songs. But if I could only have ever written one lyric it would be this: "There's nothing…"' And that was as far as Victor Spinetti was able to go – only two words into the lyric and eight thousand Beatles fans stood as one, held their clenched fists high in the air, and sang, 'ALL YOU NEED IS LOVE'.

And Victor left the stage to the sound of eight thousand people cheering.

My *Dogman* reward was less spectacular. But more rewarding.

*

Before we took *Dogman* to Edinburgh, I had a problem with the show and I didn't know how to fix it.

During one of the London performances, I read the thoughts of a father – a black man – sitting in the front row. His son, aged about four, was sitting on his lap, and this is what the father was thinking: 'You've got a nice show here. I like it. My son likes it. But would it have killed you to have had a black face on stage?'

I didn't want *Dogman*'s audience to think that he lived in an all-white world. Nor did I want to lose a member of the *Dogman* cast because of the colour of their skin. I didn't know what to do. But sometimes fate will lend a fortuitous hand. The white-skinned actress Suzie Aitchinson was not available for the Edinburgh run. The black-skinned actress Vicky Licorish was. Vicky joined the show. My problem was solved.

At the end of the performances in Edinburgh, it had become my habit to hang around by the stage, as, quite often, children would not leave the theatre without saying goodbye to Dogman.

After one performance a woman holding the hands of two small girls, one black, one white, came to the front of the stage and beckoned to Dogman. I went over. She said, 'Could we have a word with Vicky Licorish?'

I said, 'Sure,' then went backstage. Vicky was about to change but followed me back into the auditorium, still in her costume. I stood to one side as a little girl, aged about five, who, I am fairly certain, was either fostered or adopted, and who, almost certainly, was the only black child in the audience that day, looked up at Vicky and said to her, 'You look like my mum.'

\*

There aren't many people who enter the world of showbiz in order to become an abject failure. The more usual goals are glittering success, fame and fortune. I have nothing against fame or fortune. How could I? I've never experienced either. But if, during the course of my glittering career, I was able to help a small child feel a little less lonely, even if for only sixty fleeting minutes, then that is as much success as I'll ever want or need.

And, it would seem, a fitting place for a comedy career to end.

# CHAPTER FOURTEEN
## A Gang of Hermits & the Lady of Chinon

I'd wanted to escape the sound of my own voice and I'd succeeded. When I wasn't having solitary bike rides, I was sitting by the side of a river in Norfolk, seeing scarcely a soul – unless ducks and geese and swans have souls. (They do.) Others who lived on the same marina also enjoyed their solitude. I was moored opposite a man whom I saw at least once a day for over five years. Our lengthiest conversation consisted of:

'Good morning!'

''Morning!'

'Lovely day!'

'Isn't it?'

Sometimes, the conversation took a different turn:

'Good morning!'

''Morning!'

'Awful day!'

'Isn't it?'

Eventually, he started to avoid me. My constant chatter was getting on his nerves.

Days went by, becoming weeks, then months and then, eerily, years. Years in which I neither sought, nor had, any company. It appeared that I had passed the Hermit audition. I was now a fully paid-up member of the Hermit Gang (motto: 'Who Ya Gonna Call? Not Us We Hope'). It seemed that I would remain a Hermit for the rest of my solitary life. And be happy to do so.

But then I went on another bike ride.

*

I can't remember her face but I can still remember the emotions she aroused within me. I have only a faint memory of her figure, and of her clothes: anorak, blue jeans, black boots. She had dark hair and dark eyes. When I think of her, which I often do, I use the only name I have for her: the Lady of Chinon.

It was a warm and dry September, and I'd decided on another trip to France, this time riding alongside the river Loire. The crossing from Dover to Calais was pleasant and also short, one of the things that made it pleasant. From the station at Calais I took a train to Boulogne Ville, where a train conductor not only spoke to me in fluent English but made sure, at the Boulogne Ville station, that I caught the correct train to Paris Nord; a small gesture, but a welcome one.

*

On this, my sixth or seventh visit to Paris, I finally catch sight of the Eiffel Tower, which annoys me. I had prided myself on always avoiding it, but there it is, looming above me, all Parisian and clichéd, as I cycle past it to Gare d'Austerlitz and the train to Orleans.

In Orleans I book myself into a cheap hotel then go in search of a late-night supermarket and a bar. I buy food in the supermarket and beer in the bar, where I sit and watch young French people enjoying themselves in a carefree, happy and un-English way: i.e., nobody is being sick or starting a fight.

A young waiter pulls up a chair and sits at one of the tables, having a quick cigarette and a sip of his girlfriend's beer. He is enjoying himself until his boss emerges from the bar, leans over the back of his chair and smiles sweetly into the waiter's face. The waiter leaps to his feet and runs back into the bar. The boss takes his place, chatting up the waiter's girlfriend while finishing the waiter's cigarette.

I lean back and sip my beer and congratulate myself on choosing to make this journey.

Autumn is my favourite season for cycling, and although this is late September many campsites remain open as I make my way along the Loire. I'm heading west, from Orleans towards Nantes. My plan is, as usual, simply to keep going until the weather changes or the campsites close.

I camp in a small town, Mer, then cycle on to Chaumont-sur-Loire, where I find a municipal campsite charging only €4.50. From there I ride towards Tours, where I fall into conversation with a couple of French Canadians. As we chat about the pleasant state of the weather I happen to mention what a shame it is that the wind, although gentle, is in our faces. One of the Canadians says, 'According to the weather forecast, it should be blowing the other way.' And then, as though it has overheard, the wind changes direction. A magical moment, and one that has never happened before. Or since.

I have no wish to spend any time in the large city of Tours, and continue to Loynes then on Azay-le-Rideau. I find a nice, quiet campsite and, as it's the weekend (I try to never travel on a Sunday. Too scary), I book myself in for three nights at the astonishingly low price of €5.40.

Sitting outside my tent the next day, I amuse myself by watching two cyclists pack up and leave. It's always a pleasure watching other people pack away their tents. They either do it well and I marvel at their dexterity; or they do it badly and I gloat over their misfortune. The cyclists pack effortlessly and quickly and I suddenly realise that this is always the case. The only person who packs their tent badly is me. The only misfortune I am able to gloat over is my own. This depresses me. However, I am cheered by a surreal sight. After the cyclists leave, a woman wanders over to the vacated pitch and, crouching down, checks to see if anything has been left behind. She calls to her husband who comes over with a hammer. He bends, pulls up a tent peg, hands it to his wife and they both return to their caravan, looking pleased. And so they should: they now have a tent peg that they didn't have before. They are a tent peg ahead for the rest of their lives.

The following morning, I leave the campsite and have a pleasant ride to Chinon, arriving at lunchtime to find the whole town seemingly closed. I trudge around looking for a shop to buy food in, but find nothing, so give up and follow signposts that lead to the town's only campsite.

She is behind the desk in the reception. As I walk in she looks up and I am instantly smitten. I don't know why. She is not conventionally beautiful but there is something about her that grips me, holds me. As we go through the usual formalities of signing in, I ask her if she knows of a supermarket nearby. She does and, taking out a map, shows me how to get there. She looks up at me. I find myself gazing into twinkling eyes. Unaccountable feelings are stirring within me. I tell myself this can't be happening and go off to buy some cheese.

Later, I'm sitting outside my tent when she walks past and gives me a smile. My heart skips a beat. I then spend the rest of the night sitting outside my tent hoping she'll pass by again. She doesn't. I am bereft. As night falls I give up and crawl into my sleeping bag, sleeping fitfully through the night, waking from time to time, wondering if I should extend my stay and, if I did, if anything might happen between us.

Next morning I tell myself I am off my head and prepare to leave. My feelings aren't real – how can they be? Also, Chinon is a tiny town and there is little point in staying there. I decide to move on. Having packed away my gear, I am pushing my bike towards the campsite exit when she appears, walking towards me.

'*Au revoir.*'

'*Au revoir.*'

I walk on for a few paces then turn to take one last look at her. As I do, she turns to take one last look at me. Then we both turn away. I continue pushing my bike towards the exit. She walks further into the campsite grounds.

I cycle away, every turn of the pedal taking a chunk from my heart. Then I tell myself not to be so stupid. I do not know this woman. I am only feeling like this because I have been alone for so long. This is not real and in twenty kilometres she will be a distant memory.

Twenty kilometres later and I'm thinking about her even harder. I come to a town called Saumur. I can only find one campsite, which has three stars and charges accordingly. I decide against it and cycle on, passing more campsites, all of them charging €12 or more. Soon I am running out of campsites and patience. I finally find a campsite in Gennes, not too far away, which is good, because it's about to rain. I'm pitching my tent, with one eye on the weather, when I hear, for the second time in my life, the horrible crack that means a tent pole has snapped. I carry a roll of gaffer tape so I'm able to rig up an emergency splint, but whether it will last the night, I have no way of knowing. I crawl inside my fragile tent. The rain begins hammering down. God, I find myself thinking, I wish I'd stayed in Chinon.

My emergency splint lasts throughout the rainy night. But next morning, as I sit hunkered over my breakfast coffee, I look behind me and see that the tent pole has broken in two. Rainwater is flooding into the tent. I toss my coffee aside and start frantically packing. And then a fire alarm goes off. I am now meant to stop what I'm doing and assemble at a designated point by the campsite's office. Like everybody else on the campsite, I don't bother. I am not going to watch my possessions being swept away by floods, just to satisfy somebody's lust for a fire drill. Especially as, if there actually is a fire, those same floods will take care of it. That's what floods do.

Finally packed, I take the broken tent, dump it in a bin, set off to Angers, have a long and boring ride to the city centre, find the Tourist Office, get directions to a camping store and buy a new tent.

And through all this, I'm still thinking about the Lady of Chinon.

As I leave Angers and reach St Florent-le-Vieil – a pleasant little town with a massive campsite with nobody in it – I plan a daring move. I will write to her, I decide, addressing my letter to the Madame of the Campsite. I will say that I am the Englishman on the bicycle who rested on her campsite for one night only. I would like to see her again. Would she meet me for an assignation? If so, I will be at the railway station in St Florent-le-Vieil. I will wait there from nine in the morning till seven at night, every day, for a week. I will carry a red rose so that she will know me.

Yes, I think. That will do it. That will work. I'll post my letter, I'll wait at the station, day after day, clutching a red rose, until, at last, a train from Chinon will arrive; then her husband and his mates will get off it, carrying baseball bats, and beat me to a bloody pulp.

I think again.

In Nantes, I consider taking a train to Chinon. There isn't one. Also, the end of the camping season is approaching. I don't want to get back to Chinon only to find the camping site closed and abandoned. And even if I made the trip, what happens if she doesn't remember me? Or didn't have any interest in me to begin with? I'm pondering on this when I happen to catch sight of my grey and ageing face in a mirror, and the idea of someone finding me remotely attractive becomes preposterous.

I make my melancholy way to Calais and begin my journey home, taking comfort in one thing: of all the relationships I've ever had, the one with the Lady of Chinon, was, at least, mercifully short. It was also one of the more unlikely. Not because it was unreciprocated. I'm used to that. But because I thought the emotions that she had raised in me were long since dead and buried. And not just dead and buried, but buried deep, face down, and underneath concrete with a block of flats on top.

My heart was broken for, I hope, the final time, when I was fifty. At that time I wrote a weekly column in a daily newspaper. Following in the tradition that if a journalist has had a bad day then everybody else has to read about it, I wrote about my then heartbreak, beginning by giving Cat Stevens (the artist later known as Yusuf Islam) an undeserved kicking:

Cat Stevens wrote a song in the 1960s, 'The First Cut Is the Deepest'. If you're reading this, Cat, let me tell you that you got it wrong. The First Cut Is the Slightest would have made a better title. Certainly a more accurate one. Oh yeah, adolescents fall in love, and it all goes horribly wrong, and it hurts. But not for long. Like hangovers, they get over it, and quickly.

But when you're in your fifties, hangovers and broken hearts not only hurt like hell but it's a hurt that never stops. And it hurts far more than any twenty-year-old singer/ songwriter could possibly imagine.

When a fifty-year-old man finds himself at the end of a broken romance, he acts in a way that would embarrass any lovelorn adolescent. He cries. He lies around, refusing to eat, or wash, or go out. He sits by the phone waiting for her to call and say she made a terrible mistake, she was wrong about everything and can they please get back together, now?

That doesn't happen. Instead, he gets a letter saying that it's 'really important that we can be apart so we can grow as individuals', and he thinks, 'No, what's really important is that we get together and I smash you in the face with a cricket bat.'

He loses all his friends because they can't bear his relentless misery any longer. He sits in bars and bores complete strangers with interminable stories about what she said and what she did and what she looks like naked. They, if they get the chance to speak at all, console him with helpful phrases such as, 'snap out of it', or 'there's plenty more fish in the sea'. He responds to their helpful advice with a phrase of his own: 'fuck off'. He smokes and drinks till 3 a.m., and then decides to ring her, hanging up as soon as she answers so she'll know it was him. He goes to places she's likely to be, then is thrown into heart-lurching panic when he sees her from behind, walking arm-in-arm with another man, until she turns around and she's somebody else, but it's too late now, the adrenaline is coursing through his system, he's shaking, and the rest of his day is shot to hell. But he can spend it walking in a world full of lovers, usually younger, sometimes older (and that makes it worse), holding hands, kissing, laughing, being in love. And there is absolutely nothing he can do except look at them with sick, unending loathing and wish either he or they were dead.

A few days after my article was published I received a letter from a retired vicar in Somerset. 'If you think a broken heart is hard work when you're fifty,' it read, 'try having one when you're seventy-five.'

I'm now much closer to seventy-five than I am to fifty. Perhaps I will learn, in the unfortunately not too distant future, whether that vicar was right. It would be nice to learn something.

The only thing the ageing process has taught me is that the older I get the less I know. We do learn some things, as we age. We learn how to feed ourselves, clothe ourselves and to take care of our sanitary needs. Then senility hits and those are the first things to go.

The snobbery of ageing means that the older we become, the wiser we think we are. I'm sure that's not true. I'm sure that people in their nineties are almost certainly saying, 'Well, you know what you're like when you're eighty-seven. You think you know the bloody lot.'

And the one time of our life when we really think we know the bloody lot is when we're in our thirties.

I was in my thirties when I wrote and performed a thirty-minute television pilot for the BBC. One of the sketches, which featured my encountering the Devil, seemed more special than the others. And as it was a special sketch, we reasoned, it required a special actor to play the part of the Devil. 'How about Max Wall?' I suggested. 'Good idea,' said the producer.

Max Wall's career began in the music hall of the 1940s, fell into decline during the 1950s, and was revitalised in the 1970s with performances in plays such as *Waiting for Godot* and *Krapp's Last Tape*, very often directed by their author, Samuel Beckett. Max Wall, therefore, was not going to appear on some aspiring comedian's television programme for money. The only thing that would motivate him would be him liking the script. Word came back that he did; he liked the script and he'd accepted the part.

At that tine, Max Wall was in his eighties. The first thing he told us was that he'd spent two weeks learning the script. The first thing we told him was that we'd changed it. We could have filmed the sketch that Max had learned, and edited the tape. But no. We chose to edit the script and thus waste two weeks of Max Wall's life. We then went merrily on, compounding the damage. The programme was filmed before a studio audience. Max was called at 5.30 p.m. He was taken to the wardrobe department, where he was dressed as a pantomime devil. He was then taken to make-up, had rubber horns glued to his forehead and a weighty tail attached to his back. He was then kept waiting, in discomfort, until about 9.30 when it was time to film the sketch.

By the time Max Wall got onto the set he was exhausted. He was unable to remember any of the lines. The only way the sketch could be filmed was for Max to be prompted by a floor manager, one line at a time. This did not make for a sparkling performance. The sketch died a death, the show suffered accordingly and the series that I hoped would be commissioned was cancelled. To which I say, thank God.

Neither I nor the director nor the producer had the decency to treat Max Wall as if he were a human being in his eighties. Why? Because we were blinded by the light – the limelight.

The limelight – also known as the Follow Spot – illuminates the performer to the exclusion of everything else. The audience can't see anything except the performer. And the performer can't see a bloody thing. So I didn't see Max Wall as an eighty-year-old man. I saw him as a comedy commodity, nothing more than an object to further my glittering showbiz career. And if that was the attitude I had while filming a mere pilot, what would I have been like if I'd been given a series? At the very least, I'd have been too monstrous to imagine.

*

I regret quite a few of the things that I have done over the years. But I will never regret the decision I made at sixteen to be a comedian. I wasn't the best of comedians. I wasn't the worst. But I would rather be the worst comedian ever to set foot on a stage than wake up one morning, in my sixties, suddenly redundant and wondering what happened to my 'job for life'.

Nor do I regret my decision to stop being a comedian. I might feel the occasional twinge of jealousy when I learn of the successes of contemporaries (all of whom I classify as 'lesser talented'). But then I read their biographies (always published in time for Christmas) and learn that they, like so many other performers, had a childhood lacking in parental love. Or I read that they have lost someone close to them, probably to cancer, and have to cope with that loss while the media feeds on their grief. I see them having to live their lives forever in the limelight and then those twinges fade.

Or I remember the way we treated Max Wall and I feel no twinges at all.

'I travel not to go anywhere, but to go,' wrote Robert Louis Stevenson. 'I travel for travel's sake.' A philosophy I follow every time I set off on my bicycle. Often, I have no idea where my ride will take me. The best I can hope to do is enjoy the journey. As children do when they take a ride on a London train. As, I would imagine, a snail does.

In Brighton, I lived in a house which had a front path paved with flagstones. Very often, after it had rained, I would set off, probably heading for the Park View Pub, only to have my setting off ruined by crunching underfoot; crunching which meant that, for another snail, whatever journey it was on was over. I asked my Park View pals why this kept on happening. Why were snails always crawling about in the front garden just after the rain had stopped? One of them told me why.

Normally, a snail travels by exuding a path of slime and moving along that path. When the pavements are wet, the slime becomes unnecessary. The snail can travel without it, freely and unaided. The human equivalent being, perhaps, of riding a bicycle downhill. And not just downhill but downhill with the wind behind you.

What a dismal thing the life of a snail can be! The rain has stopped. The snail finds itself sailing along on a surface suddenly, and miraculously, smooth. 'This is wonderful,' thinks the snail. 'I can coast along like this for the rest of my life.' And then the Big Black Boot of Reality Comes Down and Everything Is Over For Ever.

There's a moral in there, somewhere.

I don't want to be the one who finds it.

I used to write poems for my sons, when they were young. At first, as a way of entertaining them; later, and more realistically, as a form of punishment: 'If you don't be quiet and go to sleep your father will come upstairs and read you some of his poems.' It seemed to me that the things I'd learned about snails might make a poem. I filled an entire notebook with ideas before the poem finally appeared. It was a difficult journey but I got there in the end.

> The rain has left the pavement wet
> Snails appear and quickly get
> From place to place without a trace of slime
>
> The lowliest of entities
> Moving in a state of bliss
> To walk upon the water is Sublime
>
> Humans come with heavy tread
> Very soon a snail is dead.
> Not pleasant when your world ends with a crunch.

But if the fate of snails must be
To meet the feet of you or me
At least it's independently and seldom in a bunch.

Throughout my life, I have had relationships with women –
beautiful, funny, intelligent and sexy women – and I lost every
single one of them. Even though it was nobody's fault but my
own, I decided, following my final broken heart, that enough
was enough: no more relationships with women. I had made
my single bed and now I would lie on it. And happily. And all it
took to alter that decision was a fleeting meeting with a woman
on a campsite.

What other decisions have I made that might be overturned
so easily?

My journey continues. I have no idea how or when it will
end. But it will. And it won't be long now, either. Not as I enter
my late sixties, with the odious breath of old age, death and decay
panting at my neck. But then again, I think, with a bit of luck
and a following wind, I might have twenty-five years left. The
Golden Years. Years in which I have the best of times, the best of
sex, and, more important, the best of bike rides. And why not?
What is there to stand in my way? Nothing. Nothing except failing
eyesight, hearing, knees, hips, lungs, colon, bladder, kidneys,
penis, heart and brain – and then the Big Black Boot of Reality
Comes Down and Everything Is Over For Ever.

I'd rather that didn't happen quite yet.

# *EPILOGUE*

It is a bright and sunny day as I wheel my bike out of Folkestone station. I am on my way to Hythe and a long-delayed ride through Romney Marsh. It's over a decade since I first attempted to make this ride. And if I've learned only one thing during those ten years, it's this: there is no railway station in Hythe, Kent.

Except there is. The independently owned Romney, Hythe & Dymchurch Railway runs from Hythe, passes through Dymchurch and goes on through Romney Marsh, before terminating in Dungeness, which is pretty much the route I'll be taking. Indeed, as I cycle on, I catch an occasional glimpse of one of the engines, exactly a third the size of a regular engine, chuffing along, pulling elegant carriages behind it as it rattles through the Romney countryside. Once again, the sight of the steam train makes me think about buying a ticket; once again, I remind myself that watching the train go by is more enjoyable than being on one.

I cycle the small and winding lanes of Romney Marsh, reminiscing about my childhood hero, Dr Syn, alias the Scarecrow. Even though it's daylight, it is easy to picture hooded phantoms riding the desolate, windswept marshland. I am enjoying the combination of imagination and nostalgia until I reach Dymchurch, where, instead of the tiny thatched cottages and dark cobbled streets I'd hoped to find, I'm greeted by a funfair, chip shops and men with no shirts on. I cycle past them, shuddering at their tattoos and nipples, before continuing along the coast towards Dungeness, once the home of a filmmaker, the late Derek Jarman. The thought of living, as he did, in an isolated cottage on the deserted shingle of Dungeness, has often appealed to me. This appeal disappears a mile or so away from his home, in nearby Lydd-on-Sea. Some sort of sporting event is taking place, and virtually every house has a flagpole in the garden, from which hang either the Union Flag or the Cross of St George, the sight of either of them never failing to make me feel sick. 'Patriotism,' said George Bernard Shaw, 'is the belief that your country is superior to all other countries because you were born in it.' I'm with George Bernard on this one. The only flag I'd consider flying is a white one.

I spend a few brief moments in Dungeness, admiring Derek Jarman's cottage and his peculiar, but weirdly beautiful garden, which is still intact. But the winds are fierce so I leave Dungeness, turning inland and soon reaching the nearby town of Lydd. It is lunchtime. I hope to find a nice pub and a nice pub lunch but fail to do either. Cycling aimlessly around the tiny village, I spot a sign to Lydd Airport and 'The Biggles Bar'. This seems promising so I make my way there.

Lydd Airport opened in 1954, and The Biggles Bar, I am pleased to see, appears to be unchanged since then. This is also true of their salad. Sitting on top of a pile of iceberg lettuce (the most boring of all the lettuces) are three slices of cucumber, two onion rings, a grated heap of cheddar cheese (the most boring of all the cheeses) and, bizarrely, half a tomato. It is unpleasant, inedible and, as the old joke doesn't go, there's far too much of it.

Leaving Lydd Airport and most of its salad behind, I cycle on to Rye, where I spend the night. Rye is more than picturesque, with its winding cobblestoned streets, its antique shops and its buildings, both Georgian and medieval, the town lacking nothing except, perhaps, a few bingo halls and a brothel. Of more interest to me is nearby Winchelsea, a place so small that I'd have called it a village. But no. According to the people who live there, it's actually a town. The smallest town in Britain. Others disagree. Notably the people who live in Fordwich, in Kent. Fordwich, they claim, is actually the smallest town in Britain. Fortunately, the two towns are forty miles apart, meaning their inhabitants rarely meet and can't take part in the most boring argument ever.

But I haven't cycled to Winchelsea just to see how small it is (or isn't). I'm here to visit a grave. It lies in the grounds of the Church of St Thomas the Martyr. It is the grave of Spike Milligan.

The headstone reads, 'Love, light, peace. Terence Alan (Spike) Milligan. Writer. Artist. Musician. Humanitarian. Comedian', and then, below that, a phrase in Gaelic which translates, famously, as 'I told you I was ill'. This was Spike's preferred epitaph and one that the diocese of Chichester refused to allow, presumably because English-speaking Christians might read the epitaph and be offended. Whereas, any Gaelic-speaking Christians can simply fuck off.

As I stand at Spike's grave, I am surprised by a feeling of genuine sadness. I never knew the man and I have a feeling that we wouldn't have much liked each other if I had. I don't think Spike would have liked my own attempts at comedy. And I would certainly not have enjoyed his irascibility, or, in his later, frailer years, his (I thought) increasingly desperate attempts to still make people laugh.

But then I remember the kindness he showed to a seventeen-year-old boy on the streets of Birmingham in 1967 and these thoughts seem churlish.

I also remember a story that Barry Cryer once told. He happened to be sharing a table with Spike at some literary event. Spike was clearly in a bad mood, which, Barry thought, would not make for a pleasant evening. Deciding to try and cheer him up, Barry said the first thing that came into his head. 'Spike,' he hissed, 'have you noticed how many paedophiles there are in the room?'

Spike looked at Barry with his mournful eyes and said, 'Why do people hate us?'

I surprise myself by reaching over and patting the granite cross on the top of Spike's gravestone, as though I am saying goodbye to an old and much-loved friend. Then I leave the church and return to my bike. Below me, a long straight road runs directly downhill to the thin blue ribbon of the sea. I get back on my bicycle. And then I fly.

# ACKNOWLEDGEMENTS

My sincere thanks to everyone who pledged to this book and made it possible. My thanks to Richard Collins and Steve Cox for their elegant editing and to everyone at Unbound, in particular to Imogen Denny and to Mathew Clayton, who first welcomed me on board. For helpful comments on early drafts, thanks to Arthur Dowie, Harry Scott-Moncrieff and to Claire Smith. For organising (and inspiring) book-readings, thank you, Dave Cohen and David Olrod. From the past, my thanks to the Big Girls Blouse crew – Jim Bates, John Mostyn, Dick Nelson and Rob the Roadie; and, likewise, my thanks to everyone at Birmingham Arts Lab, Tower Street. For help and support in even earlier days, thank you to Chris Bolstridge, Michael Casey, Rose Firth and Margaret Priddy. And, finally, to Timothy Smallwood, fellow pupil at Park Hill Primary School, thank you, Timothy, for the loan of your handkerchief.

# *SUPPORTERS*

Unbound is a new kind of publishing house. Our books are funded directly by readers. This was a very popular idea during the late eighteenth and early nineteenth centuries. Now we have revived it for the internet age. It allows authors to write the books they really want to write and readers to support the books they would most like to see published.

The names listed below are of readers who have pledged their support and made this book happen. If you'd like to join them, visit www.unbound.com.

Moira Adams
Keith Adsley
Richard Aickin
Richard Allen
Mark Appleton
Ian Backhouse
Danny Barbour
Keith Barnes
Eve Barrett
Alexia Bartlett
Paul Bassett Davies
Matthew Bate
Jim Bates
Brian Batson
Alasdair Beckett-King
Martin Bellwood
Elizabeth Bennett

Steve Bennett
Tony Bennett
Julian Benton
Steve Best
Robin Beste
Bill Bingham
Debbie Bird
Cathy Blackburn
Colin Blackburn
Chris Bolstridge
Dave Bowers
Mike Bradwell
Julia Braham
Rory Bremner
Yael Breuer
Arnold Brown
Shirley Brown

Curt Buckley
Joseph Bunyan
Trent Burton
Matt Butler
Neil Butler
Steve Caplin
Gillian Capper
Grace Carley
James Carr
Danny Child
Mathew Clayton
Pepe J Cleaver
Mike Clement
Vivienne Clore
Dave Cohen
Tom Conti
Jacqueline Cook
Audrey Cooke
K.G. Cooke
Nicolas Cordier
Lee Cornes
Peter Cowley
John Crawford
Luke Cresswell
Paul Curran
J-F Cuvillier
Nick Davey
Daniel M. Davis
Mark Davis
Steve Day
Tony De Meur
Hannah Dee
Ivor Dembina
Paul Dick
Ian Dickson
Les Dodd

Steve Doherty
David Dowden
Arthur Dowie
Beverley Dowie
Claire Dowie
James Downes
Jenny Eclair
Kirsten Edwards
Simon Ellinas
Hunt Emerson
Jools Emerson
Emma Erswell
Simon Evans
Tom Evans
Sharon Eyre
Michael Facherty
John Farquhar-Smith
Alan Fentiman
Susanna Ferrar
Lorena Field-Boden
Ed Finch
Rose Firth
Clare Forrest
Steve Forster
Hilly Foster
Martyn Foulds
Andrew Foxcroft
Aldo Framingo
Tom Fry
Rupert Gavin
Steven Gee
Jo Gibson
Charlotte Glasson
David & Christine Glasson
Ged Gleeson
David Goldin

Sarah Gorman

Nick Gough

Dave Gowland

Peter Grahame

Kenneth Gray

Ian Gregg

Mike Grenville

Gavin Hackett

Rick Hall

Andy Hamilton

David Hamilton

Anthony Thomas Hanlon

Tony Hannan

Helen Haran

Jeremy Hardy

Tim Hardy

Patricia Harrow

David Harry

Miranda Hart

Ian Hartley

Steve Hayes

John Hegley

Stu Henderson

Jimmy Hibbert

Mark Hibbett

Adrian Hickford

Jez Higgins

Gerry Hoban

Lew Hodges

Phoebe Hollins

Pierre Hollins

Rollo Hollins

Jim Houghton

Adrian Howe

Alex Howell

Ernie Hudson

Elizabeth Hutchison

Robin Ince

Neil Innes

Phil Inthekitchen

Michael Jackson

Christopher Jaeger

Diana James

Luke Skyscraper James

Nick Jeffrey

Ric Jerrom

David Johnson

Mark Jones

Paula Jones

Toby Jones

Juanjo

Shirley Judd

Rob Jukes

Dillie Keane

Steve Kearley

Mark Kelly

Sophie Kelly

Dan Kieran

Wendy Kingon

Sara Lambert

Mark Lancaster

Mike Lance

Sharon Landau

Anne Lane

Jimmy Leach

Helen Lederer

Caroline Lee

CP Lee

Dave Lee

Sarah Lee

Stephie Lee

Rhodri Lewis

George Lloyd
Lisa Lovebucket
Eric Ludlow
Chris Lynam
Calvin Carson Ma
Gari MacColl
Charlotte Mackay
John Mackay
Dirk Maggs
Adrienne Mann
Patrick Marber
Andrea Marutti
Phelim McDermott
Mac McDonald
Karen McMillan
Cornelius Medvei
Andrew Miller
Lynn Ruth Miller
Bruce Mitchell
John Mitchinson
David Moloney
Brian Montague
Alan Moore
Paul Moore
Fraser Morrison
Jim Mortleman
Angela Morton
Emilee Moyce
Jeanette Muff
Linda Murray
Tina Murray
Alison Mussett
Craig Naples
Al Napp
Keith Nash
Carlo Navato

Michael Naylor-Hodgkinson
Phil Nice
Peter Nicholson
J Nightingale
Joe Norris
Stephie Nuttall
Bernard O'Leary
Jan O'Malley
Kirsty Oliver
David Olrod
Maxine Ostwald
Iain Pattinson
Heather Peace
Rob Pearson
Mike Pennell
Craig Peppiatt
James Perryer
Neal Peters
Andy & Elaine Pickering
Nigel Planer
Valerie Plant
Justin Pollard
Ian Potter
Kathryn Power
Steven Pratt
Lawrence Pretty
David Quantick
Leisa Rea
Michael Redmond
John Reeves
Nick Revell
Wendy Richardson
Glenn Richer
Gary Rimmer
Jamie Rix
Keith Robbins

Annie Rodgers
George Root
Lizzie Roper
Lyle Russell
Annemarie Rutherford
Loretta Sacco
Carol Sarler
Linda Sayle
Mark Schofield
Simon Scott
Lucy Scott-Moncrieff
Craig Seeley
Linda Shoare
Lee Simpson
William Simpson
Ewan Sinclair
Jonathan Sloman
Andy Smart
Alan Smith
Bob Smith
Brian Smith
Claire Smith
Richie Smith
Rowan Smith
Peter Stark
Natasha Steel
Steve Steen
Alex Stefanovic
Rosalind Stern
Michael Stevens
Patrick Stevens
Rebecca Stevens
Mervyn Stutter
Mark Summerfield
Barbara Maurelet Sutton
T & T B'O'B

Tom Taylor
Woodstock Taylor
Tessa
Jasper Henry Thomas
Mark Thomas
Roger Thomas
Ann Thompson
Neil Titley
Michael Topping
Norah Tracey
Louise Troest
Edward Tudor Pole
Justin Tunstall
Steve Ullathorne
Rod Upton
Suzy Varty
Sarah Vernon
Richard Vranch
Paul Wakefield
Martin Walker
Steve Walker
Adam Walsh
Jonathan Walsh
Phill Warren
Jack Watts
Norm Waz
Peter Wear
Robert Wells
Paul West
Dave Westerby
John White
Heathcote Williams
Paul Williamson
Richard Willis
Richard Wise
Dendi Wolffsky

Jo Wood
Marcus Wrigley
David Jackson Young
Martin Young